American Singers

Books by Whitney Balliett

American Singers
TWENTY-SEVEN PORTRAITS IN SONG

Whitney Balliett

New York   Oxford   OXFORD UNIVERSITY PRESS

Oxford University Press

Oxford   New York   Toronto
Delhi   Bombay   Calcutta   Madras   Karachi
Petaling Jaya   Singapore   Hong Kong   Tokyo
Nairobi   Dar es Salaam   Cape Town
Melbourne   Auckland

and associated companies in
Berlin   Ibadan

First published in 1988 by Oxford University Press, Inc.,
200 Madison Avenue, New York, New York 10016

First issued as an Oxford University Press paperback, 1990

Oxford is a registered trademark of Oxford University Press

Library of Congress Cataloging-in-Publication Data

Balliett, Whitney.
    American singers : twenty-seven portraits in song / Whitney
  Balliett.
      p. cm.
      1. Singers—United States—Biography.   2. Jazz musicians—United
States—Biography.   I. Title.
ML400.B25 1988
784.5—dc19
[B]   88-4866
                                                         CIP
                                                         MN

The essays in this book (with the exception of "Go to
Macy's! Buy!") appeared in somewhat different form in *The
New Yorker* magazine.

ISBN 0-19-504610-2
ISBN 0-19-506573-5 (PBK)

10 9 8 7 6 5 4 3 2 1
Printed in the United States of America

For Berton Roueché

Note

This book is a revision and expansion—from twelve chapters to twenty-five—of my *American Singers*, first published almost ten years ago. It was written between 1970 and 1984, and contains twenty-seven biographical studies of one or more of almost every kind of American non-academic singer—the vaudeville singer, the jazz-novelty singer, the blues singer, the ballad singer, the cabaret singer, the Broadway singer, the instrumentalist who also sings, the movie singer, the songwriter-singer, and the jazz singer. (The most popular definition of a jazz singer is that there is no definition. But there is. A jazz singer simply makes whatever he or she sings swing. Ethel Merman was not a jazz singer; Doris Day is.) The book is not comprehensive, although it would be difficult to find many singers superior in their category to those included. One non-singer is present—the songwriter-composer-lyricist Alec Wilder. He accomplished two marvelous things. He wrote beautiful songs, and he published a classic pioneering study, *American Popular Song*. His book made it possible for Julie Wilson to close her chapter in *American Singers* by saying: "The great American songs will one day be like Shakespeare sonnets. All they will have to do to be perpetuated is to be used. The songs will always be there. It will simply be a question—as it is even now—of where and how and when they will be performed." And by whom, she might have added.

New York
February 1988

W. B.

Contents

American Singers

The President of the Derrière-Garde

Alec Wilder

In the spring of 1972, Alec Wilder committed his finest ironic act: he published *American Popular Song: The Great Innovators, 1900–1950*, in which he examines, with wit and grace, some eight hundred of the three hundred thousand American songs submitted for copyright in the first half of the century, and in which the work of Alec Wilder is nowhere mentioned. But irony has long been a way of life for Wilder. He is a man of Johnsonian principles and persuasions, who is extraordinarily timid and almost completely lacking in self-confidence. He lives a semi-nomadic existence, even though he is steadfastly responsible and loyal to his friends, and he has avoided the limelight so assiduously that he has become famous for it. He is sixty-six years old and delicately constructed, but he has the vitality and curiosity and strength of a child. He detests violence, but, full of Martini courage, he once challenged Benny Goodman to take off his glasses and step outside. He has repeatedly run away from opportunities to make sizable sums of money, not because he dislikes money per se but because he refuses to blow his own horn or sully himself in the marketplace. And now he has written a book which, because it is probably definitive, threatens to send his popular songs into oblivion. (An appendix dealing with Wilder's work and written by a sympathetic critic would not have been unseemly; Wilder, though, would have roared incredulously at the notion.)

That the book was completed at all is a miracle. It was edited, with an introduction, by James T. Maher, a writer and man of imposing patience, erudition, and intelligence. He talked of how the book came into being:

"Alec had had the idea for years, but it didn't jell until 1967. He applied
for a grant. Silence. Then he contacted me, and since I'd had some experience with foundations, I wrote an exhaustive backup letter, full of cost
estimates and couched in mahogany academese, and we got the grant.
This was in 1968. I suggested the structure of the book and got together
the raw materials—sheet music, what shows songs had been in, what
movies, whether or not a song had been dropped from a show, and so
forth. We screened some seventeen thousand pieces of sheet music, and
after that we interviewed those composers who would talk to us. Richard
Rodgers was polite and I think not a little fascinated, and Harold Arlen
was marvellous, but Irving Berlin was—let us say—intractable. Then,
whenever Alec was in town, we'd retire to Howard Richmond's office, on
Columbus Circle—he's Alec's publisher, and a saint—and Alec would sit
down at the piano and shout, 'Come on! Come on! Let me get going!' I'd
lay out all the tunes by a specific composer, and he'd play through them
and make comments. I'd jot them down and ask questions in return.
When he'd finished, I'd type up what he'd said and send it to him, along
with the appropriate sheet music. Writing like a madman, he'd fill spiral
notebook after spiral notebook, which I'd transcribe. Then we'd revise. I
was terrified when he came to my apartment to go over the Jerome Kern
chapter, which is the first big one. I had a query every two sentences, but
he took it with pleasure and fun, and in two days and two nights we had
it done. It was the initiation, and after that the sailing was smoother."

The book is a fair, positive, scholarly celebration of American songwriting which comes down hard but graciously on the insufficient and
applauds the good with lyrical aplomb. Wilder writes of Jerome Kern's
"The Song Is You": "It is, I'm afraid, one of Kern's self-consciously elegant 'art songs'; it attempts too dramatic a statement on too small a stage.
And it suggests a grander voice than that usually associated with popular
theatre music. It borders on the vehicle-for-the-singer more than the
song-in-itself, and, to carp one last time, it employs rubato as opposed to
steady tempo." Later on, he embraces Harold Arlen: "His songs made me
feel that I had a friend in court, and that were we to meet, he would be
sympathetic and even encouraging. I envied his talent, but, strangely, I
never tried to write in his fashion. I sensed that he lived at the heart of
the matter, where the pulse was, and that I was an enthusiastic outsider.
And I was right." Wilder continually demonstrates the insight that only a
first-rate composer could have into the work of his peers. On Cole Porter's
lyrics: "They seldom risked or indulged in tenderness or vulnerability.
Even when concerned with emotional stresses, they often managed to
keep at a polite distance from true sentiment by means of a gloss, a patina
of social poise. . . . Or else they resorted to melodramatic clichés. The light
touch, the mordant turn of phrase, the fingertip kiss, the double-entendre,

the awareness of the bone-deep fatigue of urban gaiety, the exquisite, and the lacy lists of cosmopolitan superlatives—these were the lyrical concerns of Cole Porter." And he puts the score of *South Pacific* in focus: "I'm sorry to say that the melodies from *South Pacific,* immensely popular though they were, took on a kind of self-consciousness that is akin to . . . Kern's . . . I almost feel as if I should change into formal garb before I listen to them. Or it may be that I've stopped believing. Something's missing: fire, impact, purity, naturalness, need, friendliness, and, most of all, wit." And a passing but highly perceptive comment: "Of all the better songwriters, I can think of very few who have any emotional kinship with the jazz musician and his bittersweet, witty, lonely, intense world." Along the way, Wilder sets down his principles, which are lofty and ringing: "I should make clear that my criteria are limited to the singing (melodic) line and include the elements of intensity, unexpectedness, originality, sinuosity of phrase, clarity, naturalness, control, unclutteredness, sophistication, and honest sentiment. Melodrama, cleverness, contrivance, imitativeness, pretentiousness, aggressiveness, calculatedness, and shallowness may be elements which result in a hit song but never in a great song."

Wilder has steadily applied these principles to his own work, which comprises an astonishing canon. He has, with amusement, called himself "the president of the derrière-garde," but he is a unique and adventurous composer, who has written a huge body of music, both popular and formal, much of it nearly unknown. Among his works are several hundred popular songs, three of which became hits in the mid-forties and are now standards—"I'll Be Around," "It's So Peaceful in the Country," and "While We're Young." His songs have an airy, elusive quality quite unlike that of any other American songwriter. The melodic lines flicker and turn unexpectedly, moving through surprising intervals and using rhythm in a purposeful, agile, jazz-based manner. The songs have a sequestered, intense gentleness, a subtle longing for what was and what might have been that eludes most ears and that demands singers of the rank of Mabel Mercer and Frank Sinatra and Mildred Bailey. (Wilder is obsessed with the need to have singers sing his popular songs *as written.* This does not often happen. Sometimes singers consciously change notes, perhaps thereby improving the melody, and sometimes they accidentally change or omit notes and warp the song. The trouble with this, in Wilder's view, is that other singers pick up these alterations and in turn are imitated. Yet—another Wilder irony—he is an impassioned student of jazz.) In a rare way, Wilder's melodic lines savor the lyrics at every turn, and, indeed, they are often written to fit the words, which have been done by Wilder himself and by such craftsmen as William Engvick and Johnny Mercer. In the early fifties, Wilder, after hesitating for years, plunged with vigor into the world of formal music, and the variety and scope of his compositions are bewildering.

Trying to place him in the world of formal music is equally bewildering. A first-rate music critic who has observed Wilder closely for the past fifteen years has said of him, "One must, in Alec's case, let uniqueness be unique. He occupies his own space in the world of formal music and that's it. He writes mainly for wind instruments, and the academic community tends accordingly to look at his pieces as divertissements, as entertainments. They also regard him as frivolous because he is primarily a melodist, a composer who thinks in terms of timbres and coloristic things. You see, he had little formal training and his gods have always been Bach and Debussy and Fauré and Ravel. But if he is wholly outside the academic community, he is revered by the great performers, like John Barrows and Harvey Phillips and Bernard Garfield. He is a major figure to them, and they gossip about him the way the English gossip about the Queen." He has written for full orchestra and for wind ensembles, he has written choral works and chamber music, and concert songs. He works at enormous speed. In a matter of six months, he completed two trios for bassoon, clarinet, and piano; a suite for French horn and orchestra; a suite for flute choir; his eleventh woodwind quintet; a euphonium concerto with a woodwind ensemble; and a dozen piano pieces each for Marian McPartland and Ellis Larkins. His love of chamber music is boundless. He has written for every instrument in the orchestra, and in extraordinary combinations. There are woodwind-and-brass quintets; trios for oboe, clarinet, and bassoon, and for clarinet, French horn, and piano; suites for string bass, tuba, and piano, for three guitars, for trombone choir and clarinet choir, for French horn, tuba, and piano, and for two oboes and two English horns; sonatas for bassoon and piano, for alto saxophone and piano, for tenor saxophone and strings, for euphonium and piano, and for tuba and piano or orchestra; and concertos for baritone saxophone, French horn, and woodwind quintet, and for tuba-and-wind ensemble. All these chamber works have been played and some have been published, but very few have been recorded. One that has is a suite for French horn, tuba, and piano. It was written, as all Wilder's formal music now is, for specific players, in this case John Barrows (horn) and Harvey Phillips (tuba). Bernie Leighton, who appears often on Wilder's records, is on piano. The piece, in five movements, is of a high lyric order. It easily converts the tuba from a two-by-four into a soaring gable; it demonstrates Wilder's singular melodic gifts and it makes it clear that Wilder has succeeded where so many have failed—in making jazz and formal music work hand in hand. (His pop melodies and formal melodies are sometimes almost interchangeable. He thinks of them this way: "It's mainly a matter of degree. The seed of a song grows into a small plant with a single flower, but a concert piece has as complex a root system as a tree.") Of particular note in the suite are the second movement, which is mournful and elegiac, and in which the two horns move in subtle, close counterpoint in such a way that it is sometimes difficult to tell one from the other, Wilder having written high for the tuba and low for the horn; the third movement, which is built around a cheerful seven-note riff, and in which the horns, swinging very hard, pursue and echo one another; and the last movement, which starts as a fugue and dissolves into long, intertwined melodic lines that are capped by a clapping, dual harrumph.

When Wilder was contacted at his pied-à-terre, the Algonquin Hotel, about being interviewed he said in a roundabout way that the dental crisis of his life had arrived and that he would not be able to talk to anyone— if, indeed, he was ever able to talk again—for several weeks. He said the deed—the installation of false teeth—would be done in Rochester and that he would recuperate at a friend's house in Cambridge. But he is not a quiescent man, and a week later a letter from him arrived. Then came another, and another. Before he got back to New York, they were coming almost every other day, and they formed a marvelous overture that made one impatient for the principal work. The letters had a fine, eighteenth-century timbre. Some were broadsides, some were inchoate, some were confessional, some were mystical and some very funny. And they were rhetorical; no answer was expected, or even possible. Putting subject titles on the letters did not seem amiss:

ON BEING A CURMUDGEON

In spite of my need of the leavening of laughter, I am hourly infuriated by stupidity, indifference, lack of style, obeisance to faddism, obsessive competitiveness [and] middle-class concepts such as relevance, the meaningful, and the significant.

My only ambition is to be a better person and a better creator. It's increasingly difficult, but I attempt to keep an open mind and a hungry heart, a constant need for wonderment and magic. While I acknowledge the validity of honest giving, I'm also aware of the grace of receiving (not taking). I'm a fiend for order, self-discipline, and morality. I despise anarchy in living as much as art. I do not equate the new or the original with the superior. I believe in interdependence, and, therefore, tradition.

I gave up alcohol primarily to avoid the risk of false-courage anger, and have, thus far, managed to maintain a degree of benignity, except for ill-timed boiled eggs—and that new grotesque hero: the common man. Civilization, such as the dear sickly creature is, lies in the ditch starving to death and waiting not for the wise man, the creator, the forest ranger, the anthropologist, the entomologist, the philatelist, the numismatist, the dancer, the leprechaun, the bird-watcher, or Evangeline Adams but for that indulged, cosseted, adulated, protected, and idealized idiot—the common

man! Who in hell started this macrocosmic love-in? Schweitzer? Burns?
(Didn't he come up with "man's inhumanity to man"?) Steichen, with his
"Family of Man"? What about the deserving, the *un*common, the excellent,
the striving, the visionary, the come-hell-or-high-waterer? Must he sigh
patiently, lovingly, understandingly, waiting . . . until the new, compla-
cent, vainglorious hero stumbles into sight? [But] I suppose the nobility
who were privileged to listen to the premières of the Brandenburg concerti
were a pretty vapid, unwashed lot.

A less congested letter came the following day. Wilder's diatribes are
like line squalls—wild, intense, loud, and over almost before they have
started.

ON PRIVACY AND MONEY

As the giant spring coils tighter, people, even good friends, listen less
and less. And strangely, not just because they, too, want to talk. I watch
their eyes glaze; I don't believe they're spinning fantasies to themselves or
plotting devious deals. It's some dreadful form of autohypnosis, turning on
without drugs, their conscious mind blocked by too many garish
likelihoods.

I ask myself: Is privacy (in these turbulent times) like keeping a line
warped to a dock because if you release it the motor may fail, the sails jam,
the oars break? Those who revel in publicity and being written about are
delighted with the high seas and no charts, for they know they'll be surrounded by all their buddies in a similar situation—not, to them, a plight
or a crisis, rather the great roiling arena. I'm a small-pond person: I hate
danger and am horrified by violence. I've never sought more excitement
than can be found in an amusement park, and that only after others'
insistence.

Judy Holliday, while listening to some new quintet or sonata [of mine],
would suddenly point at me and say, "That's the special passage, the secret
love, isn't it?" And of course she'd always be right. Yet they weren't secrets
to be hidden but secrets to be shared, secrets because they were very delicate and needed stern and unremitting protection.

Years ago I solved the problem of publicity by playing the buffoon
whenever I was interviewed, and by means of hyperbole I gave the writers
what they wanted: the label of eccentricity. It didn't require much effort.
When you live alone most of the time, avoid groups, parties, public func-
tions, I guess you do develop odd ways. But I never told them much, very
simply because I knew they were only half listening and would be exas-
perated and possibly angry if I persisted in presenting my true self. Mine
is not a large landscape; I live like one of Sally Carrighar's bugs in a pond.
Those plate-passing young men on the moon failed to stir me; yet I delight
in the infinity of space.

One further comment on my possibly neurotic need for privacy: I've
written verse for forty years. All of it has been sent to a remarkable man
in Rochester, Dr. James Sibley Watson, who was once the co-owner and
deus ex machina of the Dial Magazine. I have no interest in publication; I
simply wish a respected and loved friend to have it all. I've made no effort

to persuade publishers to accept my hundreds of non-pop compositions; in fact, even when my kind of pop song was fashionable, I never played half the songs for those Brill Building charmers. I enjoy the act of creating and, much as I love and depend on my friends, I am not impressed by contemporary exposure. What about money? Frankly, it's a miracle I've managed to support myself all these years. My more practical friends are disgusted with my, to them, scatterbrained generosity. For example, I met a remarkable string-bass virtuoso, Gary Karr. He had minimal music to perform, mostly transcriptions. So I wrote him a sonata for bass and piano. I didn't charge him for it or for copying the parts. I was honored that such a talent was interested in having me write something. My friends chided me on the grounds that only he could play the piece. "That's the point," I told them, "I wrote it for him." "But," they snarled, "no one will publish it, etc., etc."

Wilder has never asked for a cent for any of the hundreds of formal pieces he has written. He has done this out of fear that a piece might be rejected, and, more often, simply because he has composed all his formal music voluntarily for people he admires. But this extraordinary largesse has caught up with him. Not long ago, he said, "I've decided to write no more music unless I am paid for it. This is against my most profound convictions. But I'm broke. I know this decision will not bring solvency, as all those who love my free music shall easily be able to do without the boughten stuff. It's very, very sad (for me)."

Which reminds me of my only Hollywood adventure. I was hired for fifteen hundred dollars a week to write the score for a version of *Daddy-Long-Legs*. The film was never made, which was too bad, as it was the best score I ever wrote. The lyrics were glorious, by the man who wrote the lyrics for my song "While We're Young"—Bill Engvick.

The producer was also the writer. He sensibly wanted the songs to fit the situations. After we had written over half the songs, he was called away on another film. He told us to sit tight, collect our money, and wait for his return. I refused, on the premise that we wouldn't be earning our salaries. He considered us demented. We came back East and didn't hear from him for three months. At fifteen hundred a week, that would be ugh, ugh . . .

The letters got shorter and more peaceful as they went on. Perhaps Wilder was adjusting to his dental ordeal, or perhaps it was the salubrity of his Cambridge hideout.

ON HIS ABHORRENCE OF POSSESSIONS

Quite a few otherwise friends consider my minimal possessions a quaintness bordering on affectation. My profound need to move constantly, my loathing of leases, and my deep fear of loss I offer to them as adequate reasons for my possessions being limited to the contents of three suitcases. They're seldom convinced. Then I tell them of my Aunt Emma, a most witty and engaging lady whose collecting mania included olive pits. Once, at a funeral, after the coffin had been removed, she wandered from where we sat into the room where the coffin had been. I knew why: to pick up a few scattered flower petals. A salty little man, her brother, called out, "What'cha lookin' for, Em? Olive pits?" Some time later, I was forced to break open one of her many trunks. There, on the top tray, lay about twenty olive pits which had been dipped in gold paint. That could be sufficient reason for limiting my possessions.

Although he detests sentimentality, there is a strong strain of nostalgia in Wilder. But it tends to be a healthy, pastoral nostalgia—the sort that such Romantic poets as William Collins and William Cowper indulged in.

ON HIS DISREGARD FOR THE RECORDED PAST

I've written music for almost fifty years. I've kept no records (or recordings), reviews, interviews, programs, or original sketches of my music. I've kept only a few letters, no books, and have given to others all the presents that were given to me. Indeed, the books I've given away constitute a kind of huge, floating, national library. I have much greater pleasure in recalling an afternoon I spent in Towanda waiting for a westbound Black Diamond (a *real* train with a *real* steam locomotive) than I do a concerto première or a film recording. I remember reading a Thomas Beer novel in a deserted campus somewhere in Maine and the first time I heard Crosby sing "Penthouse Serenade" on a romantic tropical night. In the days when it was rare for a record to reach the million mark, I had a song on the back of "Paper Doll" which did just that. I was glad to get the ten thousand dollars and indifferent to all the noise about it. When someone enthusiastically tells me he still has my first Octet record, I want to reply, "Have you heard anything I've written since then?," knowing he hasn't.

By the time this letter arrived, Wilder had returned to the Algonquin and was spending most of his evenings at the Cookery, in the Village, where his friend Marian McPartland was appearing. An acquaintance of Wilder's ran into him there one night, and he was startling company. He'd listen intently for minutes, but when the pianist got off a particularly felicitous phrase he'd smite his brow and say in a booming voice, "God *dam*mit! That would have taken me three *weeks* to write, and she does it in three *seconds!*"

ON HIS DISLIKE OF HIRSUTE APPENDAGES

I'm back in the Cookery being distracted by grotesque and Halloween-like hairstyles. There's one gray-haired gent (none on his head) who should know better. His sideburns are attached to his mustache by a very narrow bridge of hair, which, in the Cookery's dim light, gives the illusion of the lower part of his face having been shot away. Another fellow, younger, has a perfectly pleasant, even gentle face. But his mustache looks as if it had been drawn on his face with burnt cork while he was sleeping. I keep being told they do no harm with their affectations. I disagree, since they markedly offend my visual need for symmetry. I say "symmetry," but I mean much more. I have found, as has another friend, that we know no man with an affected hairstyle whom we completely trust or respect. This doesn't apply to young men, though I admit to a constant inner battle required to fight my way past the outer unattractiveness to the face and the self behind the hair.

Wilder's last letter arrived the day before the interview. It was sombre but fitting.

ON DEATH

The approach to extinction in my case has caused me to become obsessed with the clarification of all obscurity, sharpening of all dullness, truing of all warp, cutting away all the rot of self-deception, knowing as clearly as I can who and what is doing the dying. I am in a kind of brooding awe of all those who manage to maintain such a powerful self-importance that they truly consider themselves superior beings. Long before I became old, I wept at the sight of death; of all that miraculous energy and affirmation turned to dust. I found myself suddenly against cremation simply because the sight of any but a big city cemetery brought the dead back to a kind of half-life for me. They were not skeletons lying in boxes. They were very faint shadows hovering above their graves. I saw them as the old romantic poets did. So I changed my will from a cadaver gift to a hospital to an old-fashioned corpse to be put in the ground in a box—preferably on a New England hillside. This does not mean that death is my constant companion but that Life, except in its most corrupt and dissolute forms, is a miracle to be all but worshipped. . . . Would the religious need God as much as they do if they comprehended the unique phenomenon of Life?

Wilder said on the telephone that it would be "indecent" to meet in the "riotous confusion" of his hotel room, so the meeting took place in a mutual friend's midtown office. Wilder is a tall man with a big head and small feet. He was wearing a sports jacket, gray slacks, and loafers, and they had the resigned look of strictly functional clothes. He has a long, handsome face and receding gray hair that flows out from the back of his head, giving the impression that he is in constant swift motion. His eyebrows are heavy and curved, and when he has finished making a point— often punctuated by his slamming his fist down on the nearest piece of furniture—they shoot up and the corners of his mouth shoot down. He has piercing, deep-set eyes cushioned by dark, doomsday pouches—diamonds resting on velvet. His face is heavily wrinkled—not with the soft, oh-I-am-growing-old lines but with strong, heavy-weather ones. He has a loud baritone voice and he talks rapidly. When he is agitated, his words roll like cannonballs around the room. He laughs a lot and he swears a lot, in an old-fashioned, Mark Twain manner, and when he is seated he leans forward, like a figurehead breasting a flood tide. A small, serene mustache marks the eye of the hurricane.

He smiled brilliantly, "Well, what the dentist did hasn't changed me too much," he said. "And all my friends have been very well-mannered. None have looked away from my mouth and none have stared at it—a bit of subtle eyework for which I'm grateful. I can whistle better than before. In a way, fear and my terrible teeth—those two things—have controlled my life. Somewhere along the line, it was discovered that I'm made largely of glass. I've very little calcium in my bones and none in my teeth. As a result, nothing mends. It's the reason I walk in the hunt-and-peck way I do. I'm in constant fear of banging into something and breaking a leg or falling down and breaking an arm. I broke my leg in the thirties by jumping off a Fifth Avenue bus on the way to meet my mother, and I spent six months on my back and six months in a polio splint. I started out with a bad dentist in Rochester—the kind who washed his utensils in the kitchen sink and drilled holes just to have something to fill. When I finally found a good one, also in Rochester, we had a system whereby I had to go every three months for a checkup. I'd take him books and think of jokes to tell him, and I even wrote a piece of music for him, 'A Molar Expedition'—all in hopes that he'd be nice to me. And once in a while, as a precaution, I'd take his hygienist and her boyfriend out for a drink. Whenever the dentist said everything was O.K., I'd go out and get drunk. I keep mentioning Rochester because I was born there and I still spend a lot of time there. I was born into a family of bankers. My father was a banker, my grandfathers were bankers, two uncles were bankers. They lived that whole ambience of voting Republican and hating the Jews. They didn't really *hate*, of course. They just maintained the proper prejudices. My father died when I was three. My mother didn't know anything about meat bills and coal bills. She wasn't married until she was thirty, and she wasn't ready then. She had been a belle who had been spoiled by her family and by men. She was a Chew, and she had grown up in a Colonial house surrounded by English boxwood in the beautiful upstate town of Geneva. It was a conventional, proper, Henry James life—a safe life, where there was safe talk and cheerful people and no arguments. The Wilders, on the other hand, were eccentric and untrammelled. But my mother was a good woman. After she died, I found a letter in her pocketbook from me saying a string quartet of mine might be performed. But she was embarrassed by my becoming a musician. Musicians were still regarded as servants. When musicians performed at the Eastman house, they came in the side door. I was the youngest of three children. My Edwardian brother lives in New York and can see again, thanks to an eye operation I had to practically force him to undergo. My sister is gone, but I am still indebted to her for singing me early Jerome Kern songs when I was a child. One of them, 'And I'm All Alone,' is still a knockout. I learned very early that I was perfectly happy to be left alone. So I suppose I became a threat in my own house—an odd boy who was always reading books and who never fought or even played much with other children but who made people laugh. I used the device of foolishness to get by. A while ago, I ran into a childhood friend who has become a self-important tycoon. I used to make him laugh uncontrollably in Rochester. I reminded him of the time we had sneaked into the bishop's house through the milk door and trailed toilet paper all over the place. He didn't even smile. I suppose that is what money does to you. I spent more time with cooks and servants than with anyone else. I even played lousy piano and banjo in an all-black band at a hotel dance in Bay Head, where we went for summers. Since the musicians were all sons of waiters and cooks, it didn't matter my playing with them.

"I went to a couple of private schools in Rochester, and then we moved to Garden City, Long Island, and I was put in St. Paul's School there. I felt *horrible*. So I went to Lawrenceville, and I felt even worse. I finally ran away. Then we moved to Park Avenue—a safe street, of course—and I went to Collegiate.

"A year or so before that, we lived on West Seventieth Street, where, as I recall, I slept in the same bed with my brother. He insisted I whistle 'The Missouri Waltz,' which invariably sent him into a heavy slumber. It does whistle well in thirds. I'd go to a nearby record store to pick up Isham Jones' records, and discovered that the store was near the Sixty-third Street Theatre, where Noble Sissle and Eubie Blake's all-black show, *Shuffle Along*, had just opened. I don't remember how many performances I saw, but it was before the carriage trade found the show. The theatre was so empty I could slip down to the apron to watch Mr. Blake. It was a revelation. It had the same impact that 'Afternoon of a Faun' had on me. I had thought, until I heard Debussy's piece, that the 'Poet and Peasant Overture' was concert music. I went down to *Shuffle Along* to hear all those friendly songs and all those exciting people onstage the way another boy would have hung out at the candy store.

"I graduated from Collegiate, but failed my Regents and never got to Princeton. Instead, I went back to Rochester and studied privately at the Eastman School. I had already started writing music. In fact, the first songs I wrote—for a friend who was giving a show in his family's house at the Jersey shore—were filched from a Princeton Triangle Club show. Nobody caught on until the choral director at Collegiate heard them. The year in New York before I went back to Rochester was a jumble, and largely a lovely one. I spent most of my time with two great friends—Carroll Dunn, whom I'd met in Bay Head, and Lavinia Faxon, now Russ.

We talked the nights away in Chinese restaurants, and Lavinia and I still do. I'm going to take her to the Ritz, in Boston, for three days to celebrate her birthday, and I'll have phlox put in her room. I tried, under Carroll's tutelage, to be a writer for a time, and I have a dim recollection of enrolling briefly in a dramatic school. At Eastman, I studied composition and counterpoint with Herbert Inch and with the son of Josiah Royce, the philosopher. I wrote concert songs and a piece for orchestra, and, after hearing Mildred Bailey for the first time over a radio in a speakeasy, I started writing songs for her and Bing Crosby and Ethel Waters. And—by God!—Crosby and Mildred eventually sang them. And at the Eastman I got to know such other students as Mitchell Miller and Goddard Lieberson and John Barrows, the great French-horn player, and Jimmy Carroll, as good a clarinettist as ever lived. They were my first professional friends. They made it possible for me to stop sidling in my shyness down the halls of Eastman.''

Wilder put out his cigarette and immediately lit another one. He stared moodily into space, and for an instant he looked like that famous brooding photograph of Eugene O'Neill. "I've always been a great coffee drinker, but I'm an even greater one since I quit the booze. A succession of trivia finally made me stop. One day, bowed down by a *monstrous* hangover, I successively lost in twenty minutes my wallet, which had five hundred and forty dollars in it that I had saved for a trip, broke a pair of glasses, and stepped on my favorite pipe. That did it. My drinking never stopped me from working, but it made me a lot of enemies. I was one of those deceptive drinkers who don't show their condition. I invariably got venomous and nasty and rude when I was drunk, but I didn't *look* drunk. On top of that, I never remembered a thing the next day, so it was very difficult to apologize adequately when some kind friend called and recounted my atrocities. But I'll say one thing: I never once bought a bottle and holed up in my hotel room. I did *all* my drinking in bars. I guess I started in earnest in the late twenties. I had begun voyaging back and forth between Rochester and New York, and I was writing a lot of popular music. Most of it is on file up at Bill Engvick's house, on the Hudson. I keep meaning to go up there and look at it, but I never seem to. Then, in the late thirties, partly at the behest of Mitchell Miller and partly because of the late Morty Palitz, an A. & R. man and songwriter, I wrote my first woodwind octet pieces. I had been fooling around with the harpsichord, and of course Mitchell was an oboist. So I added a clarinet, a flute, a bass clarinet, a bassoon, a string bass, and drums, and we made some records for Columbia. It must have been around 1938. I gave the pieces nutty titles, like 'A Debutante's Diary,' 'Sea Fugue Mama,' 'Neurotic Goldfish,' 'The House Detective Registers,' 'The Children Met the Train,' and 'Jack, This Is My Husband.' As afterthoughts. The pieces were not program music. When the records came out, they were gunned down by the jazz boys because they had a classical flavor and they were gunned down by the classical boys because they had a jazz flavor. Now, I'm told, they are beginning to be thought of seriously, and there is even talk they may be reissued. Ha! Anyway, I kept my head above water by writing arrangements for the big bands and by arranging songs for people like Frank Sinatra and Mildred Bailey. I was hip-deep in the pop-music world, and I *hated* it. In the mid-forties, I wrote my first and probably last song hits, and then, in the early fifties, a marvellous thing happened. John Barrows arrived in New York, and I started writing chamber music. He believed in me, and that was all I needed.

"Well, I've got to head back to the Algonquin. I told Marian McPartland I'd stop in tonight with a new piano piece, and I still have to finish it." It was a seven- or eight-block walk down Fifth Avenue to Forty-fourth Street, and at least once a block Wilder, who talked the whole way, interrupted himself to make judicious comments about the passing hairstyles and about another fond aversion—the new-style clown-sized bow ties. He walked advisedly, as if each pedestrian represented a potential fracture or contusion. "I prefer slightly seedy surroundings to work in," he said. "Then I'm forced to create a little loveliness. I've worked all over the country—in Chicago and San Francisco, at the University of Wisconsin, in a big room full of Chinese porcelain just off Brattle Street, in Cambridge, in a hotel in Brunswick, Georgia, and Abingdon, Virginia, in Key West, in a studio at the Eastman School, upstairs at the Algonquin, in my publisher's office, on Columbus Circle. I can't work in Los Angeles and I can't work in Maine. Maine is my Achilles' heel. I go there and slough off everything. I go there without guilt. I let Maine take over—the smell of the kelp, the rocks, the bay leaves, the fogs, the tides, that marvellous relationship between the land and the sea. I work in terrific spurts. I've written a four- or five-movement piece in three weeks. One year, I wrote twelve long pieces. I try and keep myself where I'm just finishing up one piece and starting another. I do this because I'm terrified of the dry spells I occasionally have. I had one six months ago in Rochester in the little hotel I stay in there, and it was a beaut. When it used to happen, I'd go out and drink, but now I read. In Rochester, I even went to the library and took out a thesis analyzing my music. I read it to try and find out how I write, but it didn't do any good. I couldn't even understand what the writer was talking about. I'll be going back to Rochester in June, though, because the University of Rochester is giving me an honorary degree." Wilder's initial, horrified reaction to the news of the honorary degree was that he would tell the university he could not possibly accept, because he would be on an essential business trip in Liechtenstein at the time. He finally accepted, but immediately afterward gave the citation to a friend for safekeeping. "I work almost wholly intuitively. I have a few little technical things I use, but I believe that technique is a composer's secret; any composer who talks about technique is simply offering a substitute for content. I have an innate sense of order, balance, and shape. I know most of the rules of counterpoint, although I never studied theory. When I start a piece, I try and find a melodic idea that I consider seminal, that I think will hold up. Then I find secondary themes as I move along. I work at the piano more often than not. I will play the parts I've written very slowly, and I'll work as hard on eight sixteenth notes, trying to get that right balance and flow and feeling, as I will on an entire piece. It's a process of searching and searching. Once in a while, I'll finish a passage where I *know* something is wrong. So I'll look and look until I've found the trouble and made it *right*. There was a time, years ago, when I'd get clever and simply skirt the trouble by throwing up a persiflage of counter-notes or a fancy rhythmic turn, but it never worked. The performer would spot it the second or third time through, and I'd get scolded. I still have technical gaps. A while back, I had to ask John Barrows what a passacaglia is. It turned out I had used one in a piece I'd done for him and didn't know it. Then he told me that as a child his mother had played a certain Bach piece for him, and that it shocked him. He didn't understand it. Twenty years later, his musical training finished, he went back to the piece and found that all his schooling didn't make the piece any easier for him, even though he now understood the complex musical and intellectual games Bach was playing in it. I love the act of composing, but when I finish a piece that's it. I don't really care if it's performed; I can't stand listening to many of my pieces more than once. I put the piece out of my mind. If I'm told it's not good, I'm not shattered because I'm already free of it. If I'm told it *is* good, I don't pay any attention. Self-adulation would just get in my way. So it's a clearing-house process in which I make continual room for new things. If I was protective of my work, storing it all up in my head, I'd probably stop writing. I'd be too busy contemplating my navel. Players tend to like what I write; composers don't. Composers think of performers as necessary evils, and it's the same with playwrights and actors. But I consider the written music only a guide. The notes sug-*gest*, they tell only part of the story. I'll take half the credit, and all the rest goes to the performer. Performers! Those great, beautiful people are my saviors.

"People have often compared composing and improvising, saying that composition is improvisation in slow motion and that improvisation is instant composition. Well! Composing is a slow, arduous, obvious, inch-by-inch process, whereas improvisation is a lightning mystery. In fact, it's *the* creative mystery of our age, and I wonder how many people know that. I wish to God that some neurologists would sit down and figure out *how* the improvisor's brain works, *how* he selects, out of hundreds of thousands of possibilities, the notes he does and at the speed he does—*how*, in God's name, his mind works so damned fast! And why, when the notes come out right, they *are* right. Maybe we'll just have to go on thinking of it on the folk level as a series of secrets paraded in public. Musicians *talk* to one another when they improvise, and they say things they wouldn't *dare* say in words. It's all a terrific act of confession."

Wilder turned in to the Algonquin, and it was as if the squire were returning to his country house at the end of the London season. Smiling and bowing his head, he called the doorman and the bellmen by name, greeted the people behind the desk, and, after saying hello to a waiter and inquiring about his cold, selected a table in a far corner of the nearly empty lobby. He ordered a cup of coffee. "This place is the nearest thing I have to a home," he said, leaning back in his chair and surveying his domain. "I've been coming here since I was a child, and there are still people on the staff who have been here almost as long as I have. They take care of me. They send out my laundry without my having to fill out a laundry slip, they hang a few suits for me when I'm away, they forward my mail, and they shepherded me through my drinking days. I sat here once with someone I couldn't abide—I think he had something to do with my family—and I had sixteen Martinis. He was a big drinker, and I thought I'd show him and be an even bigger one. I got in a cab to go uptown to a restaurant, and when I got there I simply couldn't *move*. I told the driver to take me back to the Algonquin, and whoever was on the door sized up the situation immediately. A bellman appeared, and he and the doorman made one of those fourhanded seats, got me onto it, and whisked me up to my room. But the important thing is I can be packed and out of my room in twenty minutes. *That* is the breath of life for me, and I guess it's one of the reasons I never got married. My sort of life completely denies the female nest-building instinct. Another reason is my terrific sense of responsibility. If I *had* gotten married—and the wedding bells *were* about to ring for me several times—I would have had a fireman, a policeman, and a doctor living in at all times. I would have worried endlessly about the house burning down, about the babies being mongoloid, about the furniture getting scratched, about the wife getting a cold. And another reason is that I don't think most women can stand music. It's too amorphous."

Wilder took a sip of coffee and looked a little apprehensive. It was four-thirty, and the lobby was beginning to fill up. "Years ago, I'd check out when I had a little money and get on a train, and I'd stay on trains for weeks at a time. I'd travel the main trunks, and I'd transfer and take all the spur lines. I loved sitting in a junction in the back of the beyond on a hot day and reading a long novel and listening to the chatter between the baggage man and the conductor. I loved talking with the engineer when he oiled his engine." Wilder barked and slapped his brow. "Can you imagine nattering with a man refuelling a jet? I remember coming down from Crawford Notch, in New Hampshire, and the train making meal stops. There would be a big M on the timetable, and everybody would get off and eat—either a full meal in the station restaurant, which was very good, or homemade sandwiches sold by a local lady. So my life has been divided between travel and music and my friends and solitude. Occasionally I just lock my door and stay alone, and that way I can refill my cup. Then, when I open the door and take off again, I have something to pass along. I hate to see people I love unless I have enough to give them."

●

Alec Wilder's dying on Christmas Eve of 1980 would have given him rueful amusement, for he did not celebrate Christmas—or his birthday (he would have been seventy-four in February) or any day except the day the skunk cabbage first came up in the spring. This was not because he had Scrooge tendencies. He simply considered such events artificial. In the same way, he abhorred cant, snobbery, fakery, egocentricity, fawning, pomp, social climbing, cleverness, and fashion. Nor could he abide bad taste, selfishness, unkindness, greed, rudeness, jealousy, or vanity— although, like any sound practicing moralist, he was guilty of them all at one time or another. He found the twentieth century in general cheap and trivial and mindless. He yearned for some sort of Kilvertian life, in which he could parcel out his time into composing his music, riding on steam trains, building gardens, writing letters, making up and solving word puzzles (at which he was expert), reading (Eudora Welty, E. F. Benson, Sylvia Townsend Warner, Peter De Vries), and endlessly talking and laughing. His longing for a pastoral nineteenth-century existence was so strong that most of what he accomplished was nineteenth-century in nature. And yet, for a man so impatient with his own times, he gave those times a great deal. He wrote hundreds of popular songs, the best of them ("The Sounds Around the House," "Blackberry Winter," "Who Can I Turn To?") gentle, graceful melodies, close to art songs in their elegance and subtlety, and matching the best of Jerome Kern and George Gershwin and Harold Arlen, who was his god. He was the first composer to attempt to break down the barrier between jazz and formal music, by writing a series of octets for oboe, clarinet, bass clarinet, bassoon, flute, harpsichord, bass, and drums, which are a larking mixture of jazz rhythms and timbres and formal forms and instrumentation. During his last twenty-five years or so, he was a prolific composer of chamber music—beautiful, unfashionable, highly melodic chamber music, which reveals his love of Bach and Ravel and Debussy, and which was coveted by such great performers as Harvey

Phillips and John Barrows and Bernard Garfield. He wrote for every instrument in the orchestra, and in surprising combinations. When he was blocked and could not compose (about every second year), he wrote prose, some of it Shavian, some of it Dickensian. He wrote thousands of letters, he wrote short stories, he wrote a still unpublished but reportedly hilarious backstairs history of the Algonquin Hotel, and he wrote a masterwork, *American Popular Song: The Great Innovators*. In it he set down acute, witty judgments of nearly a thousand of the worthiest songs published in the first half of the century. If originality is the filling of an empty space, what *American Popular Song* did was entirely original.

He gave away almost everything that came into his hands—books (bought in great numbers at Scribners bookstore), recordings, awards, gifts, photographs of himself, pens and pencils, and even his music, much of which he wrote for friends and protégés. Commercialism revolted him, and he never made much money. Yet he managed to live a reasonably comfortable nomadic life, at the Algonquin; at the One Eleven East Avenue Hotel in Rochester, the city where he was born; in Key West; and in the homes of friends. He once described this way of life in a letter:

> Though I don't feel the least bit freakish, I suppose that to even the most understanding, tolerant people . . . I must seem distinctly odd. I keep forgetting that I do very few of the things which constitute conventional living. I don't go to the theatre, movies, concerts, parties. I don't look at television or listen to radio. I have no property or stocks or insurance. I have no family but a niece and nephew I never see and a brother to whom I am as close as to a mild-mannered short-order cook. I see no friends constantly, only when I'm in their city. . . . I have no memorabilia, clippings, reviews, photographs, records, printed or manuscript music. I keep only the letters of one man. I refuse to contemplate the past or the future. I have no plans, no ambitions or infatuations. . . . I assume that the worst is likely to occur at any moment and therefore celebrate not so much feeling well as not feeling sick. . . . Since I have reduced my needs and interests to a minimum, there will be that much less to die.

He wrote letters by the dozen when he was blocked, and they were bits and pieces of himself. Whether they were philosophical or funny or hyperbolic or lyrical, they were always *Alec*. They seemed written in bas-relief. You could hear his trombone voice in them, his shouting laugh, his "No! I don't believe it!" when he was told something that tickled him. (He was an excessively shy man who camouflaged his disability with a lot of noise.) You could see him—the long, warm, tired, handsome face, the flying hair, the glittering eyes, the heedless uniform of sports jacket, gray flannels, and brown loafers. The concentration in his letters reminded you of his selfless concentration when he listened to other people's music, which he did with his eyes clamped shut, his mouth downturned, his chin held in the fork of a thumb and forefinger. He once wrote of the guitarist Jim Hall, "There is to me a strange difference [between Jim Hall and other jazz musicians]. It is as if he were so marvelously disciplined as to be able to choose his notes from a long accumulated and even hoarded *wisdom*—that kind of wisdom that is reached by having intelligently absorbed from his whole life experience. . . . His choices [of notes] seem to be transmuted from memories of joy, misery, mistakes, realizations, humilities, and wonderments."

Alec Wilder rightly considered a sense of humor the ability to poke fun at yourself, and he did that constantly, in the flesh and in his letters. He loved to tell the story of the stranger who approached him in the Algonquin lobby and praised him with such reverence that it made him feel weak-kneed and ridiculous. Immediately afterward, when he was climbing into a cab to go to the airport, he asked the bellman helping him what he was laughing at, and got this reply: "He thought you were Thornton."

Here is a typical self-snicker from a letter:

> In my fathomless (less in depth than incomprehensibility) brain, I can summon up rose trellises, tow-headed children, rocking chairs, and raffish-eyed birds which shout "Good morning!" And in that multi-circuited mess there is the shape of a slate which I wiggle designs on and wipe clean whenever new space is needed.

He had a talent for aphorism:

> I am not well-informed, but I know too much.

He could be unashamedly poetic—a Robert Louis Stevenson who really dug children, because he was, in many ways, still a child himself:

> The slice of sky I once cut out and gave to a three-year-old who carried it off to a hiding place . . .

From time to time, nostalgia seized him, the unflappable realist:

> I suppose as the years increase, one requires more and more sideshows, sleight-of-hand moments, meaningless but cheery interruptions, nonsense phone calls, expectations such as being invited to . . . visit in Sylvia Townsend Warner's English village home.
>
> Oh, how splendid it would be to look up and see a joyous group of faces, the kind one constantly saw in the twenties, foolish, innocent . . . girls' faces that were more like fiction than fact.

As Alec Wilder himself was.

Let It
Be Classy

Alberta Hunter

The singer Alberta Hunter was waiting in a studio to rehearse with her accompanist, Jimmy Rowles. A contemporary of Bessie Smith and Ethel Waters, and an immediate descendant of Ma Rainey and Sophie Tucker, she was about to resume a career she forsook for practical nursing after her mother's death in the mid-fifties. She had the time to sing again because she had recently been retired by the Goldwater Memorial Hospital, on Roosevelt Island, where she had worked for twenty years. But her return was largely accidental, and she explained it this way: "A while ago, Bobby Short had a party at his house for Mabel Mercer, before she went to sing in England, and he invited me—Lord, I've known Mabel nearly fifty years. Mr. Charles Bourgeois was there, and I saw him sizing me up, and pretty soon he asked me to sing something, which I did, real soft. He told me, 'You should be out working again, with that voice and all your experience,' and right away the next morning Mr. Barney Josephson of The Cookery called and asked was I interested in singing for him, and I was so nervous I dropped the phone. I never appeared at the Café Societys, but I always knew his reputation. I went down there a few days later and sang, and he said, 'I want you to go to work for me right away.'"

Head-on, Alberta Hunter is egg-shaped, and sideways she is Egyptian. Her face is lean and tight and handsome, and her gray-black hair is swept back into finger-size braids. Her brown eyes are clear, and she talks in a staccato, nearstuttering fashion, often tapping a listener's hand for emphasis with a sharp, woodpecker finger. She was wearing a fitted dark-khaki dress with military pockets, and she declared that she loves to dress casually. Chris Albertson, the author of a biography of Bessie Smith, arrived, and was followed by Rowles. Rowles came up to Alberta Hunter, and she smiled and asked him how he was. Sleepy and emery-voiced, he said, "Fine, baby doll."

"I was just saying how I hate to dress up, how I love to be casual. When I was entertaining, I spent a lot of money on clothes, but after my mother passed I gave them away, all those pretty gowns and slippers. I could die, because they're back in fashion. But how was I to know I'd start singing again and need them? I'll just get myself a smart cocktail dress, and I'll be all right."

Rowles riffled through a pile of sheet music, and Alberta Hunter said, "I'm going to sing songs in six languages—Italian, French, Danish, Yiddish, and German. And English. I've got the music here for the Yiddish song and the French song, but I want to start today with a blues—my 'Downhearted Blues.' I want to make it a *real* slow blues so there's plenty of time to get the story out."

"I used to work for an arranger on the Coast named Marty Paich," Rowles said, "and he'd always tell me he wanted me to play real 'fonky.'"

Alberta Hunter picked up her music and put it on the piano. She stood in the crook, next to a microphone. Rowles applied some Tacky-Finger, a non-slipping ointment, and Alberta Hunter folded her hands in front of her, raised her head, and scanned the room as if she were about to address a packed house. "Ladies and gentlemen," she said in an even contralto, "I'm going to sing a song I wrote in 1922, when most of you children weren't born. I recorded it on the Paramount label, and Bessie Smith used it for her very first Columbia recording, which sold a million copies. It's called 'Downhearted Blues.'"

Jimmy Rowles played a four-bar introduction, and Alberta Hunter began the famous lyrics: "Got the world in a jug, stopper right here in my hand. Got the world in a jug, stopper right here in my hand. The next man I get, he's got to come under my command." Her voice was steady and rich, and her vibrato betrayed none of the quaveriness that often besets older singers. Her phrasing was legato, and once in a while she used a high, almost falsetto cluster of notes which recalled Ethel Waters. There is a burnished, accreted assurance and depth and color in Alberta Hunter's singing. At first, she stood nearly motionless. She moved one knee on the beat, and occasionally she raised her right arm and smoothed the air with her hand. Then she went into a fast "When You're Smiling." She began rocking from side to side, and slapped one thigh on the after-beat. She bounced up and down, her slightly bowed legs moving like springs, her long arms walking at her sides. A slow "He's Funny That Way" was next, and was followed by another blues, "Handy Man" which starts, "That man of mine has a scheme. That man of mine has a scheme.

It's amazing the way he handles my machine." Rowles was brilliant. He paralleled her melodic lines, echoed them, cushioned them. He gave her rhythmic nudges when her time faltered, and he played rich and dense chords behind her. But he used this complexity sparingly, and it set off the purity and simpleness of her voice—a jungle framing a smooth clearing. Rowles suggested a break after a swinging "My Blue Heaven," and they sat down. He asked Alberta Hunter when she first came to New York.

"Why, it was in 1923," she answered, hooking a cardigan sweater around her shoulders. "I had got to thinking that I should look for higher ground, that I'd gone as far as I could in Chicago. So I left there on a Saturday, and by the following Wednesday I'd replaced Bessie Smith in New York in a show called *How Come?* I'd never been on a stage, but I was young and I just walked out there and had no fear. After, I wasn't sure whether or not I had cut a hog—messed up—but I knew I was all right when that audience yelled and stomped and Sophie Tucker and all them who were out there gave me a standing ovation. I was in *How Come?* about a year, and then went into a show called *Change Your Luck,* at the George M. Cohan. I went back to Chicago for a while and worked at the Royal Garden and the Phoenix and the Sunset Café with Earl Hines. I also worked in Cincinnati, at Michaelson's, and I met a waiter there named Willard Saxbe Townsend. He was handsome. He had beautiful eyes. He'd been in the Army, and I don't think he owned anything but that uniform. I married Willard and we went back to Chicago. I had a little apartment and my mother was staying with me. I was too embarrassed to sleep with my husband with my mother there, so I slept with my mother. Willard wanted to be a waiter where I was working, but I didn't want any part of that, so I took a vacation and went to Monte Carlo, where I found a job in the Knickerbocker Café. I never got back with Willard, and eventually it made a man of him. He got a degree, and when he died he was head of the redcaps' union in Chicago and the only Negro on the executive board of the C.I.O. I've never given getting married again a thought. I stayed abroad four years, and there wasn't any place I didn't go. Noble Sissle helped me get into England, and I lived in London in the same house as Marian Anderson, at 17 Regent's Park Road. She was there getting her middle register straightened out with Miss Amanda Aldridge. Marian was always a mama's girl, but she was completely unspoiled—and talk about a lady! We always got along, and she used to say God made me and threw the pattern away. But she didn't have any soul then, and we used to say things purposely to hurt her so that she'd feel things and get some soul, and she did. I auditioned for the English company of *Show Boat,* and got the part over a white woman named Maisie Ayling. I played Queenie. Edith Day was the star and Sir Cedric Hardwicke was

Cap'n Andy and Paul Robeson was Joe. My old friend Mabel Mercer was
in the chorus. Paul was unassuming, like people used to be to each other
in the South. When he sang 'Ol' Man River,' his voice was like a bell in
the distance, and people would scream. The night King George and
Queen Mary came to see us, Paul got off pitch, and he never got himself
back on, and afterward he cried like a child. I stayed with *Show Boat*
eleven months, and then I went to the Grande Carte in Paris. I learned
French at Berlitz and got a part in a show called *Vive Paris!* There was a
scene with a huge birdcage filled with women dressed like birds, and I
sang 'Les Oiseaux.' Then I went on the road—to the Natural Scholar in
Copenhagen, the Excelsior in Alexandria, the Continental in Cairo, and
the Femina in Athens. I worked Les Jardins des Petits Champs in Istanbul
and the place in Vienna where Hitler used to drink beer. I came back to
England in 1935, and I used to sing 'Time on My Hands' for the Prince
of Wales at the Dorchester. I also did some broadcasts from London to
New York, and when I came home I was on WEAF and WJZ and on the
'Lower Basin Street' show, before Dinah Shore took over. I was in a lot
of vaudeville in the thirties, with people like Seymour and Jeanette, and
Ada Brown, who was like a chubby baby. I worked at the Hot Feet Club
down here, and in 1939 I took part in *Mamba's Daughters* at the Empire,
at Fortieth and Broadway. It was Ethel Waters' show, and since she's gone
and can't speak for herself I shouldn't say a word, but she sure gave me
a hard time. I guess I outsang her, because she put everything but the
kitchen stove on me. But I forgave her a long time ago, and a year before
she died she sent me a message: 'Tell old Flossie'—which is what she
called me—'hello and take care of herself.' I joined the U.S.O. in 1944,
and was with them off and on until the day my mother died. I took the
first Negro unit overseas during the war, and when Marshal Zhukov gave
General Eisenhower a medal Eisenhower sent for me to come and sing. I
worked the E.T.O. and the South Pacific and the C.B.I. and Korea. The
last club I was in in New York was the Bon Soir, when I was studying
nursing."

Alberta Hunter stood up and smoothed her dress. "Come on, Jimmy. It's
time to work again." Rowles applied more Tacky-Finger and sat at the
piano, and they went into a rousing "Sunny Side of the Street." Alberta
Hunter's springs went up and down, her arms walked, and every eight
bars or so she snapped her head. Another Hunter blues, "Working Man,"
followed "My man is old and very thin. But there is plenty of good tunes
left in an old violin." A slow "Pennies from Heaven" came next, then an
even slower "A Hundred Years from Today," and she finished the
rehearsal with a rocking "A Good Man Is Hard To Find." Rowles jumped
up and shook her head and laughed.

"We got to pick some of those tempos up, Jimmy," she said. "They drag."

"You pick'em up, I'll be right there."

"An old lady shouldn't drag her tempos," she said.

"Old lady!" Rowles shouted. "You know what you are, Alberta? You're a *sprinter!*"

She laughed and slapped him on the chest, and Rowles put on his jacket and told her he'd call her in a day or two. Chris Albertson joined her, and she looked at him. "Do you know when I started singing? I started singing when I was about twelve years old. But I had to be born first, and that was in Memphis, around 1895. I had two sisters. One was older and called La Tosca, and one was younger and a half sister, and her name was Josephine Beatty. I used her name when I recorded in 1924 with Louis Armstrong for Gennett, because I was still under contract to Paramount—Josephine Beatty, accompanied by the Red Onion Jazz Babies. My mother was born in Knoxville. She was tall and slender and very strict, but she did everything she could for her girls. She used to carry me around on a pillow when I was little, because I was so sickly. She was a very tidy person, and she scrubbed the paint off when she cleaned. 'Get away from me, you're filthy dirty,' she'd say to me when I came in off the street. Which is where I got my nickname—Pig. My mother worked as a chambermaid for Miss Myrtle and Miss Emma in a sporting house on Gayoso Street. My father, Charles Hunter, was a Pullman porter, but he died before I ever knew him. We girls stayed most of the time with my grandmother Nancy Peterson, who also looked after all my cousins. She was a dainty little lady, who wore a shirtwaist with a velvet front. Her rent was five dollars a month, and when they threatened to raise it a quar ter she said she would move, and they backed down. She used to tell me over and over, 'Keep busy, be a lady, keep your clothes clean even if they're raggedy, stay away from whiskey, and never put a cigarette in your mouth. And do your work the best you can.'

"I went to Chicago when I was eleven, thereabouts. My mother had sent me to the store with a dime and a nickel to buy bread. I ran into my teacher, Miss Florida Cummings, and she said she was going to Chicago, had a pass for the train, and would I like to go, just like that. Well, I used to sing in little school concerts, and my music teacher had told me I could sing. I had heard you could make ten dollars a week in Chicago singing, and I had been building that up in me. So I thought I better go to Chicago and get some of that ten. I told her wait and I'll ask my mother. I ran and hid a little and came back and said yes. I knew my mother would think I was over at my friend Irma's house when she missed me, because I stayed there a lot. In Chicago, I knew enough to find the daughter of a friend of my mother's named Helen Winston. She was so surprised when she saw me. 'Sit down, Pig,' she said. 'What in the world are you doing here? You hungry? Miss Florida should have known better than to bring you up here like this'—and on and on like that. When she quieted down, she took me out to Hyde Park, where she worked, and got me a job as second cook for six dollars a week, room and board. She took the braids out of my hair and put me in dresses to make me look older. Right away, I sent my mother two dollars so she'd know where I was. I hadn't been there very long when I started sneaking out to a place called Dago Frank's, at Archer and State. It was a sporting bar, and when I tried to sing they told me to get out. But they finally gave me a chance, and I worked there a year and ten months. The hours were eight to twelve, for five dollars a week. I learned songs from the piano player like 'Melancholy,' which became known as 'Melancholy Baby,' and I also sang 'All Night Long' and 'Where the River Shannon Flows.' The next place I sang was Hugh Hoskins'. The dangerous element, like Give-a-Damn Jones, hung out there, but so did the pickpocket women, and they did everything in their power to show me how to live a clean life. Tack Annie was considered the cleverest pickpocket anywhere. She was a master. She had some sort of hook concealed in a front tooth, and by leaning over near a gentleman she could pull a diamond stickpin right out of his tie. But she was an ugly girl. Fact, she looked like a mule with a summer hat on. When I wrote 'Reap What You Sow,' I was thinking of some of those rough types.

"Hugh Hoskins' was a small place, which was enlarged because so many people came to hear me sing the blues. Then I was offered twelve dollars a week at the Panama Café, at Thirty-sixth and State. It was owned by Izzy Levine and Mr. Shaw. It was a long place, and there was an upstairs and a downstairs. There were five girls upstairs with a piano player and five girls downstairs with a piano player. Nettie Compton, Bricktop, Florence Mills, Cora Green, and Mattie Hite were downstairs, and Glover Compton, who was marvellous, was their piano player. Each one did her own thing, and the downstairs was swank, dicty. Upstairs, we had Nellie Carr, Goldie Crosby, Twinkle Davis, Mamie Carter, and me, and George Hall was the piano player. Nellie Carr did the splits, and Mamie Carter had a cute little dance. Twinkle Davis had legs like Marlene Dietrich, and Goldie Crosby had her jazzy little way. And I sang the blues. The people would pass on by Bricktop and them to come up and hear us. I worked next door at the De Luxe Café, too. Freddie Keppard played trumpet there. He was something—a big fellow. He had an old derby, and he put it over the bell of that trumpet and he'd make the hair stand up on your head. He could play loud and he could play so soft you couldn't barely hear him. Then I went across the street to the Dreamland Café, which was owned by Bill Bottoms, who later became Joe Louis's dietitian. He paid me seventeen dollars and fifty cents a week. Joe Oliver had just come up from New Orleans—this was around the First World War—and he had Sidney Bechet and Lil Hardin and Minor Hall. Oliver was big and dark, and I don't think he had any sight in his left eye. Leastwise, he sometimes wore a patch over it. But he was a lovely fellow. Later, after he brought Louis Armstrong up from New Orleans, I recall them playing 'Jerusalem' in harmony with their mutes and without any rhythm section—just the two of them floating along—and it was unbelievable. I think a little chill grew up between them when Louis began to be recognized. The Dreamland was a big square place, and the musicians played on a balcony. I'd sing down on the dance floor, and when I'd finish a song I'd throw up my hands so the musicians would know. All I'd have to do was hum a new song for them to get it. The dance floor was large, and the center was made of glass and had a light under it. There was no segregation, and every sort of person came in—the pickpockets and society Negroes and politicans and gamblers. The gamblers were kings, and they were allowed to raise a fog, which is letting people go as far as they like. Al Jolson came to hear me do 'St. Louis Blues' and 'Mammy's Little Coal Black Rose.' Sophie Tucker came to hear me do 'Someday Sweetheart' and 'A Good Man Is Hard to Find.' Later, she'd send her maid Belle for me to come to her dressing room and teach her the songs, but I never would go, so her piano player would come over and listen and get everything down. But I was crazy about her as a singer, and she influenced me. I was at the Dreamland about five years, and while I was there I started recording for Paramount, through Mr. Ink Williams. Fletcher Henderson accompanied me, and so did Eubie Blake and Armstrong and the Original Memphis Five, with Phil Napoleon and Miff Mole. I remember the thick brown wax discs they recorded on and the wax shavings falling on the floor as I sang. The Memphis Five was white, and they could *go!* I was the first black singer to record with a white band. I recorded my 'Downhearted Blues' about a year before Bessie. I never so much as said good morning to her, but I heard her sing. That voice carried from here to downtown. She was crude, raucous, and her clothes were a little clowny, a little extravagant. She just stood there, and when she started 'Nobody Knows You When You're Down and Out' you could feel her big heart going. When Bessie opened her mouth, it was the end of a perfect day. Of course, Florence Mills became just as big a star as Bessie, but she was the opposite. She was a hummingbird, and dainty and lovely. Her little voice was as sweet as Bessie's was rough, and it was like a cello."

Alberta Hunter buttoned her sweater and looked around. Her expression was serene and bemused. "I better think about getting along, go home and finish the song I'm working on. It's a blues, which means to me what milk does to a baby. Blues is what the spirit is to a minister. We sing the blues because our hearts have been hurt, our souls have been disturbed. But when you sing the blues, let it be classy. Singing a ballad, the meaning of the words runs in my mind all the time. In 'Sunny Side of the Street,' I *see* that sunshine and I'm really as rich as Rockefeller. I'm always trying to tell a story, and I want my words to be understood. I've been writing blues and songs all my life. A new song will often come to me at three or four in the morning. I'll hold it in my head and later that day dash downtown and get somebody to set it down on paper, because I don't know a note of music. Eddy Arnold sang my 'I Want to Thank You, Lord.' Dinah Washington did 'What's the Matter, Baby?' and Ella Fitzgerald did 'Downhearted Blues' and so did Mildren Bailey, who made a crackerjack record of it. My new song is called 'I Want a Two-Fisted, Double-Jointed Rough-and-Ready Man.'" She sang, "I want a man who won't let his children play with neither dog nor cat but will bring in a skunk or a lion and say, 'Here, kids, play with that.' I just got the melody to it this morning."

Scoop

Cleo Brown

Since the mid-seventies, the pianist Marian McPartland has been master of ceremonies of a National Public Radio show called "Marian McPartland's Piano Jazz." One of her most successful programs involved the long-lost pianist, singer, and composer Cleo Brown. Cleo Brown came up in the mid-thirties through the new power of radio (a weekly show that emanated from Chicago and New York) and the attractiveness of a couple of dozen Decca recordings, on which she was backed by the likes of Bobby Sherwood on guitar, Artie Bernstein on bass, and Gene Krupa on drums. She was possibly the first female pianist to work by herself in jazz (Lovie Austin, Lil Armstrong, and Mary Lou Williams were band pianists), and she sang double-entendre songs, novelty songs, love songs, and jump songs in a high, small, precise, suggestive voice that recalled Ethel Waters. Equally important, she was a choice pianist, who accompanied herself with a loose Earl Hines right hand and an aggressive, unerring left hand. (She recorded a knockout version of "Pinetop's Boogie Woogie" several years before the boogie-woogie craze.) Until Art Tatum began to take hold in the late thirties, she had the most powerful and exact left hand of any jazz pianist. She also cleared the way for such singer-pianists as Nellie Lutcher, Rose Murphy, Gladys Palmer, Julia Lee, Una Mae Carlisle, Hazel Scott, Dardanelle, Blossom Dearie, and Shirley Horn. But Cleo Brown retired from music in the early fifties, and not long after that she vanished. She is last mentioned in Leonard Feather's *Encyclopedia of Jazz* in 1960, as living in semi-obscurity on the West Coast. (She was actually in Colorado.) John Chilton's "Who's Who of Jazz" lists her as "deceased," and Roger Kinkle's *The Complete Encyclopedia of Popular Music and Jazz*, published in 1974, omits her. Here is how Marian McPartland describes finding Cleo Brown:

"When I read a couple of years ago in my friend Mary Unterbrink's book *Jazz Women at the Keyboard* that Cleo Brown was living in Denver, I got very excited. I had been looking for her for years, and some of the reference books even said she was dead. I had first heard her on records in England in the thirties and been terribly impressed by her singing and her time and her great swing. Since then, I've discovered that people like Dave Brubeck and Teddy Wilson have shared my feelings. I went through a lot of waste motion trying to call and write her in Denver, and I began to think, It's too late, she *is* dead. Then Theresa Mullen, a neighbor of mine from Merrick, Long Island, moved to Denver, and I asked her if she would search for Cleo. Well, after a lot of running around she finally found her in a black church in Denver. The weird thing is that a letter of mine reached Cleo the day Theresa found her. Theresa asked her to call me collect, and I invited her on the show, and she said yes, but that she wouldn't play boogie-woogie or anything like that, because she had joined the church, and boogie-woogie was the Devil's music. She had even changed her name. She had dropped the Cleo, and become C. Patra Brown. I told her she could play what she wanted. After all, gospel pianists can swing like crazy and still be religious. For insurance, I sat down and learned 'Just a Closer Walk with Thee' and Duke Ellington's 'Come Sunday.'"

Cleo Brown and her son, LaVern Paris, flew in from Denver on a Sunday night. The show was to be taped on Monday afternoon in RCA's Studio A, at Sixth Avenue and Forty-fourth Street. A little after noon, Marian McPartland met Cleo Brown and LaVern Paris at their hotel, in midtown, and discussed materials. Before they went to the studio, Cleo Brown had them all hold hands, and she said a prayer. She was both delighted and awed at being in New York again. The studio, the size of a basketball court, was empty except for a couple of microphones and a pair of grand pianos, stationed side by side near the control booth. The two women sat down at their pianos. Marian McPartland, in a sweater and skirt, looked svelte and delicate, and Cleo Brown, in a dark-blue print dress and a knitted hat, looked round and powerful. She has high cheekbones, a small nose, prominent eyes, and a small, bright smile. Her legs are short and thin, and her fingers are surprisingly long. Marian McPartland told Cleo Brown how pleased she was to have found her, and Cleo Brown thanked the Lord that she had. The taping began. The pianists repeated much of what they had just said, and went into the old novelty song "Lookie, Lookie, Here Comes Cookie." Cleo Brown had recorded it in March of

1935 with Perry Botkin on guitar, Artie Bernstein, and Gene Krupa, and it was one of her first hits. The two women played it as a duet, and at first there was a lot of backing and filling—Cleo Brown resisting an almost automatic impulse to swing, and Marian McPartland searching for Cleo Brown's new self-limitations. Things coalesced in the second chorus. Cleo Brown moved briefly to the fore, using Earl Hines right-hand chords and a clear stride bass. Marian McPartland asked Cleo Brown about her left hand, and she said, "Your hands kind of walk with what the ear hears." She talked about her conversion to the church, in the early fifties, saying that she began "waxing away" from jazz piano playing in 1950. Then she did two of her own songs by herself—"Fat Girl Being Blue" and "Living in the Afterglow"—and they were slow and measured and full of tremolos. She sang on both numbers, and her voice was as lightsome as it had been fifty years ago. Bobby Short, who had heard that Cleo Brown was in town, came into the control booth and sat down to listen. The pianists fashioned a laundered version of Cleo Brown's "Pinetop's Boogie Woogie," her biggest hit. Marian McPartland supplied the walking bass and Cleo Brown sang. One stanza went:

> I'm so glad that Jesus loves you,
> I'm so glad that Jesus loves you,
> I'm so glad that Jesus loves you,
> And, what do you know,
> He loves me, too.

Cleo Brown rested and Marian McPartland did an intense "Come Sunday." Cleo Brown was entranced, and said, "Praise the Lord! It's beautiful." She moved into her own "This Is My Day," and Bobby Short, his head nodding slowly, looked amazed. Marian McPartland told Cleo Brown that it was wonderful, and that she should send a tape of it to Ray Charles. Cleo Brown said, "You either play it to the glory of a bumpety-bump or you play it to the glory of the Man Upstairs."

Short, who had not seen Cleo Brown since 1949, when she was working in Los Angeles, walked into the studio, and she shouted, "Bobby! Bobby Short! My goodness! The last time I saw you you was a little old boy!" They talked, and she laughed and told him that she had just turned seventy-seven and that he should "stop working so hard in the wrong places."

Short hugged her and went back into the control room and said he was astonished that she had recognized him so quickly. "Cleo Brown was a great star for all of us when we were growing up," he said. "We got all the radio broadcasts from Chicago down in Danville, and she had a weekly sustaining show. We were attracted to her sweet, sexy voice and her brilliant left hand—and to her time, which was fantastic. Her theme song, 'The Stuff Is Here and It's Mellow,' was so popular that a minister in Danville preached a sermon with the same title. Cleo's stuff, of course, was marijuana, but the minister made it the word of God. I tried to meet Cleo Brown when I was a kid and she was at the Three Deuces in Chicago, but the night I went she was away or off. Gladys Palmer was playing, and she said to me, 'I'm so sorry Cleo isn't here. Why don't you take this photograph of her? There's no reason why you shouldn't have it. The man she gave it to is blind and can't see it anyway.' It was a photograph that Cleo had autographed 'To the greatest jazz pianist in the world,' or some such, and had given to Art Tatum, who also worked at the Deuces. Of course, I took it. I finally met her in 1942, when I was seventeen and she was at Bartel's, in Chicago. She was a bubbly person, and I played for her, and she was encouraging. I didn't see her again until the late forties, when we were both working on the Coast. She came to hear me and she played a number. We haven't met since, but she looks the same. She's just become a little old lady. I was extremely moved to hear her today. Her voice hasn't changed one bit, and neither has her playing."

Marian McPartland and Cleo Brown began a medium version of "Just a Closer Walk with Thee," and by the time they reached the second chorus Cleo Brown was swinging. Marian McPartland boosted her with off-beat chords, then took a sharp chorus full of dancing single-note melodic lines and down-to-business chords. Cleo Brown told her when it was over that she "sure got strong hands for such a delicate lady." Marian McPartland went into "You're a Heavenly Thing," and Cleo Brown joined her halfway, forgetting herself again. Marian McPartland suggested "When the Saints Go Marching In." It was played as a duet. Cleo Brown's left hand surged into view in the second chorus, and she rocked. Marian McPartland looked delighted. Cleo Brown made up for her lapse with a number of her own, "I'm So Glad Dear Jesus You Love Me." The two women closed the program by converting "Silent Night" into a kind of gospel number, letting its melody shine through only here and there, and playing passages of such contrapuntal density that forward motion almost stopped.

Cleo Brown took a cab to her hotel and found LaVern waiting in the lobby. She scolded him for taking off from the studio, and LaVern said he had wanted to have a look at the city, and, anyway, you'd never know from the way she treated him that he was a grandfather. Cleo Brown and LaVern went up to their room, and LaVern lay down on one of the beds and fell asleep. Cleo Brown sat in a chair by the window and studied the sunset—an orange gash in an otherwise gray sky. Then she talked about her life. Her hands moved constantly in her lap, as if they were shaping her words. Sometimes she closed her eyes for long stretches, and when she paused she pursed her lips.

"I was born in DeKalb, Mississippi," Cleo Brown said. "DeKalb is in Kemper County, about thirty miles north of Meridian. My parents were Dutchie and James Brown. My mother was a little country-school teacher, and she looked like me. My father was a good dad. He owned his own place, and had people to come in and farm it. He became the pastor of the Pilgrim Baptist Church in 1909, and we moved to Meridian. I was the second child, and I had four brothers—Everett, James, Leon, and Frazier. All of them are gone. My mother passed in 1939, and my dad in 1972. We went to the Meridian Baptist Seminary. When I was five, I started studying on a little manual organ. My teacher was named Ophello. I took from her until I was around seven and a half. Then I took from Nettie Pearl Reese, who was the headmistress of the Baptist Seminary and had a degree from the Boston Conservatory. I was pretty fast in music, and I did two grades in one year. I was her star pupil. In 1922, my father was called to a church in Chicago, and I studied there with Alfred Simms, of the American Conservatory. I was studying the classics, and in 1923 Mr. Simms presented me in a concert at the Antilles Club. By this time, my brother Everett was playing ragtime, and had gotten to know Pinetop Smith. I was very attracted to the music and could beat Everett playing, but my parents were dead against it. Everett was making twenty-five dollars a week, and I'd get six dollars a week playing in my father's church. When I was sixteen, I ran away and married Walter Paris, who was older than me. Walter persuaded some lady to get the license, because I was underage, and I took one of Mama's dresses. My dad got the marriage annulled, but by that time I was pregnant with LaVern. Now LaVern's a singing evangelist, and he has a lovely wife and four lovely children, and grandchildren, too. He was something when he was little. Many's the time I'd come home from work at four in the morning in a cab and find him at the curb ready to open the door for me. Later, he went on the road with me, and sometimes he'd sing and do a dance on the tabletops. I worked in the speakeasies. I ran around with Louis Armstrong and his wife, Lil, and I knew Butterbeans and Susie, the comedy team, and King Oliver, who was tall and very dark. Louis liked red beans and rice, and he was bound to keep everybody laughing. Lil was kind of fiery, but she had to be to keep Louis in line. I played in a band called the Nine Blackbirds, and we toured locally and into Canada. I was with Texas Guinan at the Chicago World's Fair, in 1933, and I worked places like the Kelshore Tea Room and the Frolic Café and the Lake Villa. I was at the Three Deuces in 1934, and I got to know Art Tatum and Teddy Wilson. Then I was brought here to take over Fats Waller's CBS radio broadcasts, because Fats had to go to Hollywood to make a movie. I did that for a year or so.

I also signed a Decca contract and made my first records. Then they started booking me to the Coast and back to St. Louis and Chicago, and it was two weeks here, two weeks there. I settled on the Coast in the late thirties, and I worked everywhere from Oakland to Palm Springs and San Diego. But I was going down, down, down. I used to keep a fifth at my bedside. I was in the hospital in the late thirties, and I was sick in the forties. I got married again in 1946, because I thought I needed a travelling companion, but I discovered he wasn't the one. Then, in 1949, I had a visitation from the Lord—what I call a chastisement. I was playing at Jim's Steak House in San Francisco, and living in Chinatown. I was in my hotel room, and this voice started telling me all the things I had done wrong. It told me to go on down to Los Angeles, and I got on a bus, and every time that bus stopped the voice started again. When I got to Los Angeles, I ran two days and two nights, until the police caught me up and put me in jail. I went to a sanitarium, and I thanked the Lord for giving me relief. The nurses had me to help them with rehabilitating people when I was better, and they told me if I landed back there they would give me E.S.T., which means electric-shock therapy. I went to work in San Francisco when I got out, and after that I worked in Sioux City and Omaha and Hollywood, then Las Vegas and Denver. That was the beginning of the end of me as a jazz piano player. I took a job as a nurse's aide in 1953, at the Colorado State Hospital, in Pueblo, and I went to nursing school, and got a license in 1959. I had been baptized into the Seventh-Day Adventists in 1953, and I never looked back. I had discovered that swinging doesn't incite decency and order, and I just pray to the Lord that playing the way I did today doesn't get me into a whole lot of trouble. I was on call as a nurse in Denver twenty-four hours a day, but I've slowed up some. I tried to learn to be a file clerk a little while ago, but people don't have much patience with my age. I live in a senior citizens' complex, and I have Social Security. I've learned that I have to live on just so much a day after rent and food, and sometimes it's like somebody's got a foot on your neck. I play at a couple of churches, and that helps. I keep going, and I thank the Lord for pulling me up and showing me the way."

Something Better
Out There

Nellie Lutcher

When jazz musicians move west, they rarely come back. Nellie Lutcher, who is in New York after a seven-year absence, was away twenty years before her last visit, in 1973. She looks the same, which is good news and means: a luxurious ski-jump nose, snapping black-brown eyes, long, graceful fingers and scimitar thumbs, a Maillol shape, and a wide, swivelling smile. Her hands evoke wild images. When they are low and flat on the keyboard, they look like long-distance swimmers. When she suddenly lifts them from the keyboard, they become fighter planes peeling off. Her head moves from lower right to upper left, from side to side, from back to front, while her torso is straight as a ladderback. Her eyes blaze and droop and smile. She likes to work with a drummer, but when she has none, she claps her hands if the beat weakens, making them explode on the afterbeat or on ricocheting offbeats. Out of this dervish hustle come her unique singing and her primitive, springing piano. Her playing is the child of Earl Hines, whom she idolized in the early thirties, when Hines was holding forth almost nightly on the radio from the Grand Terrace in Chicago. She is a strong pianist, a broadside pianist, who likes big-textured Hines chords in the right hand. She doesn't much care for arpeggios or single-note melodic lines, but she likes occasional tremolos and will slip in a glissando if she has to get from one register to another in a hurry without breaking sound. She uses everything in her left hand—stride basses, tenths, offbeat notes and chords, and boogie-woogie basses. Her playing carpets her singing. She has a robust contralto, but she almost never uses it in a straightforward way. She is a master of melisma: she will fill a single syllable with six or seven notes. She is a master of dynamics: whispers and shouts and crooning continually surprise one another. Like Joe Turner, she uses words largely to hang melody on, and what she sings is often unintelligible. She steadily garnishes her melodic flow with squeaks, falsetto, mock-operatic arias, yodels, and patches of talking. Yet her singing, like Turner's and like Jack Teagarden's, is easy and seamless.

She is an encyclopedia of the black music of fifty years ago. She grew up in the Southern Baptist church, and her singing, with its overlay of vocal effects, is full of gospel music. She was exposed to blues singers like Ida Cox and Ma Rainey and to the last of the minstrel shows on the T.O.B.A. circuit, and she heard local vaudeville on the radio. She also heard the likes of Hines and Andy Kirk on the radio, and she heard the territory bands that roamed the South. She listened to recordings, and somewhere she fell under the sway of a highly specialized group of musicians who were a compound of jazz and comedy, of improvisation and clowning. They were generally pianists, guitarists, or bassists who sang novelty songs and sometimes used a variety of comic devices—Bronx cheers, growls, sighs, basso profundo, falsetto, roars. They sang scat style, and they made up their own languages and sang them. They were expert, swinging musicians who had discovered early in their careers that their comic gifts outpaced their improvisational skills. Joe Venuti and Fats Waller probably got this cheerful movement started, and they were followed by the Spirits of Rhythm, which included the Daniels brothers on tipple, the mad scat singer Leo Watson, and the guitarist Teddy Bunn; Slim and Slam, who were Slim Gaillard and Slam Stewart; the Three Peppers, led by Toy Wilson on piano and vocals; the pianist and singer Harry the Hipster Gibson, who wore gloves when he played; Louis Jordan and his jumping Timpany Five; Cleo Brown; the pianist Dorothy Donegan, gifted with an exceptional technique and a serpentine body; the pianists Loumell Morgan and Maurice Rocco, who stood while playing; and Rose Murphy, who is sometimes confused with Nellie Lutcher. (Rose Murphy's playing is similar, but she sings in a high, tiny Betty Boop voice decorated with buzzes and trills and bird sounds.) These musicians performed for the delectation of black people, and occasionally what they did was two-edged: it made blacks laugh not only at themselves but at the Cap'n, too.

Nellie Lutcher lives in Los Angeles, and this is what an old friend and neighbor had to say about her the other day: "Nellie owns a fine small apartment house with six units, and she lives in one, and Lawrence Brown, the old Ellington trombonist, rents part of that. He says he feels safe and comfortable there. Nellie's apartment is big and beautiful, and she has everything she needs or wants, including a luxurious garden. She's on the board of directors of Local 47 of the musicians' union, and sometimes she goes over three or four times a week. It's an elected office. She still plays, and she never plays alone. She uses Billy Hadnott on bass and Ulysses Livingston on guitar, and a drummer named Gene Washington. She drives herself everywhere in her Cadillac. She's a big woman and she needs a big car. She does a lot of charity work, and Mayor Sam Yorty gave her a special award. There's not a wrong one among her seven brothers and sisters still alive. Nellie is a conservative in politics, and it's the only thing we disagree on. She has an international following, but the odd thing about her music is that you care for it passionately or not at all."

Nellie Lutcher likes to talk. "My life turned around in 1947," she said between sets at the place where she was working. "I'd been plugging along in Los Angeles for over ten years when—wham!—Dave Dexter, Jr., of Capitol Records, heard me sing on a March of Dimes radio show. I did 'The One I Love,' and a couple of weeks later he signed me to a contract. I recorded 'Hurry On Down' and 'He's a Real Gone Guy,' both of which I wrote, and when I woke up I had a couple of hits. I was paid a hundred dollars a side and no royalties, so the only money I've made from the records has been from the tunes themselves. Barney Josephson brought me to New York to Café Society Downtown, and I went to Europe, where I did very well. Carlos Gastel, who handled Nat Cole and Peggy Lee, took me over. I had no trouble until the sixties, when rock knocked things out like disco's doing now. It makes me cry to think of all the musicians disco is putting out of work. But I have my little apartment house on the west side of Los Angeles, and my union position, which came my way in 1968, when I replaced Harvey Brooks after he passed. I went to Los Angeles in 1935 from Lake Charles, Louisiana, where I was born—oh, in 1915. Lake Charles is twenty-eight miles from Texas, the last little city in Louisiana going west. It's got rice fields and pecan groves, and it's on the Calcasieu River, which connects directly with the Gulf of Mexico, thirty or forty miles south. So it's a seaport town, too. Everything was segregated when I was little, but I don't think I could have come up in a friendlier town. The Caucasian people were very considerate of the Negro people. The main trouble with Lake Charles, it has sickening humid heat in the summer. When I stopped to see my father on his birthday a year or two before he died—he died in 1961—I discovered I couldn't tolerate that heat anymore. My father was born in St. Joseph, in Tensas Parish, right up by the Mississippi. His mother was Nellie Johnson, and I was named after her. My father was tall and skinny and his nickname was Skinner. He was a truck driver and stockman for the Houston Packing Company. He was mild-mannered but stern, and whatever he said he wouldn't budge from. He played all the stringed instruments but concentrated on the bass. Weekends and some weeknights, he played in the Imperial Jazz Band, a local group that did dances and picnics and the like. He loved the comics, and he'd go to every minstrel show that passed through, and just sit there and laugh and laugh. He'd had a son by a previous marriage, and he had fifteen more children by my mother. She lost five in infancy before I was born, so I was the eldest. David died in infancy in the twenties, Charles died in the Second World War, and Vydha, who was the baby, in 1971. All the rest are left: Eugenia; Florence, who married a little while ago; Florida, who designs all my gowns; Margie, the youngest; my brother Joe, who plays saxophone; James, who is religious and has a beauty-supply business; and Isaac, who was named after my father—we call him Bubba. Most of them live around Los Angeles. My mother's desire was to play the piano, but starting a family stopped that. She was born in Charenton, Louisiana, and she passed in 1972. She was a beautiful lady—short and stout and a marvellous mother. She never bothered about going anyplace except church. We children didn't know what it meant to have a key to our house, because Mother was always there. We had a frame house, raised up off the ground, and she always saw to it that we were well fed and there was enough food to share with our neighbors when they needed it. I knew both of my grandmothers, but no grandfathers. The grandmothers lived in a little extra house we had—Nellie, and my mother's mother, Ellen. Nellie was even-tempered, but Ellen was cantankerous. They managed it together until they died. We had a piano, and when I started to tickling it, that thrilled my mother. I was six or seven when she arranged for me to have lessons with the wife of the junior-high-school principal—Eugenia King Reynaud. Money was short, naturally, so my mother told her, 'I'll do your laundry. I want my daughter to have the best piano lessons possible.' Mrs. Reynaud couldn't improvise one note, and if there was a fly sitting on the sheet music, she'd play that, too. She wanted me to have correct fingering, and she wanted me to learn to read. She discovered right away that I knew how to fake things, and she watched my ear all the time. If a student wasn't interested, she didn't waste time on him, but if he showed promise, she knocked herself out. She touched my life forever with her marvellous way of teaching. She was the pianist of the little Baptist church we went to, and when I was eight she allowed me to play for Sunday school. I got two dollars a month for that. I studied with her six or seven years, and eventually I was good enough for the lady who owned the Majestic Hotel in town to send word that she wanted me to play for her guests—'The Blue Danube Waltz,' and things like that. I also played for Ma Rainey, who came through town without her piano player.

"When I was fifteen or sixteen, I was asked to join the Imperial Jazz Band. Al Freeman had been the pianist, and he went home to Columbus, Ohio. They could have gotten someone to come from New Orleans, but the leader, Mr. Clarence Hart, talked to the men in the band and then he asked my father would he consent to *my* playing with them. My dad said it would be all right with him but he didn't know what my mother would say. He wasn't in the church, but she was, and at that time the church people in the South looked down on jazz music as the work of the Devil. My mother said I was too young, and this and that, but my father finally won her over. We played mostly on weekends, because the men in the band had jobs and families, and we travelled as far as Texas. We played a lot of head music—improvised music—but we also used some stock arrangements put out by Frank Skinner. We never knew how much we were going to be paid—one or two or maybe five dollars a night. Bunk Johnson was in the band then. He was from New Iberia, Louisiana, about a hundred miles to the east, and he didn't have any job except to play with the Imperial. He must have been about fifty years old, and everyone called him Mr. Bunk. He told a lot of jokes, and my father, who wasn't much of a joke teller, did most of the laughing. Bunk had a staccato style. He never missed a note or jumbled anything, and he played very clear. We were exposed to fine music. A lot of regional bands—Don Albert, Alphonso Trent, Papa Celestin, from New Orleans—came through town, and we listened to the radio every chance we got. We didn't have electric lights in our house, but a neighbor had lights and a radio and one of those two-sided toasters, and we'd go over most nights and listen to Earl Hines from the Grand Terrace in Chicago. I was very, very impressed by Earl Hines' style, and I liked everything else about him—his immaculate clothes and how much he liked music. I love people who love what they do."

Nellie Lutcher sat down at the piano. She was dressed in a fitted red velvet gown with puffed pink silk sleeves, and she looked around the audience as if she were about to address a stockholders' meeting. Then she smiled, lifted her chin, blazed her eyes, and announced "Alexander's Ragtime Band." It was fast and stomping, and was full of skimming legato rhythms, slamming dynamics, flattened vowels, and wild Leo Watson nonsense phrases. A swaying, medium-slow "The Lady's in Love with You" came next, and she sang it almost straight, except that she accompanied her piano solo with operatic humming. This was followed by a speeding "Caravan," in which fragments of melody raced across the room like puffs of wind across open water. She did "Hurry On Down" and "Real Gone Guy," both of them simple and jivy and swinging, and she did "St. Louis Blues" as a knocked-out blues. She got off a lot of falsetto humming and operatic high notes on her own "Lake Charles Boogie," and she didn't sing on "Mack the Knife." She sang "This Can't Be Love," and then she did a rocking, subtle "Bill Bailey, Won't You Please Come

Home," stretching her vowels like rubber bands and indulging in some
heavy mock-turtle weeping. She made the lyrics of "A Chicken Ain't
Nothing but a Bird" clear, and she sang "The Pig Latin Song" in pig Latin.
She closed with a fast "Perdido" and a meditative "Fine Brown Frame,"
and spent ten minutes signing autographs and making the heads surrounding her laugh.

She ordered coffee and caught her breath. Then she said, "I stayed in
the Imperial five or six years. I even married one of the musicians. He was
twenty years older, and my parents were bitterly opposed. It only lasted
two months. I got a little bored in the Imperial, so I joined the Southern
Rhythm Boys. It was a sixteen-piece group put together by Al Wilson and
Paul Barnes, who had both been in the Imperial. Barnes had played with
King Oliver in his last days, and Wilson had brought him into the Imperial. Al Wilson taught me arranging, which I had gotten interested in. All
the musicians in the band were older and well-seasoned, and it was marvellous to be with that calibre of player. We did one-nighters all through
Louisiana and Mississippi—that was all we could get. I quit and went
home, and then I went to California. I knew there must be something
better out there. My mother had two sisters in Los Angeles, and Mr. Clarence Hart had moved out and tried to get my daddy to follow him. I
stayed with one of my aunts. A cousin knew someone at the Dunbar
Hotel, on Central Avenue, in the black neighborhood, and he'd told them,
'I want you to hear my cousin, fresh in town.' I auditioned, and they hired
me for the lounge, 8 p.m. to 2 a.m., two dollars a night. I didn't consider
myself much of a singer, but they kept after me, so I sang. I admired Ethel
Waters and Louis Armstrong when I was growing up, but I don't know
how much I learned from them. I sing what I feel, I sing the story of each
song. The 'St. Louis Blues' is a sad song. The woman in it, her man is
gone and she's a little bitter. It's not a happy-feeling blues to me, so I try
and make that clear. But certain songs don't mean a thing to me, and I
won't, or can't, sing them. 'Star Dust' is one. I love the melody, but there's
nothing in the lyric for me, and I'll never sing it. Anyway, I stayed at the
Dunbar six months. Sometimes I'd go to breakfast dances at six or seven
in the morning. They had breakfast clubs all over Los Angeles. I married
for the second time—to Leonel Lewis—and that ended a long time ago.
He was from my home town, and we had a child, Talmadge. Talmadge
lives in San Francisco, and works for Standard Oil, and we're close. After
the Dunbar, I worked in all kinds of groups. One was led by Dootsie Williams, a trumpet player. It had trumpet, piano, guitar, and drums, and we
did vocal arrangements. We were the intermission group at the Little Trocadero for a while, and that was where I met Lena Horne, who was just
getting herself together. Another group had Doug and Wilbur Daniels.
They'd been in the famous Spirits of Rhythm with Leo Watson and Teddy

Bunn. A man named Herman Pickett was on piano, and he took sick and I joined them. Then the Daniels brothers got fired, and I took over. This was at the Club Royale. I met Sid Catlett there in 1944. He had a group at the Streets of Paris, and I think he had Allan Eager on tenor. Sid was a marvel. He loved people and they loved him. Talmadge has always said that if Sid had lived he would have tried to be a drummer, he was that crazy about the way he played. We never got any further than the romantic department—maybe because of his gambling. He was compulsive; he'd bet on *anything*. One time, he took me out to the track near Hollywood—I'd never been at a race track in my life—and before I even figured out where the horses were, he'd lost two hundred dollars. Then he got real downhearted. The trouble is, I never heard of him winning. He admired Duke Ellington more than anyone, and when he was on the Coast he sat in for Sonny Greer when Sonny took a spill and hurt himself. That set Sid up.

"I love coming to New York, but it's not easy getting here. I took the train, because I won't fly, and it was fine except there was a fire and they had to move us into another car. I checked my Oshkosh trunk through in Los Angeles the day before I left. I bought it in the thirties, and it weighs about seventy-five pounds when it's empty. One side has drawers, and the other is a closet where I can hang my gowns. Everything packs in so perfectly that when I get where I'm going I never have to send anything to the dry cleaner for pressing. Of course, the days when they picked up your trunk at your door and delivered it to you at the other end are gone. Two men and a neighbor with a truck took it to the railroad station in Los Angeles, and when I got here I had to look in the directory to find someone to bring it from the Pennsylvania Station to where I'm staying, on Central Park West. When I called, they said 'Will it fit in a van?' I said, 'No, it's too tall.' So they said, 'Can you lay it on its side?' I said, 'Yes, the clothes are packed that tightly.' So they brought it, and they charged me forty-five dollars, which wiped out any advantage I had from not using the dry cleaner. I brought clothes for all weathers. The coat I'm wearing tonight weighs eight pounds alone. So to bring down some of the weight of my clothes I'm going to mail back the heaviest things bit by bit as the weather get warmer. Then it won't be so bad when I come to ship that trunk back the day before I leave."

Majesty

Joe Turner

Joe Turner looked more like a wayfarer resting by the road than a per-former in a night club. The master Kansas City blues singer was seated on a low stool next to the grand piano in Barney Josephson's Cookery. He held a microphone in his right hand, but he rarely used it. He waved it in small circles above his knee, he marked time with it, and sometimes at the end of a stanza he brought it to his mouth and delivered a shaking basso tone. He had a cane in his left hand, and he leaned on it and occa-sionally tapped the floor. His clothes were a motley of Kansas City and Los Angeles, where he lives: a dark-blue suit with high-waisted pants and a broad belt, an orange sports shirt with a black design, and huge new sensible shoes. Turner was sitting down because he had gained a lot of weight during the preceding decade and wasn't able to stand for long. "It was all that travellin', all that eatin' heavy food on the road for thirty years, that put this weight on me," he has said. "I guess my legs won't take it because of an accident I had in Kansas City when I was twelve years old. There was a fire, and I had to jump out of a second-story win-dow of the apartment we lived in, and I broke everything. Doctor said I'd never walk again. I was in the hospital two months, and after that I crawled around on the floor a year until I got sick of it and grabbed onto chair backs and pulled myself up and started learning to walk again. But some weakness must have been left, and that's what's botherin' me now." The rest of Turner, who is over six feet tall, is unchanged. His black hair is combed flat, and his face is still a boy's face—a collection of round shapes arranged around large laughing eyes. His voice is the same, too, except that it has deepened. It is a huge voice, a pre-microphone voice—a Bessie Smith voice that was trained a long time ago to carry across fields and down streets and through ballrooms. Turner has been called a blues "shouter," but shouting implies effort and even strain. All Turner has to do when he sings is open his mouth and get out of the way.

Turner is probably the greatest of blues singers, stretching from Blind Lemon Jefferson and Big Bill Broonzy through Jimmy Rushing and down to the white English rock singers. Not all his compeers have understood the blues. Some have treated them as dirges. Some have chanted them. Some have sung them as if from a pulpit. Some have intoned them the way Carl Sandburg did his poetry. Some have laughed at them. But Turner has invariably sensed that this simple twelve-bar (not always), three-chord (not always), tonic-subdominant-dominant (not always) form is capable of assuming all sizes and shapes. He sings of every human condition—loneliness, comedy, death, irony, fear, joy, desperation—and he does so in a godlike manner. He hands down his lyrics with his great voice. Sometimes they are intelligible and the passions harbored in his words stare through, and sometimes he pushes his words together, lopping off the consonants and flattening the vowels so that whole lines go past as pure melody, as pure horn playing. Before Turner, most blues singers recited their words. The melodic content of their blues remained unchanged from stanza to stanza. They used the same notes, the same inflections, the same rhythms. But Turner improvises, for he was raised among the great musicians who lived in or passed through Kansas City in the twenties and thirties: Lester Young, Ben Webster, Pete Johnson, Count Basie, Buster Smith, Jo Jones, Clyde Hart, Walter Page, Mary Lou Williams, Dick Wilson, Ben Thigpen, Hot Lips Page, Jack Washington. He speeds up his time and slows it down. He hustles his words along and spaces them out. He roars, then drops to a soft rumble. On a fast blues, he quickly and repeatedly raises and lowers his voice a tone or a tone and a half, and a line like "You so beautiful, but you got to die someday" jiggles and jumps past so quickly that we almost miss *what* he is saying—the story of humankind in nine words. On a slow blues, he bends his notes into domes and parabolas, lets them glisten briefly before he cuts them off, pauses, and starts the next line. There is no waste in Turner's singing. He rarely indulges in the luxury of a vibrato, and if he does it is short and flat. He is a percussive singer, and his lines fall like blows. The colors in his voice match his brevity and rhythmic force. It is a slate-gray voice that pales at faster tempos and grows almost black when he slows down for a line like "It's three o'clock in the morning, and the moon is shining bright." His voice has heft and agility and streamlining. Turner's imperturbability and cool give his singing a don't-give-a-damn air, but that seeming insouciance is the secret of his majesty.

So Turner sat and sang, an extraordinary presence, whose only motions were small and sporadic. As the numbers went by—some of them anthems like "Roll 'Em Pete" and "In the Evening When the Sun Goes Down," and "Cherry Red" and "Every Day" and "Wee Baby Blues"—he nodded almost imperceptibly, or kept time with his cane, or marked the afterbeat with the microphone. There was no hint of his discomfort ("Sittin' on that stool half the night makes you want to almost cry") or of his nervousness at not having sung much in New York since 1942, when he last worked for Barney Josephson, at Café Society Downtown. He kept his eyes lowered; he looked at the audience between numbers quickly, but after he had counted off the time for his pianist, Lloyd Glenn, and his guitarist, Wayne Wright, he dropped his eyes again. At the end of the set, he heaved himself to his full height, bobbed his head at the audience several times, and made his way toward his table at the far side of the room—a house being moved down a road.

Most days, Turner and Glenn, who were sharing a room at the Gramercy Park Hotel, loaded themselves into a cab and went to The Cookery for lunch. One afternoon, when the lunch people had cleared out, Turner pushed the table away to make himself comfortable, and Glenn, who had eaten with him, moved to another table and studied some sheet music. Glenn is slight and smiling, and the white hair at his temples flashes. He is a remarkable blues pianist—a special breed that is all but gone. His accompanying stays out of Turner's way, but his melodic lines and chords frame and embellish Turner's sharply different moods. Through a judicious use of blue notes and tremolos and a strong and original left hand, he rocks. If he is asked a question, he talks fast and is happy to say that he was born in San Antonio in 1909 and learned to play boogie-woogie and blues piano from such local masters as John and Pudson Harris (who were brothers), Little Archie and Big Archie (who were unrelated), Bubber Howard, and Will Woolrich. Turner doesn't recall having worked with Glenn, but Glenn is positive they recorded together in Los Angeles in the fifties in an upstairs studio for a label that had a picture of Liberty on it. Barney Josephson put away some silver he had dried and sat down and said, "Joe, I remember walking into Café Society one night and there were Albert Ammons and Meade Lux Lewis and Pete Johnson and you—four giants—lined up at the bar. I must have looked glum, because you said, 'What's the matter, Pops, you down?' You reached in a pocket and took out a bean and said, 'Now, in my hand is a bean and in that bean is a face as alive as you and me, and you can talk to it and tell it your troubles.' You made a fist and then opened it and slapped your hand down on the bar so that the bean landed under it. 'Everybody cover my hand with your hand,' you said, and we did—Ammons and Johnson and Lewis and me, a pile of black and white hands. Then you started mumbling something like 'Bajabajeboojiborumbayahoojie,' and you stopped and said, 'All right! Take away your hands. You got nothing to worry about now. Everything's just fine.' Well, I laughed like hell and suddenly I realized I felt wonderful.''

Turner looked at Josephson and smiled and let loose a descending ''Yehyehyehyeh, man'' that sounded as if he were singing. Indeed, there is little difference between his speech and his singing: one walks and the other lopes. ''Walter Winchell gave me a flash on his radio program about that bean and what it could do for people,''Turner said. ''I got the bean from an African who worked in a place where he walked on broken glass and swallowed fire and didn't hurt himself. He told me to rub it and say that mumbo-jumbo and the bean would do anything, as long as I believed in it. After Winchell gave me the flash, people started asking me to rub the bean and help them do this and cure that, and I went wild, it was causing me so much trouble. Finally, it scared me to death to have so much power, and I put the bean in the toilet and pulled the chain. But I believed anything in those days. I thought New York was out of sight. John Hammond had heard Pete Johnson and me at the Sunset Club in Kansas City and sent for us to come to New York and play at that Carnegie Hall concert. I believe it was 1938. We met Albert Ammons and Meade Lux and we all got to be great friends. John Hammond gave us money every week, and we stayed up on Seventh Avenue at the Woodside Hotel. He told us to have a good time, and that he'd get us a job, but he didn't. So we went back to Kansas City, and waited for John Hammond's call. Everybody laughed when we got home—'Hey, you couldn't make it in New York City, man.' We'd say, 'Yeh, yeh. We just waitin' for John Hammond to call us back,' and they'd shake their heads and laugh again. Then John Hammond called, and we went to work at the Café Society for four or five years, and I didn't get back to Kansas City until 1950.''

Turner ordered a sugarless black-cherry soda and swung one leg up on the bench he was sitting on. ''I was born in Kansas City on May 18, 1911, and I was the baby of the family. My sister Katherine Turner—now she's Katie Bryant, which is her married name—is three or four years older, and she used to say my mother spoiled me. My mother made her take me wherever she went. But I like to bug her all the time because I was devilish. My father was a cook at the Baltimore Hotel and the Muehlebach Hotel, and he was a fisherman, too. He caught crayfish in the lakes and ponds and streams, and they had claws almost as big as a lobster's. But I don't know too much about him. He was killed by a train when I was three or four, and I was raised by my mamma and my grandmother. Raised, I guess—'cause I run pretty much from the time my daddy was killed. My mother was a tall woman, and a very beautiful lady. She was real light. She died five years ago in the house I bought for her in L.A. She was from La Belle, Missouri, and my father was from San Antonio. I never did ask where they met. After my father died, my mother worked in a laundry, pressing shirts. Until I went to school, which was the Lincoln, about ten blocks away, I stayed with my grandmother, who lived across the street. She was tall, too—a reddish-looking woman, like an Indian. She was my mother's mother, and I knew her as Mrs. Harrington. She had ten daughters. I never heard my mother sing a note, and she didn't play no music, and my father didn't, either. But ever since I was a kid I had singing on my mind. I started singing around the house. We had records—Bessie Smith and Mamie Smith and Ethel Waters. Ethel Waters is the only singer I ever adored, and I met her after I got to be a man. I used to listen to an uncle by marriage named Charlie Fisher. He played piano in a night club, and he also played on a piano in the hall downstairs in our house, which was like an apartment building. He taught me the new tunes, and I listened to two other uncles, who played guitar and banjo and violin. I was about thirteen by then and had gotten over my accident. We'd duck school a lot—I didn't get past the sixth grade anyway—and go down to the river and fish and swim. Or I'd go down from the house a block or two in the morning and find one of the blind blues singers standing on a corner. I'd stay with him all day and we'd cover the town. He stopped on corners and sang and I passed a tin cup. We went into restaurants, too, and when I was old enough I sang along. I made up words—blues words—to go along with his guitar music, and later, when I was singing with a band, I could sing for two or three hours straight and never repeat a lyric. Those blind blues singers would make quite a bit of change during the day, and they'd pay me fifty cents. I did that off and on for two or three years, but I can't remember those singers' names. My mother didn't worry none about me when she found out—only did I have a hat on under that hot sun. I did all kinds of jobs. I shined shoes and sold papers and worked with a man had a double team and a wagon and hauled paper boxes and like that. I'd lead horses around the stockyard and make a couple of bucks, and I had me a job in a hotel cooking breakfast for the waiters. I learned how to cook from my mother and grandmother—least from watching them. I'd cook bacon and eggs, and fried potatoes, and grits, which we called mush. They kept it on ice until it got real hard and then I'd slice it and cook it like potato pancakes. I sang a lot on the streets, me and a bunch of the boys. They played gas pipes with one end covered and an old banjo and big crock water jugs. They blew across the mouth of those jugs and made that bass sound to keep the beat—boom, boom, boom! When I was sixteen or seventeen, I started hanging around the Backbiters' Club, which was on Independence Avenue. I sat outside and listened to Pete Johnson play the piano. The windows were painted over on the inside, and during the day I sneaked in and scraped off enough paint so me and my buddies could watch the people dancing at night. My brother-in-law was the doorman, and his job was to shake down the customers, search them to see if they were carryin' guns—anything like that. I couldn't get in at night with him around, but when he took another job I drew a mustache on my face with my mother's eyebrow pencil and dressed up in my daddy's hat and one of his shirts. I was already tall, and I'd slip the hat down over my eyes and go in with a crowd. The musicians would tell me, 'Go home, little boy,' but I'd bug them and say I could sing, and finally one night they let me. There was no mike in those days, but I got up there and sang blues songs, and they were surprised I could keep time so good and that I had such a strong voice. I sang a couple of songs and the man who owned the joint liked them and the people liked them. The man asked me how old I was, and I told him twenty, and he looked at me and said, 'Your mama know where you are?' and I told him my sister did, and I started working there on weekends. He paid me two or three dollars."

Turner yawned and examined a watch on his right wrist, which had Los Angeles time, and at a watch on his other wrist, which had New York time. "I got to walk me around some before my legs die," he said, and worked himself to his feet. He rocked down to the front of the room, his shoulders sloping like eaves, turned, and rocked back. When he reached his bench, he looked at it for a while and swung himself down with a swift unbroken spiral motion. "Oh me, oh my," he said, then shouted, "Glenn! Hey, Glenn!" as if he were on one side of Grand Central Station and Glenn on the other. Glenn looked up and smiled and came over. Turner peeled a twenty off a wad of bills and handed it to him. "Get me some change for that, please, Glenn. You said you got to go to the drugstore, so find me three big Vicks nose drops. They got that other stuff, the other jive, don't let them talk you into it. But don't come back with nothin', without some kind of nose breather. My throat dries up with all this singing and carryin' on."

Turner rested his hands on his cane. "The Backbiters' Club had an upstairs and a downstairs," he said. "The bar was upstairs and the music downstairs. I sang with Pete Johnson, and he had Murl Johnson on drums and a saxophone player. We moved to the Black and Tan club, which had been a furniture store and had a balcony and all. An Italian named Frankie owned the place, and he wanted to make me the manager. I said I didn't want that but I would get the entertainers and the waiters if he'd let me learn to tend bar. The bartender was Kingfish, and he was older. Part of my job was to get the bootleg whiskey and part was to take off my apron and sing with the band when things were quiet. Kansas City was wide open, and sometimes the last show would be at five in the morning. After Prohibition ended, we moved to the Cherry Blossom, at Twelfth and Vine. It had been a theatre, and it had a great big dance floor. George E. Lee had a band there, and his sister Julia Lee played the piano and sang. She was a beautiful brown-skinned woman with personality plus. The floor show had a comedian named Rabbit and a shake dancer, which was like a dancer in burlesque. Me and Kingfish still tended bar, and we had a ball serving beer in those big heavy glasses. We were at the Cherry Blossom two or three years, and then I left town with Pete Johnson's band and travelled to Chicago and St. Louis and Omaha and back to K.C. again. We moved around, back and forth and in and out, but we never went too far from home. My mother was running an apartment building at Eighth and Charlotte then, and I'd show apartments for her, but I always kept one back for me and my gang. I went into the Sunset Club. Piney Brown ran it, and I was a bartender and still sang. When the place was empty, the band would play real loud and I'd go outside and sing through one of those big paper horns, up and down the street, and the people would come. I thought I was somebody when I got enough money together to buy a paper horn and a baton so that I could direct the band when I wasn't singing."

Glenn gave Turner his nose drops, and Turner checked his New York watch. "Hey, Glenn. I believe there's still time for you to take your nap." Turner's voice sank, and he went on talking, almost to himself. "You get out there and flag a cab and get in and when you pay the man he got to have his tip, too, and then you get in another cab and come back here to go to work and you pay again and tip him, and it's startin' to cost a lot of money." His voice trailed off. He peered around the room and his gaze stopped at the piano. "The reason I look down at the floor so much when I'm singing is if I look at the people I forget what I'm doing, which bugs the devil out of me. But I can see the people out of the top of my eye and see how they take what I'm doing. If they don't look happy, I change things around and sing something different. When I push the words together, it's because the piano player might be playing too fast and I don't want to get left behind. I'm in trouble if they go on without me. It's like the merry-go-round. I don't want to fall off the horse and have to wait until it comes around again." Turner was silent. He was running down. He looked at Glenn, who had got up and put on his coat. Turner stood up and headed for the front door of The Cookery. "I settled in L.A. in the fifties, but I been on the road pretty much ever since. Paul Williams, Dusty Fletcher, bands like that. I worked with Helen Humes, and we got to be big rock-and-roll stars. It wasn't but a different name for the same music I been singing all my life. By the fifties, Pete Johnson, who was my buddy, went his way and I went mine. He finally settled in upstate New

York before he died. I been married three times. I had a little boy, but heart trouble took him. Whatever money I've made the wives about got it all. I'm married again, to Patricia Sims. We been married five or six years, and I still work around L.A., and Norman Granz has had me to make some records for him, so I keep busy. It's my life. Singing's all I know how to do."

Just a Singer

Helen Humes

Helen Humes bears comparison with Mildred Bailey and Billie Holiday. But Bailey and Holiday and most of their compeers are dead or retired or poking around in the ruins of their voices, while Helen Humes is singing as well as ever. That is a sufficient kindness, but she is also sharing with us a style of singing and of performing that is almost gone. She came out of the pre-World War One South, mostly self-taught and with the sounds in her head of horn players like Dicky Wells and Jonah Jones and of singers like Bessie Smith, whom she heard twice at the Lincoln Theatre in Louisville. It was a kind of singing that we can barely imagine learning now. It preceded the microphone and demanded a strong voice, Ciceronian diction, and an outsize presence. The singer was *alone* onstage. It was also a kind of singing that relied on embellishment and improvisation, on an adroit use of dynamics, and on rhythmic inventiveness. The singer jazzed his songs.

Helen Humes had fifteen minutes before going onstage at the midtown night club where she was working. She was wearing a sleeveless black gown whose halter top was emblazoned with sequins and a lot of gold brocade. She is a pretty woman. Her features are regular and arranged just so, and her lifted chin italicizes them. She wears her hair in a short, dark cloud, which is lighted from beneath by her classic smile. Her hands and feet are small, though the rest of her is mapped out in expansive meadows, sharp drops, and roomy valleys. But extra pounds are to singers what nimble feet are to boxers; they add depth and range to the attack.

Unlike many Southerners, Helen Humes has a loquacity that is frequently tempered by thought. "This is the first long gig I've had in New York since I worked for Barney Josephson more than thirty years ago, at Café Society Downtown," she said. "It was 1942, and I had just left Count Basie. I was tired and my health was getting bad. I was nervous with all that bus travel, so I went home to Louisville to sit around and rest. Then I went to work at Café Society, where I stayed into 1943. Then I went up to Fifty-second Street, I think at the Three Deuces, and then I was down at the Village Vanguard with Eddie Heywood. While I was there, Derby time came around and I wanted to be South, so I got Pearl Bailey to take my place for a few weeks. Well, I haven't returned to New York for any time until now, and Pearl went on from the Vanguard to the Blue Angel to Lord knows where. Me, I went out to California with Connie Berry, who was a piano player. I did five seasons with Jazz at the Philharmonic. I worked in Hawaii in 1951, and in 1956 I went to Australia with Red Norvo. I went back to Australia in 1962 and again in 1964, when I stayed ten months and they tried to make me a citizen. I travelled to Europe my first time in 1962 with a raft of blues singers like Brownie McGhee and Sonny Terry and T-Bone Walker and Memphis Slim, and in 1967 I was at Shelly's Mannehole and Red Foxx's club, in Los Angeles. But Mama got sick and I went home. When she died, not long after, I decided to quit singing, and I took a job in a munitions factory in Louisville. I was there two years and I made gunpowder. You had to stand on wet concrete floors and there wasn't a lot of heat in the winter, but I was having the best time. Being an only child, which I am, you like crowds, you like people. Then, in 1973, Stanley Dance came to Louisville and invited me to the Newport Jazz Festival, but I told him I didn't know if I could sing anymore. I was scared to death to even try. But I came up and I stayed close to Nellie Lutcher the whole time, and she pulled me through so good that five days after I sang at the Festival I was on my way to France to work for four weeks. A year ago, I went back to France and sang at Newport again and did a week here at the Half Note.

"Talking about my mother, I was blessed in both my parents. My mother was a schoolteacher named Emma Johnson. Her father and mother had come from Lancaster, Kentucky. He was a full Cherokee and a medicine man, and she was half Cherokee, half Irish. My father was from Knoxville, Tennessee, but I didn't know much more than that about him. He just died, at the age of ninety-six, so I think his parents, who I never met, must have been slaves. I was in New York doing some business when he passed. He was in the hospital in Louisville, and he'd had a seizure of the flu but was recovering real nice. I went over to Jimmy Ryan's the night before I was to leave, but I felt strange. Roy Eldridge hollered to me from the bandstand, 'Hey, Humes, come up here and sing.'

But I told him I just didn't have it in me, and I went back to where I was stopping to go to bed, and found out the hospital had called and my daddy had died just when I was at Ryan's. My father was known as Judge, or J. H., for John Henry. He was one of the first black lawyers in Louisville, and he was always doing something for other people. 'You have to have friends. You can't live in this world by yourself,' he'd always tell me. My mother never worked again after I came along. We had so many good times together—popping popcorn and making ice cream and playing games. When she died and I made up my mind to quit singing, I sold my piano and my recordplayer and my records so I wouldn't be reminded or tempted, and that was it. Or I thought it was.''

Helen Humes laughed and pushed herself to her feet. She went over to the piano. Her accompanists—Ellis Larkins and Benny Moten—were already warming up. She said something to Larkins, who immediately leaned back and released one of the sprays of hand signals that he prefers to words. He played several left-hand chords, and Helen Humes turned around, took the microphone out of its cradle, smiled, and, standing easily by the piano, began "There Is No Greater Love." During the first chorus, her voice and the song kept missing one another. Her vibrato ran a little wide, she cracked a couple of notes, and her dynamics were uneven. But everything settled into place in her second chorus, and she fashioned an impressive series of embellishments. She started phrases behind the beat and then caught up. She used melismatics. And she worked her way back and forth quickly and cleverly between near-shouts and langourous crooning. She has a light voice strikingly reminiscent of Ethel Waters, but she insists that no singer influenced her. Humes' voice has a dark, fervent underside, which appears when she sings the blues and which Ethel Waters lacked. Her phrasing is hornlike. She takes daring liberties with the melody, particularly in her second choruses, and she keeps close guard on her vibrato. Like all pre-microphone singers, she can shout at will, and she can also slipper along just above a whisper. She is a master of rhythm. When it pleases her, she drags behind the beat, passes it and falls back on it, and unerringly finds those infinitesimal cracks that exist between beats. But there is nothing deliberate or contrived in her style. It is elegant primitivism, and it has a sunny, declarative quality. Her next number was a medium-tempo, shouting version of "Please Don't Talk About Me When I'm Gone," and then she did an attentive "Every Now and Then," a song she delights in and renders much as it was written. A hymnlike "Summertime" was followed by a cheerful "Birth of the Blues," complete with its verse, and a rocking—and for her—quite moody "Gee Baby, Ain't I Good to You." She kept accumulating and then sweeping away little piles of notes all through "I Can't Give You Anything But Love," and she finished her set with a dramatic reading of "If I Could Be with You One Hour Tonight."

She sat down and wrapped a sweater about her and mopped her face. She cleared her throat and banged her chest with her hand several times. "I think I still have some of that cold I toted up here from Louisville," she said. "But I feel better singing now than I ever did before. My voice used to be so clear when I was younger, and people tell me it's gotten real clear again. I'm happiest when I'm singing—particularly if I have a good accompanist like Ellis. I just sing the way I feel. Most of my songs come out differently each time, but there are some I try and do the same way each time. I've been called a blues singer and a jazz singer and a ballad singer—well, I'm all three, which means I'm just a singer. And I've always been myself. I didn't model myself on anyone when I started out. Somebody'd tell me to listen to So-and-So's record, but I'd only listen, if I listened at all, *after* I had learned the tune myself.

"It got started as a singer almost by accident. After I had graduated from high school, I took a two-year business course and got a job as a secretary in the First Standard Bank, which was the first black bank in Louisville. During my vacation, I went to stay with Margaret and Luke Stewart, in Buffalo. They were Louisville friends, and Luke was one of the greatest guitarists I ever heard. I went up there for two weeks, but I didn't get home for two years, because I took my first work in Buffalo as a professional singer. I'd been singing and playing the piano most of my life. I fiddled with the piano as soon as I was tall enough to reach the keyboard, and after I had tried the clarinet and the trumpet, which I didn't care for, I took piano lessons from a very good German teacher, who had me going in the classics. I sang in church from the time I was little, and I sang and played piano in the Sunday school Bessie Allen ran at the Booker T. Washington Center. You could learn any instrument there, and that's where Dicky Wells and Jonah Jones and Bill Beason started. When I was fourteen, Sylvester Weaver heard me sing. He was a blues singer who had recorded on the Okeh label. He told Mr. Rockwell at Okeh about me, and Mama took me to St. Louis and I recorded 'Black Cat Moan' and 'A Worried Woman's Blues.' I believe J. C. Johnson was on the piano. A while later, I made some more records in New York, including 'If Papa Has Outside Lovin'' and 'Do What You Did Last Night,' both of which I'd like to hear now so I could sing them again. But I never kept any of my records, because I never thought they was as good as they could have been. That was all the recording I did then, except the Okeh people asked me would I like to go on tour. But Mama said no.

"I worked at the Spider Web, in Buffalo, and then over at the Vendome Hotel, where I was with Al Sears' band. He's retired now and doesn't do *nothin'* but play golf. I must have been in Buffalo a year, and then I went on to Schenectady, where I did my first radio program, with two white girls, and on to Albany and Troy. I went home after that, and a few months later I rejoined Al Sears at the Cotton Club in Cincinnati. This was in 1937. One night, Count Basie stopped in and offered me a job. He said he'd pay me thirty-five dollars a week, but I was already making that without having to travel, and Basie wasn't much yet anyway, so I said no. Well, Al Sears *did* go on the road, and we ended up at the Renaissance Ballroom, in Harlem, where John Hammond heard me, and this time I *did* join Basie. Billie Holiday had just left him, and I went with the band at the Famous Door, on Fifty-second Street, in 1938. That was when Basie really exploded, and when he had Buck Clayton and Dicky Wells and Lester Young and Jo Jones. I didn't have any trouble being the only woman in the band. I did my singing and went home and read a book and went to sleep. When we went on the road down South, the chances were good we wouldn't be allowed to eat in any decent place, so I started doing the cooking. I had my pots and my hot plate with me, and I cooked backstage. When I'd left the band and was at the Café Society, the phone would ring and it would be somebody from the band passing through, and he'd say, 'Hey, Humes, this is So-and-So. What you got cookin', honey?' Jimmy Rushing was my best friend in the band. He was full of fun and had stories in his head twenty, thirty years old. We'd sit on the bandstand together and he'd tell me things and we'd start laughing, and Basie would get mad. Later, when I was in L.A., Jimmy'd call when he was in town and I'd cook and we'd spend the day eating and drinking and playing cards and laughing."

Ellis Larkins and Benny Moten were in the middle of an intermission set, and Helen Humes paused to listen for several minutes. "This is the first time I ever worked with Ellis—the first time I ever *met* Ellis—and he is something else," she said. "People told me before, 'Look out for Ellis, he's difficult.' But he's all right. Since I don't have anybody in my family left to look after, I might as well spend the rest of my time singing. But I'll keep Mama and Papa's house in Louisville. Thank heavens a neighbor recently moved into it to keep an eye on it! Down there in the summer, the little boys in the neighborhood make a path through my yard going after the peaches on my three peach trees. They come early in the morning and call up, 'Miss Helen, my mama wants to make me a cobbler, so can I pick some peaches?' One little boy came back and back and finally a tattletale told me, 'Miss Helen, he selling those peaches.' I've had a very happy life, and I wouldn't do it otherwise. I even got married once and survived. I married a Navy man in 1952, but I haven't seen him since

1960. He wanted to settle in Japan, and I told him, 'Fine, and I'll be right here if you ever come back.' I don't even know where he is now. I haven't made all the money some people think I have, but anytime my friends are in distress and if there's anything I can do for them, I do it. I guess I'm like my father that way, and I guess he was like *his* father that way. At least, that's what Mama always told him."

It's Detestable
When You Live It

Ray Charles

In Los Angeles, midway between Beverly Hills and Watts, there is a small, factorylike two-story building that is occupied on the ground floor by the Urban League and on the second floor by R.P.M. International. (The initials stand for Recordings, Publishing, and Management.) The building, of gravy-colored stucco, blends easily into a nondescript, old-fashioned residential area dotted with small stores and small businesses. It has windows only on the ground floor, it is rectangular and flat-topped, and, except for its partly glassed-in front, it is expressionless. But its insides, like a poker player's thoughts, are startling. A flight of stairs carpeted in Florida orange climbs from the foyer to an orange-and-white reception room containing a switchboard, a desk, an orange-haired receptionist, a leather sofa, a couple of leather chairs. Two facing doors open into yellow halls. At the end of one of the halls, off which are a dozen brightly colored cubbyhole offices, is a spacious yellow-and-blue-and-black recording studio, equipped with a piano and an organ, clusters of microphones, and a control room, jammed with glistening sound equipment and resembling the cockpit of a jet plane. At the opposite end of the hall are adjoining mogul offices. In the bigger one, three of the walls are painted yellow and the fourth is made of rough brown cork blocks. The wall-to-wall carpet is bronze. A dreadnought V-shaped table-desk, set before a high-backed leather chair, faces the door, and arranged around the walls are an upright piano, a television set, a long leather sofa, and a card table ringed by chairs. An enormous moonlike lighting fixture is set into the ceiling. The smaller office is a frenetic twin: the desk and the cork wall and the sofa are black and the floor has brilliant red carpeting. This one is occupied by Joe Adams, the executive vice-president of Ray Charles Enterprises, which is the heart and mind of R.P.M. International, and the bigger office is occupied by Adams' friend and boss, Ray Charles, the unique singer, pianist, composer-arranger, music publisher, recording executive, and promoter.

Charles *is* the American Dream. He is wealthy and world-famous and inordinately gifted. But none of this, his talents excepted, was given him. He was born in sub-log-cabin poverty in the Deep South at the start of the Depression, he went blind when he was seven, he was an orphan at fifteen, he has been harried by drugs, and he is black. Despite all this, he has solved the Midas-touch-versus-artistic-integrity problem with extraordinary grace. He is, in his naked, powerful manner, in a class with Billie Holiday and Bessie Smith and Louis Armstrong, and, in a country that has never counted jazz as one of its blessings, he is widely admired. There is no one explanation for this. Perhaps it is because Charles almost *touches* his listeners with his voice, perhaps his wild, to-the-bone singing offers a safety valve, a purgative in a turbulent time, perhaps the iron honesty of his voice helps offset our haywire morals, or perhaps it is simply because he is a highly concentrated performer whose singing and presence and timing form a hypnotic force.

Charles can sing anything short of lieder and opera. He has recorded standard popular songs, country-and-Western music, down-home blues, American anthems such as "Old Man River" and "America," novelty numbers, rock and roll, the Beatles, and folk music. He works with equal ease in front of a small jazz band, a big band, vocal groups, choruses, and strings. (The sound of his pinewoods voice tearing along over violins and a choir is one of the wonders of music.) He can shape his baritone voice into dark, shouting blocks of sound, reduce it to a goose-pimpling whisper, sing a pure falsetto, yodel, resemble Nat Cole at his creamiest, and growl and rasp. He is always surprising. Yodels follow deep-throated rasps, he dwindles from stark recitative to a soft, fleeing moan, he rocks along way behind the beat and then jumps into metronomic time. He yells asides to his accompanists or the audience between words, he bends and cracks and splits notes in treasonous places, and he is a master of melismatics. Insofar as it is humanly possible, he never repeats himself; every performance of "Georgia on My Mind" is minutely different. He is his own best accompanist, playing a piano that ranges from the country blues to a clean, Nat Cole single-note style, and he is a competent alto saxophonist. His compositions, gospel-flavored and often funny, are a natural extension of his singing, and so are his arrangements, with their economy and their affecting voicings.

His appearance is deceptive. From a distance, he looks frail and spidery. He has a shuffling, bent-kneed walk, and at the piano he sways wildly from side to side or rears back to the point of falling over. A steady smile and big, ever-present dark glasses mask his face and make him seem smaller than he is. But close up he is tough and compact. He has wide, boxers' shoulders and a flat, trim waist, a high forehead, close-cropped hair, flaring cheekbones, and a jutting, stony chin. His speaking voice is deep and guttural and hand-hewn. He talks quickly and his language moves between sunny, sprawling Southern colloquialisms and lofty Northern abstractions. He is startling on the telephone; he literally barks and grunts. And he is in constant motion—reading from a Braille notebook with one hand and holding a telephone with the other, lifting his head and shooting out his chin, wringing his hands or clapping them softly together, and standing up for no reason to do a little hopping dance and then abruptly sitting down.

In recent years, Ray Charles the singer has become the cork bobbing on top of the Ray Charles Show, which appears, on a concert basis, in night clubs and concert halls around the country and in Europe. This generally opens with his big band, a seventeen-piece group that is the equal in precision and fervor of any current big band. The band plays a batch of instrumentals, and the Raelets, a comely female vocal quartet, sing several numbers. After an intermission, and with the audience kneaded and ready to rise, Charles himself appears, and sings and talks and plays his way through a dozen or more numbers.

In January, February, and March, the Ray Charles Show rests. But Charles spends most of this time in his office at R.P.M., arranging bookings for the coming year, managing his small stable of young talents, memorizing lyrics, walking down the hall to record, consulting with Joe Adams, holding staff meetings, editing tapes, considering new songs to record, talking on the telephone, and granting interviews.

"Most days, I get here late, but I stay late, till nine or ten," he says. "I can get more done between 5 and 10 p.m. than I can during the day. Actually, one of these days I might run for senator or governor and get a bill passed to make the working day from about 11 a.m. to 7 p.m. The way it is now, most people don't go to bed until twelve or one anyway, and the next day they walk into that office at eight-thirty or nine evil. My way, you'd read your papers and drink your coffee and leave your house nice and new about nine or ten. You couldn't pay me to live in New York, which is just the nerve center, the money center. I like the slow pace out here, which is more like the pace of Europe.

"I've never been able to understand why the people where you live should be any problem. Anyway, what the hell difference does it make if you're colored or white? I just want to be treated fair. And I don't want to be treated better because I'm blind. When I went to school, there just weren't any books about us. It was George Washington and it was just like a dictatorship. We were told what we could learn and that was it. Hitler couldn't have killed all the Jews he did by himself. He had to condition other people. It's the same with black people. That nappy hair. You've been taught it's bad. You're conditioned. Same thing, why is it *black*mail instead of *white*mail? I've seen a commercial on television where they have these two cars testing gasoline, and the white one always goes the furthest. When you have people who have been *made* to feel imperfect, the problem is how to teach them they *are* good, that it has nothing to do with color. After all, a lot of the whites who first came over here were outcasts, religious or from prisons, but people just want to control other people. Now the Northern people always say, 'Did you see what they're doing to the Negroes in Alabama or Mississippi?' but they're doing the same thing up here, only they're sneaky about it. Down South, at least they're open. They *tell* you. I wonder what would happen if Christ *was* black. 'His face shall shine like patent leather and His hair be like the wool of a sheep,' it says somewhere in the Gospels. I would like to see what would happen if He came back and He came in the wrong color. I'm not one who worries about coming back. I don't quite believe God is going to take the good people and raise them from the dead, but if He did I don't picture Him needing to take the nothings of the world and raising them, too. The bad people would just be the dust the good people walked over.

"When I'm on the road, I'm home in pieces—two or three days here, a week there. It's not so bad. It used to be a lot worse. I'm fortunate enough to have my own plane. I can do four hundred miles to a gig in an hour instead of spending the whole day in a bus. We have a Viscount turboprop—a four-engine prop jet with Rolls-Royce engines. The way we have the configuration of it, I have a lounge and sleeping area in the back, and in the rest of the plane we took out a lot of the seats and spaced the remaining ones plenty far apart. There are roughly thirty-five of us on the road, but the plane could hold sixty-four. Before that we had a Martin 404, a two-engine job, which could carry about forty. And we have a little twin-engine Cessna 310, which holds about five people. I like to fool with radio and engineering when we're flying, but I believe I could set down a plane if I had to without killing myself. I might tear a wing off, but I don't believe I'd kill myself. Anyway, we have two full-time pilots, and we've been lucky. Once, we were in the Cessna—there was the pilot and co-pilot and a couple of friends—and we were coming into the Oklahoma City airport. It was freezing outside and the heater that is supposed to defrost the windshield broke and the windshield was coated with ice and we literally couldn't see a damn thing, even when we got down to two hundred feet. So we circled and circled, and of course the more we did the more ice the plane picked up and the heavier she got, and on top of that we were running out of fuel. Then suddenly a hole appeared through the ice on the windshield. It looked exactly like somebody had taken an icepick and made it. It was a miracle. So the pilot could see the strobe lights and he brought us in. The pilot I had then, Tom McGarity, like to broke his neck on the ice on the ground when he got out of the plane, but he didn't panic up there. We've never had any trouble with the Martin and the Viscount. Lightning hit the Martin once and went straight through the plane. It made a *bang* and scared the hell out of everybody, and you could see it come out the other side."

There was a knock on the door, and Joe Adams came in. He is over six feet tall and slim and Broadway-handsome. He has arching eyebrows and a small mustache. His hair is combed flat. He is a clotheshorse, and he was wearing a green V-neck sweater, a turtleneck shirt, and olive pants. His voice is low and even, and he speaks with B.B.C. precision.

"I have the band list," he said to Charles. "Contract time is coming up. You want to put your thoughts on who you want and who you don't?"

"Go ahead,". Charles said.

Adams sat down on the edge of the desk, swung one leg slowly back and forth, then began to read the roster. (Some of the names have been changed.) "Leroy Cooper."

Charles nodded.

"Wallace Davenport."

"He's all right," Charles said.

"Lionel Gilbert."

"I'd like to do a little research on that."

"Henry Thomas."

"Yeh. I'd love to have him back. He's a preacher, that one."

Adams read the rest of the list, Charles made his yeas and nays and maybes, and Adams left.

"Out of seventeen guys in a band, it always works that you have just six or seven who are the key men—the men who concentrate and work with the younger cats and keep the outfit straight and sharp. It's very hard for a guy in the band to skate on me. I can hear every horn, every note. Musicians are not the easiest people to handle. A lot of times I make people nervous in the band, so I try and be a little close with them. If there is something personal a musician has on his mind and he can't handle it, he can come to me, and fine. I've always wanted a big band to work behind me. I like the sound. You can make a small band from a big band, but you can't make a big band out of a small band. I'm a person who takes his time, and when I could afford a big band I put one together. And

I've been fortunate enough to maintain everything new I've tried. It was my mother who taught me that patience.

"Her name was Areatha and my father's name was Bailey Robinson. My name is really Ray Charles Robinson. Sugar Ray Robinson was a powerful man when I was coming up, so I took my first and middle names and dropped the last. Then, of course, later I ran into the other Ray Charles, the choir director, but it hasn't been any trouble, outside of getting each other's mail once in a while. I was born in Albany, Georgia, in 1930. September 23rd. But my parents moved to Florida when I was two or three months. We moved about forty miles east of Tallahassee to a little bitty place called Greenville. My father worked for the railroad, cutting and repairing the crossties and connecting the steel. But he was also a mechanic and a builder. He could build anything. In the South in those days, you learned to do many things to make a living. We were poor people in every sense of the word. My father taught me if you ever get your hands on a dollar you always keep enough to get home on and you never let that dollar become your word. If your word is no good, your money isn't, either. He could go downtown and give his word anywhere, and that was it. If he said he'd be somewhere on Monday at eight in the morning, it was Monday at eight, not Tuesday at ten or eleven. I try and do that. I work maybe three hundred jobs a year, and in the last fifteen years I've missed just three jobs and I've only been late six times. My father was what they used to call a 'good nigger.' But he was no Uncle Tom. He just wanted to be left alone, and he was not interested in chasing some white woman. He was very well respected. If a white man liked you, he liked you and he'd do anything in the world for you, and that was the way my father was treated.* My mother was a sweet lady. She cooked and worked for white families, and she made all our clothes. And she had a strong feeling about independence. Just because I was blind, she'd tell me, didn't mean I was stupid. 'One of these days I'm gonna die and you're gonna have to take care of yourself,' she'd say. So I was taught to wash and scrub and cook and rake the yard and make my own bed. I'd cut wood, too, which caused a situation in the church, where they got to saying that my mother was making that poor blind boy cut wood when a piece of wood might fly up and hit him in the face, so she went and told them that even when a man with sight cut wood sometimes a chip flew

---

*In *Brother Ray: Ray Charles' Own Story*, by Ray Charles and David Ritz, published by Dial in 1978, Charles says this of his father: " . . . To tell the truth, I wouldn't bet a lot of money he and my mother ever were married. . . . The old man wasn't part of my life. He was a tall dude—I remember that. But he was hardly ever around. . . . Sometimes he came to see Mama, but not very often. He was so big and she was so small that people often confused them for father and daughter."

Ritz feels that the Charles in his book is authentic and that the Charles in this chapter is, by Charles' design, for white folks.

up and hit him in the face and even if he saw it he couldn't move fast enough, and that quieted them. If I hadn't of been taught by my mother, I wouldn't be anywhere. I was brought up not to beg. Even now, I wouldn't beg nobody for *nothing*. If we had a little extra, we knew it, and if we didn't, we knew it, and nobody said a word. I think my mother killed herself working with my father to make ends meet, and I'm sorry she didn't live long enough to see me become something.

"I was born with good sight and I didn't start having trouble with my eyes until I was five. It started by my eyes running like hell all the time. Not tears—it was too thick. It was more like mucus, and when I'd wake up in the morning it was so thick I'd have to pry my eyes open. The pressure began to build up behind my eyes and there was a pain like the pain you get in your head when you stay up for two or three days and don't sleep. Then my horizon began to shorten up. The local doctor was not a specialist, but he did the best he could. He gave me drops and told me to stay out of strong light. But it got worse and worse, and when I was seven I was stone-blind. I often think of my parents having to watch all that. It was probably glaucoma. At least, that's what doctors I've talked to since say it sounds like. Glaucoma used to damn near kill people, but now thirty per cent get their sight back and forty get partial sight. I remember many things about seeing: the way the sun looks, the moon looks, my mother looks, and the colors, the standard colors, the mother colors—red, green, black, white. I remember the sunsets. I only use my memory of seeing if an occasion calls for it. If I want to buy some clothes, I can get a true picture of the colors using my memory of the mother colors. Normally, I don't look to the past for instruction. There are so many things you can see without the eye, and ninety-five per cent of seeing is unimportant anyway. I know what this desk is like and what this chair is like and what a woman is like. I don't have any trouble with food or taste, and I've never been a heavy eater anyway. I like a good cup of tea and about a gallon of milk a day. And there are things I don't want to see, like people lying in the street with their heads bashed open. I see as much through touch as most people do through seeing. The majority of the time there is someone with me, but I'm not sure that wouldn't be the same if I could see. The first time I came to New York, I came alone, and before I had money I did everything by myself. Now, I don't drive a car, but I don't ever care about driving a car. I ride bicycles and motor scooters. I've been known to do that. I'd love to ride a bicycle in Central Park when I'm in New York next time—go out with two or three people and they'd ride right near me and talk. We used to ride bikes in the hills around home, but I don't recommend it for everybody. Your senses don't become better by theirselves. You develop them. I used to shut myself up in a hallway and take a golf ball and throw it against the end of the hall and try and catch it before it passed me coming back. I'd judge where it was by the way the sounds bounced off the walls, the same way when I was walking down the street by myself, my step would make an echo and the echo would get louder and louder when I approached something big, like a building. *Everything* makes a sound, even crêpe-rubber soles on a rug, but you have to train yourself to pay attention all the time. If I came to a very busy intersection, where the traffic sounds got mixed, I'd get myself in among a bunch of women, and when they crossed I'd cross with them. And I caught the trains and buses and planes by myself. If you hand the ticket man a one-dollar bill for a five-dollar ticket, he'll let you know, and I'd always ask for my change to be counted out in singles. I don't think in all the years I was out there by myself that anybody beat me for a penny.

"We were tough kids then, stuck in that little town in the woods in the South, where they gave you castor oil for everything. It was different from now and it helped you later in life. If we fell out of a tree and knocked our wind out, we got up and kept running. If we got cut, we'd stick some clay dirt in the cut, or a cobweb, and that would clot it. If we had boils, we'd take the thin skin from just inside the shell of an egg and put it on the boil, and it would burst, or we'd take a hot brick from on top of the stove and pee on it and create steam and the steam would burst the boil. We'd make tea out of honey and lemon and sassafras, and it would sweat out a cold, and if we ate too much candy we'd take castor oil and a few drops of turpentine, and, baby, it worked. And we ate a lot of hard foods—raw sweet potato and hard pears and coconuts and the meat from sugarcane. They'd exercise your gums."

Charles leaned back in his chair and lifted his glasses slightly, rubbed his eyes, and pushed the glasses back in place. He seemed to be staring at the light in the ceiling.

"I love to work with young people. I wish that one day a week, Sunday or something, the big newspapers would devote space to what the young people do *right*. Let the young people *know* that they don't have to rob a bank to get in the news. If I was in charge of a newspaper, I'd find out what the young people are doing that's *good*, and print it, so they'd know we care about them. It's like my feeling about drugs. What I did is done and that's that. I've been talking about drugs to the papers and everybody for a long time, and I could continue to talk about it for thirty more years. But if you make a mistake and rectify it, you don't want to hear about it the rest of your life. I'm no missionary or pope and I'm not trying to reform anybody. I did it and it's done and over and that's that.

"Well, I didn't start school until I was seven, when my parents sent me to the St. Augustine School for Deaf and Blind Children, in St. Augustine. It was a state school. Before that, my mother, who was not the most educated woman in the world, taught me. She taught me the ABCs and a little arithmetic, and she taught me how to print. I can still print today. I can't write, but I can print. I was treated very fair in school. I was normal there, happy there. In September, the state bought your train ticket to get you there, and in June they bought you another one to get you home, but at Christmas your parents had to buy the tickets. The school went through the tenth grade, which is what I was in when my mother died. I was fifteen. She had some sort of gastric disorder. She'd eaten a sweet-potato pie or sweet-potato bread and she blew up like a balloon overnight and she died the next day. I came right home. I couldn't cry right then, and I couldn't eat for three weeks, and I almost died for it. My father was never the same after that, and he died—they said from diabetes—not long after.* My mother was thirty-three and my father about forty. There were just no medical facilities outside of the local doctor. The nearest hospital was forty miles away, in Georgia. If you got sick you went to bed and Mrs. Reynolds or Miss Jones or Miss Williams, ladies in the area, they took turns and stayed up with you at night.

"My mother had brainwashed me to the point where I had to be independent. There was no point in living off this aunt or that uncle, and anyway they was mostly living in places like Baltimore, which was a *long* way away. But I knew some people in Jacksonville through my mother—Lena Mae and Freddy Thompson. I agreed to live with them because I could pay them something. I'd go out and play piano at tea parties and such and make five dollars and give half to them. They fed me and took care of me. I had picked up my first piano at home. There was a little café next to us and it was run by a man named Wylie Pitman. He had a piano there and he was of the boogie-woogie school—Meade Lux Lewis and Albert Ammons and the like. When he played, I'd run in and listen. He must of taken note. He would let me sit on the piano bench next to him and bang on the keys. I didn't know *nothing*. He would tell me, 'Play it, play it. You're doing fine.' I'll always love that man for that. He just let me bang on the piano, and one time when I was about six and I was losing my sight and there were some other people in the café, he called over to me and said, 'R.C.'—which is what people called me—'I want you to play like you played yesterday.' I had the nerve to get shy when I couldn't play a damn thing anyway, but I sat there moving my left hand back and forth and banging with my right and they clapped just to make me feel good. From that point on, I loved to play music. By the time I was seven I could play little tunes, one finger, then two fingers, and I had always loved to sing from the time I was tiny. Mr. Pitman had a jukebox and I'd hear those blues by Big Joe Turner and Tampa Red and Big Boy Cruddup

*See note on page 61.

and Sonny Boy Williams. When I got to school, I started studying. I was an excellent musical student. I studied Chopin and Mozart and Bach. Beethoven had a lot of feeling, but Bach was nervous, with all those lines running against each other. Classical music is a great foundation for playing jazz. You play correctly, with the right fingering. With classical music, you play exactly what the man wrote, but in jazz, when you get rid of the melody, you put yourself in. So every time I thought my teacher wasn't listening, I played jazz. And I listened to Goodman and Basie and Ellington and Erskine Hawkins and Andy Kirk and Lunceford and Tiny Bradshaw and Artie Shaw. Shaw got me interested in the clarinet, so I took it up, along with the alto saxophone and a little trumpet. Shaw had more feeling than Benny Goodman, and I loved his sound. And of course my favorite pianist, then and now, my idol, was Art Tatum.

"I stayed with the Thompsons about six or seven months. I had worked a little in Jacksonville in Henry Washington's big band, but he didn't need me, so I went to Orlando and got a job with Joe Anderson, who had a sixteen-piece band. I wrote arrangements for him and I sang. I've done a lot of arranging and occasionally I still do one. I can hear the whole arrangement in my head, note for note, and I just sit down and dictate it. We didn't work too often, and there were times when I was sustaining myself on beans and water and crackers, and it came to be a heavy proposition—a malnutrition thing. I can really understand how people can get chained into situations like that, how people can get stuck in a web and can't get out. Men sit and stare and women become prostitutes. I was one of the fortunate ones. I had this little profession and I did get out of it. But it was total hell twenty years ago, with the race thing and being blind, too. It's easy for people who eat warm food and sleep in warm beds to talk about it, but it's detestable when you live it. I stayed with Anderson three or four months, then I went to Tampa. I knew a guy worked in a music store, and one night he took me to this little club and I sat in on piano with a hillbilly group, the Florida Playboys. Their piano player was sick and I got the job. It was a strange thing. They were white, but they were always nice to me. Every night, they took me home, and when the girls came up and talked to the fellows I didn't feel left out. I wasn't interested in chasing no white girl. My only interest was music and getting my hands on some money. I always loved hillbilly music. I never missed the *Grand Ole Opry*. It was honest music, not cleaned up, and it still is. They don't sing, 'I sat there and dreamed of you'; they say, 'I missed you and I went out and got drunk.' I learned how to yodel by being around the Florida Playboys. Then I went with a small combo led by Manzie Harris, and after I had saved my money with him for seven or eight months I decided I wanted to get out on my own, go to a nice-sized city the furthest from where I was. I was afraid of New York and Chicago. I had a friend, and we took a map of the country and he traced a straight line diagonally as far as it would go and it hit Seattle. I didn't know anybody there and nobody had sent for me, but I got on the bus. I got to Seattle at five in the morning. I went to a little hotel near the bus station and I was so tired I slept twenty-one hours. When I woke up, I asked downstairs what time it was and the lady said two o'clock. I thought it was two in the afternoon. She straightened me out and I asked where could I go to hear some music and she told me about a place, a private club, called the Rocking Chair. I took a cab and knocked on the door and told the man I'd heard they was having a talent night. I pleaded with him and he said, 'O.K., you look older than eighteen. Come on in.' When I got my chance, I sang 'Driftin' Blues,' and they went wild. People from various clubs in town were there and the man from the Elks Club heard me and two days later I had a job there. I put together a trio—the McSon Trio, with Gosady McGee on guitar and Milt Farred on bass. I'd known McGee in Florida, so that was one of those strange coincidences. I never thought of calling the group the Ray Charles Trio, and when we got our first money—three hundred dollars— I divided it evenly, even though I was the leader. I didn't know anything. We worked at the Elks three weeks and then the Rocking Chair man approached me and asked me to come and work for him, and instead of giving two weeks' notice, which I didn't know about, either, I told the Elks man the whole story and he said, 'All right, you have told me the straight of the thing and I am very happy for you and you go.' I spent most of my time in Seattle in the Rocking Chair, but I also worked the Black and Tan, the 908, and the Washington Social Club. And I got married, but it didn't quite work out. We had a little trouble with the girl's mother. She thought I'd never amount to anything, and rightly, I guess. I don't blame her. But once we were married and every time there was some disagreement between us this girl she'd call her mother and her mother would lay it on me on the telephone. I didn't have any poise and I wasn't as nice as I am now. So I said some wrong things. But I think it could have worked out if the mother had said, 'Settle your own fights; it's between you-all now.'"

The phone rang. "Yehrr," he said. "Tell the car to wait. I'll be there in five minutes."

Charles went into Adams' office. A chunky, elderly man was sitting on Adams' sofa. It was Al Williams, of the old Stepp Brothers dance team. "Joe, I'm going out a little while. I'll be back in about half an hour," Charles said, and the door closed after him.

Adams sat down behind his desk. It was gleaming and completely bare, except for a couple of pens and a blotter. There was an abstract painting on one wall and photographs of Charles' plane on another.

"In 1959, Ray Charles was going out on the road and he asked me to go with him as the m.c.," Adams said, in his low, manicured voice. "They wanted a little dignity for the show. Then he asked me to go overseas with him. I went. And then he asked me to join him on a personal basis. I agreed. The first six weeks, I never heard a word from him, so I quit. Two weeks later, he sent for me, and I'm still with him. I've never been hired in the sense of a contract. A handshake between gentlemen. Eventually, he started forming his companies, and I now serve as his personal manager and the general manager and vice-president-treasurer of all of them. He's never told me what to do or how to do it. We have the kind of relationship where he's so astute that I should be paying him.

"I was born in Watts when no one had ever heard of Watts. I wanted to take public speaking in school, but they said, 'No, you'll never get a job in radio because you're a Negro.' I used to walk all over Los Angeles looking for work, and some of the people who turned me down are working for me now. I was the first Negro announcer in coast-to-coast radio, and I started with the disc jockey Al Jarvis. I was with N.B.C. ten years, and when I quit I quit at the top, with a Number One rating. It was 1957, and there was no more creativity in the work for me. Along the way, I've worked as a speech-and-diction coach at M-G-M and done a lot of pictures and television shows. I was with Pearl Bailey in *Carmen Jones*. Otto Preminger hired me. And David Merrick put me in *Jamaica* with Lena Horne.

"I design all of Ray Charles' clothing as well as the gowns the Raelets wear. I designed this building, which we built in 1963, and I did all the interior decoration. I'm kind of blessed. I have the good fortune to have good taste. I like things clean and pure. The members of the band have eight changes of uniform and we carry ninety-seven shirts, so that they have a clean shirt every day. When I hire a man for the band I give him an instruction sheet, so he will know how I want him to dress and behave. No drinking on duty, no narcotics, and I will not allow profanity in public. I teach them pride in their work. You can set your watch by the time we start our shows. Once we took a job and were told to hit at eight o'clock. There were only four or five people in the hall. The man who hired us had figured on a half-hour leeway for himself. Well, he begged me to stop the show and I did, but I gave him hell. On the road, I have a road manager and a stage manager and two bandboys, and there are outside people, like seamstresses and tailors. I have learned to fly. During the Second World War, I was with the 99th Fighter Squadron, the first all-Negro squadron, but I washed out. After I had joined Ray Charles, I was always ordering and buying airplane parts, and I wanted to know what they were for, so I took up flying. But I'm a cautious pilot, a scared pilot.

"Ray Charles is a strong man, a remarkable man. He didn't have much help, but he was a millionaire at thirty and he could have quit working a long time ago and been independently wealthy the rest of his life. People never used to think that he could even talk. But he can talk about anything. And he reads a great deal. He sees with his fingers. Once a little piece of equipment had to be replaced in the engine of one of our planes. The mechanics worked five hours on it and couldn't get it properly in place. Ray Charles said, 'Let me see what I can do with that.' In five minutes, he had the job done. He will never compromise himself or his materials. We were sitting in the office of the president of a New York record company once and the man said, 'Ray, I know how you can make a million dollars. Record an album of spirituals.' Charles refused. He felt it was wrong to tamper with religious music that way. He often works from impulse. One night, I was leaving here around eleven, and when I went in to say good night he said, 'Get me a Corvette.' 'I'm sorry,' I said. 'What did you say?' 'Get me a Corvette. That's a car, a Chevrolet, and I want it in gold.' Luckily, I found an all-night automobile dealer who happened to have a gold Corvette. And he used to drive a scooter. There are two Cadillacs sitting out there in the parking lot, but I think he'd rather ride a scooter. I would sit behind him on it and apply pressure to his shoulders to tell him what direction to steer in, and sometimes, on an empty road, we would hit fifty-five. I've seen him go in a strange building and take a flight of stairs three or four steps at a time. If he wants to wear his green tuxedo instead of his black one, he appears in the green one. He tells the difference by finding some little thing on each suit—a loose thread, a button that is a bit off center, a pocket with something different about it. He is a good cook. And he can type seventy words a minute and he plays a good game of chess. He can do more than most people with sight. When we were making a recording of a tune called 'I Believe' and the Raelets were held up by bad weather and couldn't make the session, Ray Charles sang his part and then he sang all four of the Raelets' parts, in falsetto. It turned out beautifully."

Charles opened the door from his office and stood there swaying and smiling. "I'm back, Joe." He turned, went into his office, and, skirting his desk, sat down heavily. "You know, it's *rainin'* out there. Rains here, and everything comes to a stop. But it's better than Seattle, which I left in 1950, when I moved permanently to L.A. I'd made my first records earlier in the year, for a little record company called Swingtime, run by Jack Lauderdale. We made them with the McSon Trio. I got an apartment on the west side of town, and I thought I wanted to stay. Lowell Fulson, who had the first big hit of 'Every Day,' was here, and Lauderdale thought I ought to go out on the road with him, so I did, as the added attraction. It was the first time on the road in my life. We went to Arizona and New Mexico and Texas. We went out there and tried our best to stay out there. It was exciting to me. It had a gloss. I stayed with Fulson a year and a half, and once when we were going through Texas, Howard Lewis, who was a big promoter in that part of the country, told Lowell he should have an agent. He called Billy Shaw in New York, and they arranged a contract. Not long after, we went to the Apollo, in New York, and the Shaw agency came and heard us and they signed me and Billy Shaw told me, 'When the day comes that we don't produce for you, you don't need us. And when the day comes that you don't produce, we don't need you.' It sounded cold to me. I was young and enthusiastic, but later, when I got to understand business, I understood what he meant. Lowell began having his problems of various kinds and I decided I wanted to suffer through my own problems instead of his. I wouldn't downgrade him. He was essential to me, and so was Wylie Pitman and Howard Lewis and Jack Lauderdale and Billy Shaw and the fine gentlemen at Atlantic Records, where I had my first big hit, in 1954. They were all links in the chain of my success. Shaw booked me as a single attraction, which meant they would send me to a little town and I'd play and sing with whatever musicians was there. I did it a couple of years, but it was hard. It was necessary for me to try and find out what it was like on my own, but playing one-nighters with all those different musicians . . . Man, I *love* music and I hate to hear it played wrong. Early in 1954, I went into a club in Philly and the band was so bad I just went back to my hotel and cried. That band couldn't read and they couldn't hear, either. I called the Shaw agency and told them I couldn't play the job. It was the first time I literally refused to play. They sent someone down to Philly, and the next day we found some musicians and I was able to finish the gig. I needed that job. I didn't have any pocketful of money. I couldn't afford to work with that band and I couldn't afford to work without it. But everything happens for a reason, and if it hadn't of been for that experience I might have gone another long while without my own band, because it was a hell of a lot easier to book a single at seventy-five a week than someone with a whole band. I pestered the Shaw people to death and they loaned me the money to buy a station wagon, and I had enough money to make a down payment on a car for myself. I went down to Dallas and put a band together out of people I had heard one place or another. It had Leroy Cooper on baritone, David Newman on tenor, a couple of trumpets—John Hunt and a guy named Bridgewater—and Jimmy Bell on bass. I'd met my second wife, and after I got the band together we were married and moved into an apartment in Dallas. That was a damn good band, and we had our good times and our bad. We were on the road three hundred or three hundred and fifteen days a year, sometimes travelling seven hundred miles one day and a thousand the next, through hot July, or going the two hundred and forty miles between Dallas and Houston on pure ice, at five miles an hour and getting hit anyway by a car and only being forty-five minutes late for our gig. Our first big hit record was 'I Got a Woman,' and then there was 'A Fool for You' and 'What'd I Say' and 'Hallelujah I Love Her So.' My percentage of successes was extremely good. If you can count out seventy-five to twenty-five in your favor, you shouldn't gripe too much. I dearly loved the people at Atlantic. Their engineer, Tommy Dowd, was a marvellous man, and they never told me I had to record *nothing*. They'd submit materials, but I was always my own boss and sometimes I'd send all the tunes back. But this caused me to write my own things, like 'Hallelujah I Love Her So' and 'What'd I Say,' and I did all the arranging for the band. In 1957, when I felt ready to buy a house, my wife and I moved out here. We left Atlantic in 1959 and went with A.B.C. Paramount, where we had our first million-album seller. There were no bad feelings. It was just an honest business arrangement. But I rejoined Atlantic recently. Joe Adams is my executive business manager. He's been with me over ten years. He was a disc jockey with KOWL here and he was very big. Between twelve and three every day, there was no place you could go in Los Angeles and not hear Joe Adams. He first came out on the road with us as an m.c., and I began to study him. He struck me as articulate and very intelligent. He's tight with money and he's got the business where it's manageable. I feel I'm only a small businessman. I'm content to let the business grow as long as I can see a little improvement each year. This is a very slippery business. You have to be careful. It's constantly changing, and you've got to move with it. I remember when there were only a handful of recording companies in the whole country. Now there are I don't know how many.

"I'm not even sure I'm a singer. You certainly need some luck. I've been able to take a pop song, and it paid off, and a country-and-Western, and it paid off, and a blues, and it paid off, and standards like 'Old Man River' and 'Georgia on My Mind,' and they paid off. But I've tried to find songs *I* can get feeling out of. I must please myself first before I sing a song in public. The song must strike me some way in my heart. Now, I love 'Stardust,' but I'll never record it. Every time I sing the song to myself, I can't get the feeling out of it. The same with the national anthem and Nat Cole's 'Nature Boy.' I loved that record, but I can't sing it to sink. But I like to sing 'America the Beautiful.' The lyrics of a song are vital. You become the person the writer is talking about. It's like a dramatic actor. People have come up to me and said, 'That girl Georgia you sing about must have really meant something to you.' Hell, I never had a girl named Georgia, I never *knew* a girl named Georgia. I can be very angry or very sad when I go onstage, but I love music so much I forget that. I refuse to get entangled in something that will make me perform bad. I start to work, it's like a different machine takes over. Tempos are important. I set the tempos, and 'Georgia' may be a hair faster one night or a hair slower the next and it can have a profound difference on the way you sing the words. The melody is your guideline, your radar, but music would mean very little to me if I had to sing it the same way day in and day out. What I do is try and improve on it each time. Change a note here and there, make a twist in your voice, bend a note—take liberties like that. You won't become stagnant if you can change a little each night. I'd have to *make* myself sing the same song the same way twice a year, which some people do every night without any effort at all.

"I can't give any reasons why the public likes me. Of course, one time I might be up and the public might not feel a thing, and another time they might cry and I might consider myself down. The only thing is I have tried to be honest and I cannot be a disappointment to myself. I've felt that way all my life. I've often wondered, Who am I? What am I that people would spend the money to come out and stand in the rain to hear me, come out and spend the money on tickets and baby-sitters and carfare to hear me? But if I can tell myself I did my best, I know in my heart I feel satisfied."

Two in One

Joe Williams

The singer Joe Williams says he is six feet one, but his stilt legs, football shoulders, and pedestal-like shoes (13EEE) make him look several inches taller. So does the way he stands onstage—loose and tilted slightly back, the microphone held to one side, his free arm crooked or moving in lazy arcs. He has a tall face, too. His forehead is high and is crowned by a graying, cropped Afro, his eyes are large and wide-set, and he has a long, serious nose. His big chin cups his face. Good actors are rarely good singers, but good singers are often good actors. Expressions flow across Williams' face: his eyes flash, his teeth light the back of the house, his mouth clamps shut between stanzas, making a quarter-mile curve. Williams has an enormous bass-baritone. It is the sort of voice that was developed, like Bessie Smith's and Joe Turner's, from singing in large spaces without a microphone. But it is not a Paul Robeson voice—all bottom and ballast. It is lilting and flexible. It moves swiftly and lightly from a low C to a pure falsetto. It moves through glottal stops and yodels and delicate growls, through arching blue notes and vibratos that barely stir the air. Williams is two equally accomplished singers. One is the famous blues singer, and the other is the almost unknown ballad singer. Between 1954 and 1961, Williams, having come out of near-obscurity, sang the blues with the Count Basie band, making great hits of "Every Day I Have the Blues" and "In the Evening." The always astute, tuned-in Duke Ellington, in his autobiography, *Music Is My Mistress*, wrote of Williams:

> I first heard him in Chicago. He was singing around for a while with Jimmy Noone, and at that time he was a very good ballad singer. He sang

beautiful sweet songs, and whatever he sang he sang magnificently, but he never got a real good break . . . Joe Williams was still waiting for his break when he turned to the blues. He was no imitator of other blues singers, but he sang real soul blues on which his perfect enunciation of the words gave the blues a new dimension. All the accents were in the right places and on the right words . . . Since those days with Count Basie, he's been going stronger and stronger. Held higher and higher every day in the ear of the listener, he ain't looked back since.

Williams the blues singer had modelled himself chiefly on Joe Turner, whom he first heard in 1938. "Joe Turner opened it up more than anybody else for me," he has said. "He was a handsome man then, a statue of a man, and he'd just stand there and belt it out." Williams sings the blues with great elegance. His diction is clear, and his emotions are held close to the chest. His blues offer cool jubilation. He is, despite his admiration for Joe Turner, a successor to Basie's Jimmy Rushing, whose blues suggested morning coats and striped trousers. But Williams comes down on the right beats, and he swings even harder than Turner and Rushing, who liked to be legato. The other Joe Williams is just coming into the light. His ballads have none of the on-the-mountain quality of his blues. He trims his voice to make it fit the size of the song. He sings songs as written, he uses a careful vibrato, and he keeps his voice conversational. His ballad singing has the smoothness and comfort of Nat Cole's; the melody he spreads before you doesn't have a nub or a wrinkle. That the two Williamses exist peacefully side by side is almost unique. (Billie Holiday was at ease with both popular songs and blues, and so to a lesser degree was Louis Armstrong. Ray Charles makes everything a blues.) Blues singing and ballad singing are in many ways antithetical. The blues are incantatory and have little melodic content. You can almost chant them. The best ballads come close to art songs, and they demand dynamics, rhythmic subtlety, and a high melodic sense. Blue notes and the very form of the blues carry their emotional weight, and garbled lyrics don't matter much. But a ballad's lyrics are half the reason for singing the song, and they must shine with meaning. The emotions in blues singing are primary, and the emotions in ballad singing are kaleidoscopic. A blues singer is as important as his blues, but a ballad singer should get out of the way of his song, giving the impression that it is practically singing itself.

One afternoon during a New York visit, Williams sat in his hotel room and talked about his life and his music.

"I was born an only child, on December 12, 1918, in the little town of Cordele, Georgia," he said. "My born name was Joseph Goreed, but my mother and aunt and grandmother chose the Williams for me when I was sixteen, and I adopted it legally later. When I was three, I was taken to Chicago by my grandmother. My aunt and my mother, who was working as a cook, were already there. I don't remember my father at all. My mother always told me that she was determined I wasn't going to be raised in ignorance. And she never intended to find out what my father might or might not do for me. Anyway, we never heard a word from him. There was a great exodus from the South to Chicago in those days. Most people took the train, and those who couldn't walked. At first, we lived with the Reverend Jay and his family. Reverend Jay had been a guest in our house in Georgia. We ended up on Wabash Avenue in the Fifty-six block. A Mrs. Seams lived next door—Mother Seams, she was called— and she had a tennis court and croquet, so I learned tennis and croquet. My mother was the love. She was soft and gorgeous—but strong. She was five feet two, and she sang and played the piano. She and my aunt sang in church every Sunday—St. Paul's Colored Methodist Episcopal. My mother would take me to rehearsals at church and to symphony concerts in Grant Park. I had a stepfather—James Mason. He and my mother were together over forty years. I went to the Austin Otis Sexton grammar school. It was predominantly white. I played soccer and handball and touch tackle. It was more interesting to me to elude than to use my bulk to bruise someone. I was very aware of all sports—the 1932 Olympics, the great Bronko Nagurski, what was happening in football at Ohio State and Notre Dame, boxers like Barney Ross and Tony Canzoneri and Tony Zale. Summers, I'd sell peaches and apples and eggs door to door. I attended Englewood High School. In my sophomore year, they discovered a spot on my left lung, and they collapsed the lung. I went back to school, and stayed a little over a year, but I never graduated. I had done some singing with a quartet called the Jubilee Boys when I was fourteen, and when I was sixteen I got a job in a club called Kitty Davis's—I was tall enough to get away with it. I was there about eight months, and I was the only black person in the place. I sang all the pop songs of the time— 'Once in a While,' 'For You,' 'You Can Depend on Me.' I had been listening to everybody—Herb Jeffries with Earl Hines, Perry Como with Ted Weems, Ivie Anderson with Duke Ellington, Dan Grissom with Jimmie Lunceford, Pha Terrell with Andy Kirk, and Louis Armstrong, who was playing with Erskine Tate at the Vendome Theatre when I first heard him. He was in the pit band, and the only thing you could see was the bell of his horn pointing up. But you could hear that grand sound, so full of feeling—the epitome of jazz. I listened to classical singers, like Lawrence Tibbett. I'd even try to sound like him. I didn't care for the tenors, but I did listen to Bruno Landi. And, of course, I listened to Ethel Waters. She sang with more feeling than anyone else. I first heard her in a broadcast from the Cotton Club. She was singing Harold Arlen, and Duke Ellington was accompanying her. I found out right away that it took a special perception to understand what she was doing. She was not for your typical beer-drinking crowd. I think Ella Fitzgerald sounds more and more like her the older she gets. I also sang at dances in black ballrooms. The musicians would take up a collection for me. They had winter formals and summer formals, and they *were* formals—ladies in their beautiful white gowns, men in tails. Juggs was the top club, and the Savoy was the top ballroom. Johnny Long's band played at the Savoy—not the white Johnny Long but the black one—and sometimes Basie or Lunceford. You could be assured you'd get four thousand people.

"In 1937, I joined Jimmy Noone's twelve-piece band. Jimmy would play alto saxophone in the ensembles. He was in charge. He knew exactly what he wanted. He never raised his voice but he'd frown if anything went wrong. We toured the South in an old Walter Barnes bus. Barnes had a popular band that went back and forth across the South in the mid-thirties. We played for black audiences, and we had good crowds in Tennessee and Florida—or until St. Petersburg, where the place we were supposed to play was dark. We turned around and went back to Chicago and put a sign outside the next place we played: 'After a Triumphal Tour of the South.' I was singing songs like 'Always' and 'Nagasaki' and 'You Leave Me Breathless.' We broadcast almost nightly, and because it was live you had to get it right the first time. When you broadcast, there was no amplification in the club, so you had to *sing*. And, of course, there were no monitors to check yourself on. I worked with Coleman Hawkins' big band for a while in 1941. We were on the road in Memphis when Pearl Harbor struck. Hawkins broke up the tour, and we went back to Chicago. It was the story of my life in those days—always back to Chicago. I sang with Johnny Long for a while, and in 1943 I joined Lionel Hampton at the Tic Toc Club in Boston. I replaced a singer named Rubel Blakely. That was some band—Joe Newman on solo trumpet, Joe Wilder on lead trumpet, Arnett Cobb on tenor saxophone, Milt Buckner on piano. And Dinah Washington singing the blues. Hamp paid me eleven dollars a night to start. The music held that band together. I was with Hampton four or five months, but I never recorded with him, because the union recording ban was in effect. I met Frank Sinatra around this time, at the Paramount Theatre when he was with Tommy Dorsey. I had first heard him with Harry James in 1939. He was singing 'Everyone But Me.' The Dorsey and Lunceford bands backed their singers better than any other big bands. When I left Hampton, I went back to Chicago and worked the clubs on the South Side. In 1945, I sang the blues for six months in Milwaukee with Pete Johnson and Albert Ammons.

"Then I joined Andy Kirk, and had a nervous breakdown. I was in Elgin State Hospital from April of 1947 to April of 1948. I had electric shocks—the works. I had to reorder my priorities. I had to figure out if I even wanted to be a singer. I had plenty of time to think, and some of the things you think about in a place like that are not so pleasant. Like: Who needs you? Like: I'm stopped, but everything is still going on out there. I went home six times for visits, and it was never easy to come back. Part of my trouble might have been the things you had to fight every day. When you wanted a drink, when you wanted a meal—how to do it? How to get through the breeze every day and not be burned? I used to send the *Negro Digest* to my white friends. They didn't need it. They had no need of guilt trips. My mother always told me you are your own best friend. She also told me when I was in school that if someone liked me, to bring him home. I did just that with a white football player I knew. He had a good time, I think, but he was silent at the end of the evening, because he knew he couldn't invite me home. So I was well fortified by the time all the beautiful blackness appeared in the sixties.

"When I left Elgin State, some people helped me get a job selling cosmetics door to door. You took half of what you made. It kept me busy, and it made me so tired sometimes I couldn't get my clothes off before I fell asleep. I had sung in a choir and with a dance band in the hospital, so I hadn't given everything up. Then I started singing a little with Jay Burckhardt's band. Jackie Cain had been with him, and he had Gene Ammons on tenor saxophone and Jimmy Gourley on guitar. I tried to balance selling cosmetics and singing. George Shearing came through with his quintet, and I worked with him at the Regal Theatre, and that did it. I gave up cosmetics. In 1950, I did a two-week stint with Count Basie at the Brass Rail. He had his small band then, and it could swing you inside out. He had Clark Terry on trumpet, and there wasn't anything Clark couldn't play. He had Buddy DeFranco on clarinet and Wardell Gray on tenor saxophone and Freddie Greene on guitar and Gus Johnson on drums. Basie gave me fifty dollars a week out of his own pocket. I worked with Red Saunders for nine months at the Club DeLisa, and I worked in Cleveland and Buffalo. Basie came through Chicago again in 1954, and he had his big band by then. I sat in, and sang 'Roll 'Em, Pete.' We talked in Basie's hotel room later, and he asked if I'd like to come on the band. He told me he couldn't pay me what I was worth, but as things got better for him they would get better for me. I joined the band in New York and stayed six years. We had our hits, but the main thing was it was a very lifting experience being with that band. It was made up of men who took great pride in getting their music right. It was a matter of self-discipline, and of group discipline. If someone got out of line, we didn't go to Basie. We straightened him out ourselves. We were treated like artists, so we tried to act like artists. Basie was very quiet, but he observed a lot. In a way, he ran the band by letting it alone. I left in January of 1961, and I've been a boy singer on his own ever since."

Williams had slid lower and lower in his chair, until he was sitting on his neck, his legs stretched out about eight feet in front of him. Suddenly, he pulled himself to his feet in a concatenation of vertical and horizontal movements, picked up a banana from a breakfast tray, peeled it and ate it, and sat down. He is dark, and he seemed to absorb the watery light in the room. His speech is a slow version of his singing, and whenever he mentioned a song he simply went into it, singing a half or whole chorus in a light, airy way, as if it were easier for him to sing than to talk. When he wanted to make a point, he emphasized certain words by making his mouth rectangular so that each syllable came out staccato and squared off. At first, he wore heavy black spectacles and looked very grave. The more he relaxed, the more he laughed. He has two laughs. One is slow and low-pitched. It starts as a rumble, then rocks away in slow motion. The other is higher-pitched, and it undulates like a gentle chop.

"I was married three times before I met my wife, Jillean," Williams said. "They were all marvellous, and we have remained friends. But everybody isn't livable. I don't get my dander up often. If I have a difference of opinion with someone, I try to find out his logic and match my own against it. I met Jillean in 1957 at the Waldorf when I was doing the Starlight Roof with Basie. She's English, raised in Surrey, and very much a lady. She cries over pictures of the Queen, and for her Mr. Churchill was close to God. She was a Wren during the war. I didn't see her again until 1959, when I went to England. We were married soon after. Jillean's father, Andrew Milne, was a fine man. He had this old friend Dick. They had lunch at the club every day, and when we told him we were going to get married he laughed and laughed in his booming way and said, 'Wait until I tell Dick. He does nothing but talk of his daughter who's married to a Chinese. Wait until I tell him I'm going to have a black son-in-law.' Jillean is consistently the most pleasant person I have ever been around. She has such enthusiasms. I don't think I've ever said anything by design to hurt her. I tell her she doesn't look a day over thirty-five, and she says, 'Now, darling, come on,' and I say, 'Don't forget, I'm looking at you with old eyes.' She calls me Sir: 'No, Sir is out. Can I take a message?' 'No, Sir is in New York at the Blue Note. He'll be back next week.' Or she calls me Chief Thundercloud, because I'm part Seminole. Her loyalty can take you by surprise. Babs Gonzales, the singer, came to the house once, and he was sitting there saying he says, she says, and then he started taking off on me. Jillean came pouring out of the kitchen when she heard this, and said, 'How dare you talk that way to Sir! How dare you! You get out of here!' And she opened the front door. I laughed until I almost fell down—because I knew Babs hadn't meant any harm. We lived on Central Park West when we were first married, but I got tired of seeing incinerator dust hanging over the Park, so I asked her if she would like a house in the country. She said she didn't want a house. We started looking around anyway. We thought of Spain, where we had friends, but I didn't want to be a dried-up expatriate. We thought of Northern California, and we thought of Canada, but Canada is too cold. We never discussed Los Angeles at all. She said she had always loved the desert. I had been to Las Vegas once, so we took a look and bought a house. Jillean has no inclination to make a move to any other place, although we have talked about the ocean. For the first time in my life, I have become a member of a community. I do jury duty, I play golf with judges and lawyers. We have a swimming pool, and Jillean has room for her animals. She loves animals, and will pick up a cricket if it gets in the house and take it to the front door and say, 'There, darling, go and fly.' I have worked very little in Las Vegas. I did fifteen weeks in one of the lounges with a drummer friend named Ralph Pollak. He'd tell me to come in if I wanted to tune up—that I could sing anything. I wouldn't work any of the main rooms unless I got the full treatment.

"I have a bass-baritone, and at least two and a half octaves. I have never taken singing lessons. I've learned naturally: to get the proper chest tones by pushing the air up through the chest from down here; to get proper head tones, nasal tones, up in the mask; to start my notes straight and let the vibrato follow later; to be constantly aware of diction, because there have been so many singers I couldn't understand. Onstage, my entire attention is focussed on my background. It's like a play—the interaction between you and the other instruments. Each is a separate voice. The trick is to make it seem that you are involved with the audience—to make the audience think you are singing to them—when you aren't at all. You are singing with the people onstage. Sometimes the beauty of what I hear behind me causes me to smile when there is nothing to make me smile in the song itself. There is nothing wrong with singing a song the way it is written, with making a song say, 'Please like me.' I have become more and more conscious of singing in tune, and I've come to the conclusion that any note held longer than four or maybe six beats is in excess. I've also decided, Never get loud. You can achieve great clarity without volume. I'm enjoying singing more than I ever have. I work about forty weeks a year. There's plenty of work and plenty of money. You can't but eat so much and drink so much, and you can only wear one suit at a time."

Williams laughed, and started singing "I'm Old Fashioned" in a high, loose baritone.

Moonbeam
Moscowitz

Sylvia Syms

Excellence generally parries neglect with bitterness, stoicism, or a brave and judicious narcissism. Sylvia Syms has long since chosen the last of these weapons. She has said of herself, with her wide smile, "I have no desire to be a superstar. I don't think I could stand the responsibility of having to prove myself every single day. If you don't make it, you have a ball trying. But I've made it. I don't know by whose standards, but I've made it by mine. So the only person I have to satisfy now as far as my singing is concerned is me." During the forty or so years of her career, she has sung in almost every notable night club in the country. When the night-club business began faltering, in the mid-fifties, she turned to the theatre, where she has appeared on and off Broadway in *Diamond Lil* with Mae West, in innumerable productions of *South Pacific*, in which she has perfected the part of Bloody Mary, in *Dream Girl* with Judy Holliday, in *Thirteen Daughters* with Don Ameche, in *Funny Girl* with Carol Lawrence, in *Flower Drum Song* and *Camino Real*, and as the lead in *Hello, Dolly!* And along the way she has made recordings, one of which, a daring up-tempo version of "I Could Have Danced All Night," became a hit for Decca in 1956. But time and again, just as she has appeared ready to swim into the lagoon of recognition and financial comfort, she has foundered. The causes have been myriad—an operation; a female rival; her own intransigence toward working conditions, managers and bookers, and clothes; an automobile accident; her physical construction; the twists and turns of her private life; and the tricks of fashion. But she continues to work well as both an actress and a singer. Here is the singer in two different set-

79

tings—a rehearsal for a concert appearance with the composer Cy Coleman, and sitting-in at The Cookery with her friend Barbara Carroll.

It was a sleepy New York Saturday, and Sylvia Syms was in Cy Coleman's sumptuous living room. They were rehearsing a dozen Coleman
songs for the concert, which was to take place the next day. She was
wearing one of her many djellabahs, and she looked tiny in the high-
ceilinged room. She is barely five feet tall, and is plump and shapeless.
Her legs, both broken in the accident, look spindly, as does her left arm,
which was also broken. Childhood polio has left her with a curvature of
the back. But her presence is immediately commanding, and on first meeting her one is surrounded by her rich voice, her frequent laughter, and
her rhythmical, dramatic motions. Her moon-shaped face lights up whatever it is aimed at. Her wide mouth is almost always smiling; she has
large, slightly slanted eyes, elfin ears, and an aquiline nose; and her broad
forehead ends in a helmet of short, coppery hair. She is an impulsive,
long-syllabled talker who is apt to sail into any subject *in medias res*, and
she did when Coleman excused himself to make a phone call: "Mr. Sinatra sent me his newest single this morning," she said. "I don't know why
I call him Mister when I've known him as Francis for so many years. I
guess it's my profound respect for him. I don't remember when we first
met, but *he* would know. I've watched him greet by name without hesi-
tation someone he hasn't seen in twenty-five years. He's a quiet man,
articulate and well-informed, and he's been a gracious friend. When I was
in the hospital after my operation, he called every day, or had someone
call if he couldn't, and when it became clear I'd need a respirator to take
with me wherever I went, he had the best one there is sent to me. I still
use it an hour every day. He has a good sense of humor. After my automobile accident, he sent me a pair of skates with the message 'Try these
next time,' and I returned the gesture when he opened a tour at Caesars
Palace by sending him an antique silver ear trumpet. I've never once
watched him sing and not come away with something new. I'm grateful
to have been alive during his era. All of which explains why, when I was
a guest at his home in Palm Springs and he asked me to sing at some inn
we had gone to after dinner, I couldn't. I just couldn't get up there know-
ingly in front of him and sing. All he said was, 'Sylvia, you're nuts!'"

Cy Coleman sat down at the piano again and loosed a couple of booming chords. "God!" he said. "The sound of the piano is frightening this
early." Sylvia Syms put on a pair of granny glasses. They decided on
"Witchcraft." By the third measure, her body had begun to reflect her
singing. She bounced slowly up and down, rocked her shoulders from
side to side, and swung her hips. She has a powerful contralto, but she
controls it effortlessly. Her diction is bell-like, but she does all sorts of

subtle rhythmic things with the words—sometimes piling them together, sometimes letting them drift. The next number was a slow ballad. Her voice became soft, she stretched out her hands, palms up, and raised her shoulders. The number was full of crooning turns of phrase, and one heard slow breezes and early stirrings. Then she and Coleman went into a buoyant duet of "Hey, Look Me Over" and a ringing version of "The Best Is Yet To Come," which they did in unison, in harmony, in alternating passages, and as a round.

Sylvia Syms laughed and leaned against the piano. "My! They're going to get a warmed-up lady out at the theatre in New Jersey. What time is it, Cy? I have no sense of time and I spend all day at home calling for the time. We have two shows of *South Pacific* today, and they're picking me up at three." Cy Coleman said it was just after one, and he suggested a final rehearsal at noon the next day. Sylvia Syms walked the ten blocks to the small apartment she has long had on Lexington Avenue. She took short steps and swayed from side to side, as if she were shouldering her way through the press of her talk. "For some reason, I got to reminiscing about my childhood with Cy before we started today, and it was painful. I was born the oldest of three children in Manhattan but grew up in Flatbush. My maiden name was Blagman and when I started out I called myself Sylvia Black. Then I saw the name Syms with a 'y' somewhere and I liked it and took it. My mother was a New York girl and so was her mother, but my father came from Russia. It was a great love affair between my father and mother. He yelled a lot at me, but I never heard him yell at her. My mother still lives out there. She's intelligent and funny and articulate, and she still points that finger at us children when we visit her and says do this or do that, but now we just laugh and tell her to jump in the lake. She's very into her Judaism, and I suppose she wishes I were, too. I've always been aware of being a Jewess, but my religion is people. My father designed clothes, and he died when I was seventeen, but I didn't know him as much else than a strict, hardworking family man. I was a very removed child, and it started when I sang with a full and beautiful voice before I'd learned to talk. I sang in my carriage, and later I'd sit on the front stoop and sing at the top of my lungs. But my parents didn't know how to cope with my singing. They were poor and their backgrounds had taught them that the life of a singer or actress led directly to the gutter. My father was sensitive in all areas except the one I was interested in, so I got no help, no formal training. I was born a heavy child, and I grew heavier because I was unhappy. Very soon I created a complete fantasy world. I got a reputation, and I'd hear parents tell their kids to keep away from that crazy Sylvia. I'd stay awake all night listening to music on the radio, and when I was in my mid-teens I started sneaking out of the house after everyone was asleep and going down to New York.

I'd get on the subway and go to Fifty-second Street. My father got hys-
terical when he found out, but that didn't stop me. I had long red cop-
pery-chestnut hair tied in braids and parted in the middle, and I had absolutely no fear of going out in the middle of the night. Who wanted to
make passes at a fat Jewish girl from Brooklyn? I became the first of the
groupies, and I began learning about the momentary, joyful noises of jazz.
And I had the greatest people to teethe on. I got to know Fats Waller. He
had bad feet, and I remember him playing the organ in a little church
uptown and pumping it with his bare feet. And I got to know Art Tatum.
He called me Moonbeam Moscowitz, the Jewish Indian. He'd take me
uptown after work to the Log Cabin or Tillum's, where he would play
with a tenderness and warmth he never showed downtown. Sometimes
Jerry Preston, who owned the Log Cabin, would call my mother and tell
her everything was O.K., and around seven or eight in the morning he'd
send me home in a limousine. Or else Tatum would take me even further
uptown to a grits-and-fried-chicken place, and after we'd eaten we'd walk
down the street and watch the sun come up. On my twenty-first birthday,
he gave me a little glass piano with his initials on it, but it eventually
broke. And three years before he died he had Van Cleef & Arpels make
a gold piano with a keyboard of sapphires for the black notes and fresh-
water pearls for the white notes. But I don't have that anymore, either.
Erroll Garner pestered me about it so much I finally gave it to him, and
he took it everywhere, in its original little felt bag.

"Billie Holiday became my mentor, and I copied everything she did,
excluding the drugs and booze. She said to me once, 'You know what's
wrong with you, Sugar? You love me.' She was a beautiful, dignified lady,
with an innate sense of good taste. She was drawn to singing songs you
knew she understood. She had a kind of animal relativity to the songs she
sang. I have no concept of living within a budget, but once I saved
twenty-five dollars and bought her a print gown for her birthday, and she
was so pleased you'd have thought I'd given her the moon on a stick. I
can remember her in the gown at the Onyx Club, coming down those
little stairs in the back and the lights softening and the room becoming
silent and her moving onto the stage and looking just like a panther. She
began wearing gardenias in her hair because of me. One night when she
was working at Kelly's Stable, she burned her hair with a curling iron just
before show time, and I ran down the street to the Three Deuces, where
Ada Kurtz had the checkroom. Checkroom girls sold flowers then, and I
bought a gardenia and Billie put it in her hair to hide the burned place.
Of all the men she married or knew, I think she loved Buck Clayton the
most. We were sitting around at the club on the Street where Billy Eckstine had his big band, and B said to Billie, 'Ain't I pretty?' 'Yeh,' she said,
'but you ain't the prettiest.' 'Well, who is the prettiest, then?' B asked her.

'Buck Clayton's the prettiest man in the whole world.' I got to know Lester Young through Billie. In fact, she used to tell me when I started singing that I sounded just like the way he played. He was the first person I ever heard say to his piano player, 'Just play vanilla, man. Just play vanilla,' which meant cut out the embroidery and play the proper chords behind solos. I still use the phrase when I run into an accompanist who thinks he's Niagara Falls. Lester was a quiet, inside-himself man, and he'd always tell me, 'It's hard, Baby, it's hard.' I don't recall how I met Duke Ellington, but he called me Lady Hamilton. He made every woman in the world feel beautiful. Once, when I was working in Chicago, Bentley Stegner, who was a music writer for the *Sun-Times*, took me to hear Duke. It was snowing and blowing and there weren't any cabs, so we walked and walked through knee-deep snow, and I had on an old babushka and my mascara ran all over my face, and when we got there Duke took one look at me and said, 'Lady Hamilton, I don't know where you just came from, but please save a few dried-up bones for me.' I hung out with Mildred Bailey, too. She was a wild lady, and she had a rapier tongue. I'd go to hear her at Café Society, and I went to her little house on Sniffen Court. She was a domestic lady and she loved to eat, and so did I. She thought I looked like her and she'd tell people I was her little sister. She told me I'd be a star but I'd be very unhappy getting there."

Sylvia Syms arrived at her door and pulled a key out of her bag. "Before I moved in here, I lived with the comedienne Pat Carroll in a loft right over the Fifty-fifth Street Playhouse, near Seventh Avenue. When we opened the fridge, film music came out, and we could lie on the floor and look through a little hole and watch the pictures." She put her key in the lock and waved, her stubby fingers spread like a child's.

It was eight-thirty on a Monday evening. Sylvia Syms was still in *South Pacific*, but Monday was her day off, and she was in a cab headed for The Cookery, where she was planning to sing with Barbara Carroll. As was her wont, she had spent most of the day at Elizabeth Arden getting the week's accumulation of "Texas dirt" she used for makeup as Bloody Mary removed from her face and arms. She was wearing a black-and-white cotton knit suit, and her hair was arranged tightly around her face and she looked radiant. She leaned into a corner of the seat, and her legs lifted from the floor. "I met my great friend Barbara in 1946. I'm not a woman's woman, and Barbara and Judy Holliday and Pat Carroll have been my only women friends. When I first met Barbara, it was like seeing my reflection in a mirror. We've been through just about everything together, including the automobile accident. I was about to go back to California to audition for the mother in the television series *Bridget Loves Bernie*, and I'd been visiting Barbara at her country place in South Salem. We were being driven back to New York in her little car, and Barbara insisted she sit in the front, so I got in the back with her daughter, Susie. We were coming to a toll gate and Susie and I were playing some kind of game, and the brakes failed and—whammo! I threw myself on top of Susie and she was unhurt. Barbara looks as beautiful as ever, but I don't know how many operations she's had on her face. I was in and out of a wheelchair for a year and a half. But, please God, I'm in fine shape now. I consider that I've come through smelling like a rose, which is why I spend every available minute finding out what the rest of the garden is like."

At The Cookery, Barbara Carroll finished her set, and she and Sylvia embraced. Barbara asked her if she would sing during the next set, and Sylvia said yes. Sylvia examined her face in her compact mirror. "It doesn't matter if I'm Sarah Schlepp during the day. But when I perform I have to wear the best. As a result, I've turned into a not-half-bad-looking woman. In the broadest sense, I like me. I even enjoy the things about me I'm not too crazy about. But I didn't feel that way during my first singing job, which was at Kelly's Stable. I went in there one night with a couple of Brooklyn friends and auditioned with Benny Carter's group for Ralph Watkins, the owner, and he offered me a job for the summer. I'd met dear Benny one night at Nick's, and his daughter and I hung out a lot. It was 1940, and Ralph Watkins paid me twenty-five dollars a week. The Nat Cole Trio was the intermission group and Billy Daniels was the star. The job worked out O.K., but I didn't have the right clothes and I must have looked awful. I didn't work again for five years, and then I went downtown into the Little Casino. I was there a whole year, and Ram Ramirez, who composed 'Lover Man,' was my accompanist. Mike Levin wrote about me in *down beat*, comparing me with Billie Holiday and Lee Wiley. I was a buxom, sharp broad, but I was stupid enough to resent the comparisons. I guess I thought I was Topsy and had just grown all by myself. But on the strength of the piece I was hired at the Club Troubador for two hundred dollars a week. Louis Jordan and his Tympany Five were there, and so was Georgie Auld's big band. Another singer, who shall remain nameless, was starred. Well, I was breaking it up, and she wasn't, and one night after work Mike Colucci, who ran the place and was a nice gent, told me, 'Sylvia, I have to fire you.' He wouldn't tell me why, and I was crushed. I found out later what had happened. The other singer's manager handled all sorts of big acts, like Nat Cole and Stan Kenton, and when he heard I was hurting his act he called Colucci and said, 'Get rid of Sylvia Syms.' In the fifties, when I was working in New York, this great big man came in to hear me five nights in a row, and finally he introduced himself and told me I was the best singer he'd ever heard. It was the same gent who had had me fired, and I was flabbergasted. All I could say was 'Oh yeah, how come you did what you did to me at the Troubador?' and all he said was 'She was my act and you were killing her. If you had been my act and someone else was killing you, I'd have protected you in the same way.' I had a gossamer vision of the business. I romanticized it, and I guess in some ways I still do.

"In 1946, I got married for the first time. Actors have always been my downfall, and I married Bret Morrison, who was doing *The Shadow* on radio. He's one of the nicest men I've ever known, and he's probably the only man I'd marry if I ever married again. Anyway, I was a rotten wife. I had my head in too many places. We lived in an elegant duplex on West Sixty-seventh Street, but it was a mausoleum, and it turned me off. We had all the right linen, the right china, the right crystal—and all the wrong ingredients for a good marriage. We were together until 1953. In the mid-fifties, I married Ed Begley—the dancer, not the actor—but it's not a part of my life I like thinking about.

"My being fired at the Troubador gave me a mysterious quality. It was O.K. to be fat if you were exotic. I have some pictures of myself from the mid-fifties when I reached two hundred and forty-two pounds. I looked Chinese. People didn't know what to make of me, and because of my dark complexion they started asking me if I was black. In fact, a lady television interviewer asked me the same question a while ago. I started working in every upholstered joint in New York, and I began to create a nice following. I was in the Ruban Bleu in 1951 with the Norman Paris Trio, and I worked off and on for several years at the Village Vanguard. People like Orson Bean and Robert Clary and Harry Belafonte came and went there, but I stayed on forever. I worked at the Show Spot with Barbara when Mabel Mercer was upstairs in the Byline Room. But I have always been just another name on the lists of the various managers who have handled me—mostly, I think, because they haven't known what to do with me. I even had one once who told me I should be grateful I was working because I was such a mess, which did its little damage. I was never good-enough-looking to sing with a band, and in a lot of the rooms I worked you were required to mix with the patrons, and I just didn't know how. But in 1954 the managers Pete Cameron and Monte Kay came into my life, and they got me a recording contract with Decca. Nothing much happened until 1956, when, at the end of a session, Milt Gabler, who was the A. & R. man, reluctantly let me record 'I Could Have Danced All Night.' Reluctantly! They were dead set against it. Rosemary Clooney had had a hit version on Columbia for a couple of months, and on top of that I wanted to do it at double tempo, which nobody had done. But a month later my version took off and became a hit, and so did other tunes I recorded, like 'In Times Like These,' 'Dancing Chandelier,' and 'It's Good to Be Alive.' The upshot was I got job offers all around the country in hotels and night clubs, and it nearly destroyed me. They expected Miss

America but they got me. I still didn't know how to dress, and the clothes I wore made me look like the 'Beer Barrel Polka.' It got so if Ed Sullivan wanted someone to sing 'I Could Have Danced All Night' on his show, he asked Julie Andrews and not me. But I've finally discovered that your wardrobe can be one of your most important assets. There are women in every audience who spend the first twenty minutes of a singer's performance counting the sequins on her dress."

Barbara Carroll stopped at the table and said she'd play a few numbers before Sylvia Syms sang. After she had run through five or six, she smiled at Sylvia and announced her. Barbara moved to the far end of the piano bench, and Sylvia sat down beside her. They looked like girls sharing a swing. Sylvia warmed up with Sammy Cahn's "Can't You Just See Yourself?" She smiled broadly, lifted her head, and slowly rotated her shoulders. When the number was over, she eased into Harold Arlen's "As Long As I Live." Her head bounced up and down, and she snapped the fingers of one hand. She moved right inside the song, and, heating up the words, poured them out through the runnel of the melody. Then she sang an exquisite version of Billie Holiday's "Easy Living," and that created a peculiar sensation. The way Billie sang the song ran along behind her, and the two seemed to be singing a duet. She moved with a deliberate, almost heavy ease from word to word, and her voice echoed Billie's. She finished, and, crossing one knee over the other, folded her hands on her raised knee. Her voice dropped into a low buzz, and in a gentle, staccato fashion out came the opening words of "Imagination." The staccato passage eased away, and Sylvia went into a legato bridge. The deceptive ease with which she sang made her softest phrases ring. She considers herself a narrative singer, a storyteller who happens to sing her stories, and it was easy to see why. The room was in thrall and when she was done there was a long moment before the applause. She stood, bobbed quickly several times, and returned to the table. Barbara Carroll laughed and clapped; the swing had stopped.

Sylvia Syms looked in her mirror, and ordered more coffee. People came over to the table and told her how beautiful she sounded, and she replied with a round of pleased "Thank-you-darling's." Being a performer is like suffering a chronic condition," she said after they had gone. "Performing is also the most dominating mistress in the world; I'd never have been able to give so much to a human being. Singing for me is my total cleansing. It's what keeps Mabel Mercer young and full of the gorgeous juices and adrenalin, and it does the same for me. I have to have a personal, almost physical relationship to the songs I sing, so I paraphrase them in my head for my own understanding. I can't sing 'The Boy Next Door,' nor can I sing Cy Coleman's 'Big Spender,' because it's about a prostitute. And I don't understand singers who make a swinging thing out of a tragic song like 'Love for Sale.' So lyrics are terribly important to me. My notes follow the words and they generally land in the right places, but if they don't I invariably know it. If you laugh when you're singing, an audience will laugh with you, but if you cry, the audience won't cry with you. That is Mr. Sinatra's secret: his joy, his emotion never overreach; they always stop just in time. There has to be a certain amount of improvisation in my singing. I almost always breathe a song in the same way, but the notes are given a different emphasis. I perform in a one-to-one way. I have to *see* a face in the audience, and then I'll sing to that face. It's a very personal thing, to sing *to* people and not at them. I *need* my audience, which is why I never sing to myself at home.

"Before I leave for the great beyond, I'd like to do an album of all the songs I've done before, the songs I did first and kind of feel I own. I'd like Gordon Jenkins and Don Costa to do the arrangements, and I'd sing Sammy Cahn's 'Guess I'll Hang My Tears Out To Dry' and Harold Arlen's 'As Long As I Live.' And there'd be James Shelton's 'I'm the Girl' and his 'Lilac Wine,' which only singers like me sing. And I'd do 'Mountain Greenery' and 'Imagination' and all the Jimmy Van Heusen and Rodgers-and-Hart songs I've done before. I'd call the album 'On Second Thought.' I think it would be an important thing. When you ask as much as I have of this world, you have to leave something in exchange."

Still There

Peggy Lee

Norma Deloris Egstrom, the frightened, unknown blond singer from
Jamestown, North Dakota, who was hired as Peggy Lee by Benny Goodman in the summer of 1941, still lives inside the glacéed, world-famous
blond singer from Bel Air, California. What was visible in her act in the
mid-eighties was a creation that has been slowly and carefully constructed over the years by herself and by her various image-makers. This
onstage figure has grown more intricate. When Peggy Lee appeared at the
Empire Room of the Waldorf-Astoria in the mid-seventies, she was
swathed in white robes and white makeup, and she suggested snow
queens and Icelandic sagas. Now she is apt to wear a close-fitting helmet
covered with glass beads, huge, round tinted glasses, an egg-size ame-
thyst ring, a heavy rope of pearls, and various silk robes and gowns. All
that can be seen of her beautiful face is the tip of her nose; the famous
mole adrift on the alabaster sea of her right cheek; her mouth; and her
resplendent chin. The total effect is of antimacassars and gingerbread. The
contrast between this encrusted beauty and the simon-pure voice is startling. Peggy Lee's style settled into place in the late forties. She is a
stripped-down singer. She keeps her vibrato spare and her volume low.
(She has a powerful voice but chooses to hold it in reserve.) She avoids
long notes and glissandos, and if she uses a Billie Holiday bent note she
lets it die almost immediately. Many singers confuse shouting with emotion. Peggy Lee sends her feelings down the quiet center of her notes. She
is not a melody singer. She does not carry a tune; she elegantly follows
it. She is a rhythm singer, who moves all around the beat, who swings as

intensely and eccentrically as Billie Holiday. She is a subtle and brilliant showman. She can slink, arch an eyebrow, push out a hip and rest a hand on it, half smile, wave wandlike arms, bump, tilt her head, and slouch— all to dazzling, precise effect. And her shows themselves are models of pacing and sequence. She may sing two dozen songs, and they might include Cy Coleman's "Big Spender"; "Lover," in six-eight time; "You're My Thrill"; Duke Ellington's "I Got It Bad"; "Just One of Those Things"; Bart Howard's "Fly Me to the Moon"; "I Won't Dance"; "Love Me or Leave Me"; "As Time Goes By"; and Kris Kristofferson's "Help Me Make It Through the Night." She also does her own fine songs—"It's a Good Day," "Mañana," "I Don't Know Enough About You," "Johnny Guitar," and "I Love Being Here with You." She dips in and out of her anthems ("Fever," "Baubles, Bangles, and Beads," "I'm a Woman," "Why Don't You Do Right"), but gives full, affecting readings of the Ellington and Kristofferson, of a Japanese folk song, and of the strange Leiber and Stoller "Is That All There Is?" The voice slowly subsumes her image and by the end of the show has enveloped us.

A singer, a former singer, and a pianist talk about Peggy Lee. The first is Sylvia Syms: "I first knew her in the Goodman days, when she was known by the nickname of Norma Jean, which I still call her: She's always had great humor and great sensuality. She's very articulate. She's very intelligent. She is mannered—but Peggy Lee–mannered. She has a way of making her relationship to a song seem so simple. Her sound is like a reed. She walks away from any other singer. The colors in her voice are pastel rather than the bright greens and blues and reds of so many other singers. I have never once felt stifled in a Peggy Lee show—there is always a wonderful feeling of air. She's very caring about her audiences. There is none of the it's-too-bad-I-have-to-be-bothered-with-all-this feeling that certain performers give off. She knows what an exalted thing it is to be alive."

The next is Jane Feather, wife of the jazz critic Leonard Feather: "I started out in the early forties as a singer. I called myself Jane Leslie—in honor of Leslie Howard, who was very big. I was sent up from Minneapolis, where I lived, to replace Peggy in Grand Forks, North Dakota, where she was a great favorite—Peggy Lee and the Collegians. Then we both worked in Fargo. I was at one end of town and she was at the other, in Powers Coffee Shop, and we became friends. In 1941, she got a job with Benny Goodman at the College Inn in Chicago, and I was at the Edgewater Beach Hotel, and we roomed together. When Benny went to New York for a long gig at the New Yorker Hotel, we rented an apartment in the Village. It was a basement place with a garden, and we thought it was fantastic. Peggy was still pretty much a wild North Dakota farm girl.

Instead of buying six potatoes, she'd buy a twenty-five-pound bag. And she'd make bread and put the dough to set in a warm closet—and run down to Washington, D.C., to see a boyfriend."

The third is Mel Powell, the brilliant one-time Goodman pianist who has returned to jazz after a thirty-year absence: "Peggy was brought into the Goodman band to fill the celebrated shoes of Helen Forrest, and it wasn't easy. She was supposed to sing in Helen's keys, and Eddie Sauter's arrangements were difficult. I was eighteen and she was nineteen, and plain human compassion made me take her under my wing. I'd tell her to watch my mouth, and I'd silently count off the beats until she was supposed to start singing. One of Peggy's first assignments was a record date. It was in Chicago, with John Hammond in the booth, and she had to sing 'Elmer's Tune.' She stood at the mike with the sheet music in her hands—I'm pretty sure she couldn't read it—and it shook so badly it sounded like a distant forest fire on the first take. It took her a long time to settle down with the band, and one reason was that Benny didn't subject himself to any kind of sensitivity training. He rarely took the trouble to learn the names of his sidemen, so he called most of them Pops, which was O.K., but he called Peggy Pops, too, and that didn't speed up her acculturation. So a bond formed between Peggy and me, and it's still there. We talk on the phone, we see each other, and Peggy and my wife have become very close. Whenever I hear her sing, I think of what Louis Armstrong said on the set of a movie called *A Song is Born*. It was made in 1948, and a lot of jazz musicians were in it. Somebody asked him about swinging, and he said, 'Man, if you can't swing quarter notes, you ain't going to swing.' Peggy can swing quarter notes, and all the rest—behind the beat, on the beat, in front of the beat."

When she is working, Peggy Lee collapses on her days off—but not completely: the engines of publicity must be kept running. During a New York gig in the eighties, she had a one-o'clock interview with William B. Williams, the WNEW disk jockey and maestro of the "Make Believe Ballroom." She travelled the five blocks from her hotel to the station in a stretch limo, and Greg Dawson, the proprietor of the Ballroom, and Phoebe Jacobs, her old friend and aide-de-camp, went with her. Peggy Lee wore a wide-brimmed black straw porkpie with a big black rose on one side, round rhinestone-rimmed tinted glasses, a black-and-white silk knee-length jacket, and black pants and black shoes. Her hat was tilted, and her face was in the shade. William B. had been ill, and it was his first day back. He looked shaky, but his voice reverberated nicely, and he was pleased to have Peggy Lee aboard. She told him that he was a big part of New York life and that millions of people had been praying for him, and he told her that he was a big believer in prayer and that "a cry from the heart to God is the highest form of praying." He also told her that she was a basically small-town lady yet represented the height of elegance. Peggy Lee said she lapped that up. Williams said that he didn't know what an abashed fan was but that he was an unabashed Peggy Lee fan. Peggy Lee called him Sweet William, several Peggy Lee records were played, and the interview was over. The narrow, labyrinthine halls outside Williams' studio filled with hugs, and Peggy Lee made her way to her limo on Dawson's arm. The limousine went back to the hotel. Dawson disappeared, and Peggy Lee and Phoebe Jacobs had lunch in a small restaurant off the lobby. Phoebe Jacobs is a cheerful presence who has been an amanuensis of the likes of Benny Goodman, Ella Fitzgerald, Red Norvo, Duke Ellington, and Sarah Vaughan. She has a good understanding of how show business impinges on the verities of jazz. The women ordered fruit salads, which were served in long-stemmed celery vases. Phoebe Jacobs laughed, and Peggy Lee said, "I get the feeling I don't belong here." After lunch, Peggy Lee, now on Phoebe Jacobs' arm, went back to her suite, on the twelfth floor. The view from the living room was to the south, over Murray Hill, and was dominated by the Empire State Building. Peggy Lee attended to some wardrobe matters, helped by Phoebe Jacobs and by Holly Foster, Peggy Lee's blond eighteen-year-old granddaughter, who had made the trip from California with her. (Peggy Lee has one child, a daughter named Nicki.) Then she showed Phoebe Jacobs some enormous acrylics of roses that she had painted and brought with her from California, and that Mario Buatta, the designer, was going to help her sell, perhaps to a textile company. The acrylics were soft and elegant and finished. She sat down on a sofa and talked about herself. She talked in short paragraphs. Her voice is low but not soft, and she has a big, surprising laugh. She went where her mood took her.

"I live in Bel Air, in a French Regency house," she said. "It's stucco and has a mansard roof. The foyer is two stories high and has a circular staircase. The kitchen is white. The rest of the house is in different shades of peach and apricot. The house has more than ten chandeliers. The two in the kitchen are wood, and there is one over my bathtub. I have a wonderful view from almost every room of trees in the foreground and the ocean in the distance. It's a perfect place to grow roses, and I have at least a dozen varieties, including Bing Crosby, Peace, Eiffel Tower, Mister Lincoln, Mon Cheri, and the Peggy Lee rose, which is registered with the American Rose Society and is the biggest rose I've ever seen. Even the roots are enormous. I have a green thumb, but now I have a gardener with a green thumb, too, and we planted them together. Somebody asked me recently if I always dress up, and I do—even for rehearsals. But when I plant roses or paint I wear karate clothes."

"My father and mother had Norwegian and Swedish blood. Mother's name was Selma Anderson. She was a tiny, beautiful lady, who weighed about ninety-eight pounds. My father was Marvin Egstrom. He was tall and thin, and he had light-brown hair, which never turned gray. He had beautiful gray eyes and a beautiful smile. He was a railroad man—a station agent—and we moved from town to town. He always wore a three-piece suit, even in the remotest parts of North Dakota. There were seven children—Milford, Della, Leonard, Marianne, Clair, me, and Jeannie. All are gone except for Marianne, who lives near me and is my dearest friend. I helped her run away from home when we were little. When I was four, Mother died, of diabetes. She knew she was going to die, and she made clothes for all of us. My father was totally bewildered by her death. A year later, he remarried. My stepmother was cruel, and physical violence became a daily part of my life. She was particularly cruel to me, because I was my father's favorite. Unfortunately, my father and I didn't see much of each other, even though he lived into his seventies. But I know the value of forgiveness, and I've long since forgiven her."

"The guitarist Dave Barbour was my first husband. He was very handsome and had a special, dry sense of humor. He called Louella Parsons Louella Parsnips, and one day when we were playing golf and he swung and missed the ball completely he said, 'Golf is harder than oboe.' Another time, when he was being wheeled into the operating room and I was running along beside him saying, 'I love you, I love you,' he said, 'Stop nagging me.' And when I told him we were going to have a child, he said, 'Why, Peg. I hardly know you.' We were married eight years. But he had a problem with alcohol, and he finally asked me to divorce him. It was one of the hardest things I ever had to do. He eventually joined A.A., and he didn't drink for thirteen years. We remained close, and we decided to remarry. But he died four days later. He was only fifty-three.

"I've been married three times since, but I don't consider the marriages to have existed. They were of very short duration. It wasn't anybody's fault, and there's no bitterness."

Peggy Lee went into her bedroom and came back with a doctor's reflex hammer. She began to tap her cheeks gently with the hammer, saying that she had to tone up her skin for a television interview she had with James Brady at WCBS just before six o'clock. Then she tapped her forehead, and her throat. All the while, she talked about singing: "There are layers in my mind when I sing. When I was doing 'Why Don't You Do

Right' at the Paramount, a whole poem came into my head, and I couldn't wait to get to my dressing room to write it down. What might be emotionally feeding you—a person you're involved with, a musician playing well behind you—will form another layer. Still another might be: Did I wear the right shoes with this gown? People say my voice is thin or small, but I have a lot more voice than I ever use. I ration it, and it's lasting very nicely. I've compared some of my old records with my newest record, and I don't find any lessening. God willing, I'll sing as long as there's breath. And I certainly hope that I'll be able to tell if I weaken, or that people around me will tell me if I don't know myself. My understanding of singing has expanded as my mind has expanded. There are songs that I've outgrown, that I can no longer sing. They're miniskirts now. I'm a quick study, but it takes me longer to learn a new song, because I delve deeper into the words. It took me a year to understand 'Is That All There Is?' The reason I do 'Lover' in six-eight time is that when I saw a French movie with a lot of running horses in it it occurred to me that the horses' gaits were in Latin rhythms. I thought about a song I could work the same rhythms into, and tried 'Lover.' I also decided to change keys every chorus, which gives the illusion it is going faster and faster—from trotting to cantering to galloping.''

Peggy Lee retired to put on her "television face." She reappeared at five-fifteen, shaded this time by an enormous red porkpie. A smaller limousine waited downstairs, but her entourage had grown—Phoebe Jacobs, Holly Foster, Greg Dawson, who was waiting in the lobby, and Henry Luhrman, a publicity man, who was picked up on the way to the CBS studios on West Fifty-seventh Street. The makeup man at the studios turned out to be the same one she had had when she did "The Ed Sullivan Show," in the fifties and sixties, and he told her that she knew more about her makeup than anyone else. The interview with Brady lasted four minutes. Dawson and Luhrman left, and Peggy Lee told her driver to go back to the hotel. She said that Benny Goodman had been at opening night at the Ballroom and that he was in very good shape. "After Benny hired me, he would just stare at me, and I thought I was getting what musicians called 'the ray.' But I finally figured out that that look simply meant he was preoccupied—he had become so immersed in what he was listening to or thinking about that he didn't realize he might be staring rudely. I started with the band at the College Inn. The lighting consisted of a huge single spotlight, and I had the feeling I was being run down by a steam engine. Mel Powell saved me. He taught me the arrangements, and he introduced me to Billie Holiday's singing. Sid Catlett was in the band, too. He was a sweetheart. He cried when he learned that Benny was letting him go. I was with Benny two years, and that was a long time for a girl singer. One of the good things about being with Benny was that I got to know Alec Wilder. Alec and I used to sit and talk by the hour in the lobby of the New Yorker Hotel, where Benny was playing. Or, if we had time, we'd go out and find a curb and sit on it and talk. We were great curb-sitters. We even found a curb to sit on in Beverly Hills when the band was playing in Los Angeles. I introduced Alec's 'While We're Young,' and he wrote a song for me—'Is It Always Like This?' He also wrote the lyrics, which begin, 'Are the trees always so green? Has the sea this silvery sheen?' Alec always thought I was Alice in Wonderland. Maybe he was right."

Go to
Macy's! Buy!

Margaret Whiting

No matter where the singer Margaret Whiting is or what she is doing—shopping on the Miracle Mile in Los Angeles, singing at the Ballroom in New York, walking with friends in Charleston—she looks and sounds the same. She has a big, concave English face, bold, dark, well-spaced eyes, a distinguished nose, and an inturned smile. Her short blond hair is teased. She has stubby hands and good legs and a substantial figure. She sounds the way she looks. She has an encircling, quadrophonic speaking voice and a heavy-duty contralto singing voice that is equally audible in a small rehearsal studio and at the back of Carnegie Hall. All her attributes seem to have arrived in the same place at the same time; she is one of those rare beings whose talent and confidence, imagination and taste, and appearance and personality stay in balance. Such was the case at a rehearsal held in the green room of the 92nd Street Y for a "Lyrics and Lyricists" program dedicated to Johnny Mercer. On hand with Margaret Whiting were the singers Julius La Rosa, Marlene VerPlanck, and Carol Woods, and an accompanying quartet made up of Tex Arnold on piano, Gene Bertoncini on guitar, David Finck on bass, and Richard De Rosa on drums. Some rehearsals are disturbingly climactic: what comes later is never as good. This one, though raggedy here and there, had beautiful moments. Almost fifty Mercer songs were done whole or in part, and memorable were Marlene VerPlanck's soft, almost hummed (she is a microphone singer) "Skylark," with its startling opening words, "Skylark, have you anything to say to me?"; Carol Woods' fast, swinging "That Old Black Magic," a song she had never done before; Julius La Rosa's "Satin

95

Doll," "Any Place I Hang My Hat is Home," and "One for the Road" (ingeniously arranged as a duet, with Carol Woods singing "Blues in the Night"); and Margaret Whiting's "Lazy Bones," a legato song that swings even before it is sung, "Come Rain or Come Shine," "My Shining Hour," "Moon River," and "When the World Was Young" (also sung with great effect by each of the three others).

Johnny Mercer once told Margaret Whiting that she sang like a trumpet. Although she began in the early thirties, when microphones were prevalent, she has a pre-microphone voice. She has unerring dynamics, perfect pitch, and a tightly controlled vibrato. Some singers' voices always seem a part of them, like an invisible limb. Margaret Whiting's voice floats immediately free, and it becomes one with the song she is singing. So does her diction, which buoys every word, every line. At first, her singing seems matter of fact. It has an everyday ironstone quality, an old unbreakableness. But when you get used to its muscularity and richness, you find sotto-voce phrases, patches of lullaby, barely riffling vibratos, and easy growls. She considers herself a ballad singer, and she tends to avoid up tempos—big people, often graceful and precise, rarely run well. She was handed her métier. Her father was the songwriter Richard Whiting, and she grew up in a house filled with songwriters and singers. Whiting could write any kind of song well. He wrote statuesque ballads ("My Ideal," "When Did You Leave Heaven?"); lilting medium-tempo songs, almost jazz songs ("Sleepy Time Gal," "Japanese Sandman," "Beyond the Blue Horizon," "Too Marvelous for Words," "You're an Old Smoothie," "Louise," "Miss Brown to You"); and nonsense songs ("Tulip Time in Holland," "Ain't We Got Fun?," "Hooray For Hollywood"). He was one of the first songwriters to settle in Hollywood after sound came in, and among his colleagues were Harry Warren, Mercer, Buddy DeSylva, Harold Arlen, Johnny Green, Victor Young, Burton Lane, and Hoagy Carmichael. Margaret Whiting's friend and manager Greg Dawson has said this about her: "She doesn't have star hangups. She doesn't have the craziness and selfishness that generally come with the territory. In fact, she's never appreciated her own talent. Or perhaps she's finally begun to in the past five or six years. I'd say she's become not self-centered but simply centered. I suppose her lack of self-appreciation came from the fact that she started so young. That and the fact that she was Richard Whiting's daughter and was raised in a house where she'd find Harold Arlen playing the piano and Johnny Mercer singing in one room, Judy Garland and Mel Tormé doing duets in another, and Uncle Jerry Kern holding forth in another. Intimidating. But she loves to perform, she loves to sing. She's an all-embracing person. She has enormous energy. She wears everybody out around her. She's a non-stop talker, and when she's having throat problems she goes to the movies, because she can't talk there. She loves horror movies and thriller novels, and she's crazy about shopping. She can tell you the name of every good specialty shop in the United States. She has a unique relationship with songwriters. They're always testing out new songs on her. Many years ago, Walter Gross brought her a song he had written, and played it for her. She loved it, and suggested a lyric writer, who worked out. The song made millions. It was 'Tenderly,' and Margaret never even recorded it. She's a pretty good businesswoman, but I don't think she has ever thought much about money. I don't think it means much to her. She's never really had to work, because of her father's royalties—'Till We Meet Again' is one of the great all-time ASCAP moneymakers. Performers tend not to be terribly generous about other performers. Mention a peer or a newcomer and their eyes start to glaze over. But Margaret is different. She goes to every worthwhile night-club act in town, she goes to every Broadway and Off Broadway show. She's very supportive of young talent, and of old talent. Julius La Rosa asked her if he could run down a show for her that he was bringing into Michael's Pub. When it was over, she told him it was boring. She suggested a change here, a change there, and when the show opened at the Pub it was a great success."

The rehearsal ended just before six o'clock, and Margaret Whiting made some telephone calls (to a record shop, where she was due the next day to autograph some albums, to a couple of disk jockeys: she keeps the pot boiling), and said she had been invited to have dinner with her old friends Zeta and Sam Tyndall, who own a brownstone on East Ninety-fourth Street. The Tyndalls, she said, are American-song freaks. He can quote the lyrics of almost every song written in America in the past seventy years, and she can hum the music. They know most of the good American singers, and few weeks pass without Tony Bennett or Barbara Lea or Margaret Whiting stopping in for dinner. Margaret Whiting was dressed in a fitted black-and-white blouse and a white skirt, and she was carrying a purse the size of a duffelbag. She went out to Lexington Avenue, got her bearings, turned right, and headed full steam for Ninety-fourth Street. Zeta Tyndall, who is dark and pretty, greeted Margaret Whiting at the door of her house, and showed her into the living room, which was tall and shadowy and filled with books, early American painted furniture, and contemporary paintings by Helen Miranda Wilson and Fairfield Porter. Sam Tyndall, who is short and voluble, brought Margaret Whiting a glass of iced tea. "Put your feet up, Margaret," Zeta Tyndall said. "You must be pooped." Margaret Whiting sat down on a sofa, shucked her shoes, and lifted up her feet. Zeta Tyndall arranged some pillows behind her, and Margaret Whiting said, "Oh, God! That's wonderful!" The Tyndalls asked her how the rehearsal had gone, and she said very well. She told them how impressed she was with Carol Woods, a black singer who had been in *One Mo' Time*. She had replaced the late Johnny Hartman in the Mercer show, and although she hadn't sung any of the songs before, she was already doing them as if she had sung them all her life. Johnny Mercer is never far from Margaret Whiting, and he soon came up in her conversation. "Johnny and my father taught me to sing," she said. "And so did my Aunt Margaret. My father always told me to sing the songs the way they're written. He told me to expose myself to all kinds of interpretations, but that when I sang the song myself to sing it properly. Johnny Mercer would listen to me when I was practicing, and he'd say, 'You don't *mean* what you're singing. You're cheating. You're not giving enough. Think of a ballad as a one-act play. Find the top moment in a song, and build to that.' I also studied with Lillian Goodman for eleven years, and with Harriet Lee, at Metro. I listened to Mildred Bailey and Lee Wiley for their sheer effortlessness, and to Ethel Waters and Frances Langford and Judy Garland, who knew everything there is to know about singing. I sing all the time. I walk down the street and sing to myself, and someone will pass me and say, 'Pardon, but did you say something?' I don't have to concentrate on the technical things—dynamics and vibrato and breathing. They're just there. I think of nothing but the lyrics when I sing, of setting up word pictures. Each song has its own mood, color, texture. 'My Funny Valentine' is Larry Hart at his wriest, if there is such a word—'Your looks are laughable unphotographable yet you're my favorite work of art.' I'm very in tune with Larry Hart. I don't as a rule go into the lives of the songwriters I sing—I know you two do—but Hart's songs show what he was. The most important thing for a singer—or an actress, which is what a singer must be—is to know who you are, to not be afraid to stand naked in front of an audience."

Dinner was served at a long Shaker table in another tall, shadowy room. It consisted of poached chicken with a green sauce, baked rice, and asparagus vinaigrette. The wine was a Côte Rôti. Margaret Whiting ate heartily, and after seconds she leaned back and complimented Zeta Tyndall. Zeta Tyndall thanked her but said that, actually, Sam had cooked the dinner. Sam said that he and Zeta had been talking about her a few nights before and wondered whether the reference books were correct in saying that she had been born in Detroit and not in Chicago. "Well, I *was* born in Detroit, and it was July 22, 1924. My father was running Remick Music, and he had already written 'Tulip Time in Holland' and 'Till We Meet Again' and 'Japanese Sandman.' We lived in a brown house on Shrewsbury Drive in a Detroit suburb. My sister Barbara, who's five years younger, still lives in Detroit, you know. When I was four, we moved to California, and my father went to work for Paramount. At first, we stayed at the Roosevelt Hotel, across from Graumann's Chinese. I remember the smell of orange blossoms. Then we moved into a house in Laurel Canyon, and finally into a two-story Spanish-style house on Ambassador Drive in Beverly Hills. It was behind Jack Warner's private golf course. Oscar Levant used to babysit once in a while, and, of course, he'd play for me. I went to the El Rodeo public school and to Alison Ryan's dancing school—white gloves, if you please. My father was a short, slight, soft-spoken man who wore glasses. When I was very little, he'd sit me beside him at the piano and play Kern and Gershwin. He loved to walk and he loved golf, and he was always walking down to a pitch-and-putt place near us. He'd go with Kern or Harry Warren or Johnny Mercer. There was a friendly rivalry and great affection among the songwriters and lyricists. Jerome Kern was still king. He was short, and he had a stiff, fast little walk. He always wore wing-tip shoes and a sports jacket. He was not a warm man. My father came from Peoria, Illinois. I never knew his father, Frank, but his mother, Blossom, had a great influence on me as a child. Her parents had come over from England. She was a charming little person with dainty feet. She was like heather—purple. She wore purple clothes and when it was cold she'd put a purple coverlet on her bed. She read to me all the time, and she loved playing cards and taking drives. For her time, she was chic and groovy. My mother's name was Eleanore Youngblood, or Yungblut, as it had been in Germany. She was born in Detroit. She was the youngest of thirteen children, and her father, Bernard, had come from Germany. Her mother, Minnie, was old-country. My mother's sister Margaret—Aunt Maggie—was a marvellous singer and performer, and my mother eventually booked her. When they were starting out, someone suggested they go to Richard Whiting at Remick Music—music publishers were still very important. They did, and Richard fell in love with Margaret. I don't think you two knew that. He suggested the sisters see Jack Yellen, who had written 'Ain't She Sweet?' and 'Happy Days Are Here Again.' He also developed vaudeville acts. Aunt Maggie introduced 'Way Down Yonder in New Orleans' at the Temple Theatre in Detroit. Then my mother said, 'This is it—we're going to New York.' They met Ziegfeld and Irving Berlin, and Aunt Maggie was booked into one of the big vaudeville houses. For a time, my mother managed both Aunt Maggie and Sophie Tucker. Sophie was the definitive pro—new material, new songs every time she appeared. People always took her at face value as wisecracking and loud and brittle. But she was caring and very bright. I can't count the times she came to hear me and told me later to take more time with a certain line, to do my bow differently, to walk more slowly. Sophie was always on top of everything. After my mother died, a few years ago, my sister and I found a letter she had written to Aunt Maggie that was signed, 'Your old bow-teller.' It took a while to figure out that she was referring back to the days when my mother stood in the wings and told Aunt Maggie how many bows to take. Aunt

Maggie developed eyes for a dancer named Charles Mosconi, and Eleanore went back to Detroit to go to the dentist, and started seeing my father. In her outgoing way, she told him he should either go to New York and write for Broadway or go to Hollywood and write for the movies. What they did, in due course, was get married and move to Chicago, then to Detroit, which is where your confusion comes from."

Zeta Tyndall suggested they adjourn to the living room for coffee. Margaret Whiting said she didn't want coffee, but would like a glass of water. She went on, "My mother was a pioneer woman without a frontier. She was about five foot three and had dark hair. She had a kind of American Bea Lillie sense of humor—if that's possible. She was brave, funny, strong, and giving, but life was not always easy with her. I can remember her saying to me, 'Dinah Shore is doing such-and-such a radio show. Why aren't you?' or 'Judy Garland is doing such-and-such a show. Why aren't you?' In fact, it took a long time to find out what a wonderful woman she *was*. She and my father complemented each other. My father was a nervous man, and he had high blood pressure, and in 1938 he had a heart attack and died, at the age of forty-six. Aunt Maggie came to live with us. She'd been singing at Bill's Gay Nineties in New York. She called Cliff Edwards—you remember, he was Ukulele Ike, and he was in a lot of movies then—and asked him to recommend an accompanist so she could practice, and he sent a twenty-year-old named Skitch Henderson. I'd rehearse with her. Johnny Mercer became a mentor to us. He had come out to the Coast in the early thirties, and he and my father—such gentle men—developed great affection for each other, even though my father was seventeen or eighteen years older. When Johnny had first arrived, my father said to my mother, 'Eleanore, this man is the most gifted man I know. There's Kern and Gershwin, and there will be Mercer.' Johnny wanted to continue his friendship with my father through us, and he did. We called him Big Bad Mercer. He was a good painter, you know. He loved flowers and birds. Once, when Alec Wilder visited him, he found Johnny standing next to a bird feeder with an empty fifty-pound bag of birdseed in his hand, and Johnny said, 'I hope you brought some birdseed, Alec, because I've just run out.'

"After public school, I went to Marymount, with Harry Warren's daughter, then I went to another school, with Fanny Brice's kids and Lawrence Tibbett's kids. I never sang in high school. Most singers of the thirties and forties came up with the big bands, but I came up in radio and on recordings. When Johnny and Glen Wallach and Buddy DeSylva started Capitol Records, in 1943, the first three things they put out were 'Cow Cow Boogie,' by Ella Mae Morse, Bille Holiday singing 'Travelin' Light,' and Johnny Mercer singing 'The Strip Polka.' Then I recorded 'My Ideal' and 'Without Love' and 'Moonlight in Vermont' and 'There Goes

That Song Again,' Johnny was doing the a. and r. then, and before we did 'Moonlight' he said, 'I want you to tell me about Vermont, about the trees coming to life in the spring, about maple syrup. I want a spring-winter-fall-summer picture.' I didn't know what a ski tow was, so they changed the lyric to ski trail. The record was a hit, and here's a funny thing—I've still never been to Vermont. Life seems to have got faster and faster since the Capitol days—the radio shows in the forties, the television in the fifties, the Beatles in the early sixties and the bottom falling out of everything, making country music records with Jimmy Wakely in the late sixties, and the '4 Girls 4' show, with Rosemary Clooney, Helen O'Connell, and Rose Marie, in the seventies. And now this Mercer program, which I hope we can take on the road."

Zeta Tyndall asked Margaret Whiting if she had once been married to Joe Fingers Carr, the piano player. "We had eight good years," Margaret Whiting said. "His real name was Lou Bush. He'd been an a. and r. man at Capitol, but he also played funky piano, and he took up playing full time and called himself Joe Fingers Carr. He was a very good piano player, and he taught me a lot about singing and entertaining. He taught me the science of putting an act together. The first number, they just stare at you. The second should be a ballad, which settles them down. The third, you do something faster and go get them. And so forth. Debbie is our daughter. Lou died in the early eighties. My first husband, as you probably know, was Hubbell Robinson. He was a vice-president of CBS radio—very charming, very important at the network, and he had terrific insight into the entertainment business. But I lived in California and he lived in New York, and it was a tough go. My third husband was a cinematographer named Richard Moore. He invented Panavision. He was tall and blond and good-looking, and we saw a lot of movies together. That's about all there was to it."

Margaret Whiting yawned, and said, "Dear people, we have a position rehearsal and a dress rehearsal tomorrow. I should get some rest. Thanks again for the lovely dinner. It toned me up. Sam, would you walk me to Park Avenue to a cab, please?" Ninety-fourth Street was full of tree shadows, which moved back and forth on the pavement like water. Margaret Whiting and Sam Tyndall trudged toward the avenue. He was a head shorter and a couple of hands narrower. He asked Margaret Whiting how long she had lived in New York, and she said, "I had a fire in my house in Bel Air in the early sixties. I rescued my father's old 78s of *Madame Butterfly*, but I had to throw a lot of things in the pool to save them. It all made me think, Your roots are with *you*, not in a house. I decided to move to New York. I've been here ever since. When you're coming in from Kennedy and you see that shot of the skyline just before the Midtown Tunnel—it's breathtaking. The tempo turns you on, and that's very important to an entertainer. All I have to do is go out in the street and look around. The windows. The colors and sounds and smells. I wonder so often what such-and-such a person I see is like. One day, I had a call in my head: 'Get up, Margaret. Go to Macy's. Buy!' I got on the Seventh Avenue bus and all I had was a twenty-dollar bill. The driver told me, 'Find the change, lady, or get off.' A woman sitting there said, 'If I had a twenty-dollar bill I would have taken a cab.' But a man got up and gave me the change and invited me to sit with him. Before I knew it, there was Macy's, and he was so pleasant it may have been the only time in my life when I didn't want to go shopping. Then there are the parties where you'll meet a dentist, an opera singer, an architect, a novelist. Or you'll find yourself performing in a gala at the Waldorf, which I did several years ago when they installed Cole Porter's piano in Peacock Alley. I was singing away and who should come in and sit right down in front of me but Ethel Merman. That was a moment. New York teaches you all the time. I've been lucky enough to be able to do pretty much what I wanted. I've spent a lot of time around men—songwriters, agents, performers, my three husbands. I had never realized before I moved to New York what it was like to be a woman working in an office, or behind a counter in a store, or waiting on tables in a restaurant. Learning that has been illuminating and moving to me. New York is the biggest present anyone ever gave me."

Margaret Whiting and Sam Tyndall reached the avenue, and Tyndall flagged down a cab. Margaret Whiting got in, rolled down the window, and thanked Tyndall again. He blew her a kiss, and as the cab moved away the sound of her voice poured out the window. Tyndall could hear her say good evening and give the driver her address, and he could still hear her when the cab was half a block away.

Coming Out Again

Anita Ellis

The great dramatic soprano Eileen Farrell considers Anita Ellis the best American popular singer—praise not from the mountain for the molehill but from a superb classical singer who can sing popular music very well for a superb popular singer who can sing classical music very well. Miss Farrell has held this opinion for some years, and when she was asked about it she simply said that she knew of no superlatives that Anita Ellis didn't deserve. Anita Ellis is aware of Eileen Farrell's admiration, but she has never been able wholly to accept it. It is only in recent years that she has allowed herself even to consider the possibility that she might have an out-of-the-way vocal instrument, for she has suffered all her life from acute stagefright. For as long as she can remember, she has been frightened of performing (even *en famille*), and she is still frightened. She first realized the extent of her fear in 1951, when the producer Max Liebman signed her for the *Show of Shows,* with Sid Caesar and Imogene Coca. "I opened my mouth to sing at my first rehearsal," she once said, "and nothing came out. Mel Brooks was there, and he kept whispering, 'Relax, Anita, relax,' but it didn't help, and afterward I couldn't even talk." She has reached the point of being able to will herself to perform, but it is far from easy. When, after fifteen years of semi-retirement, she agreed to come out again and sing at Michael's Pub in December, 1974, she would tell her audience between numbers what agony it was for her to be there—her deceptively loose arms ending in tight white fists, her near-sighted gaze focussed blankly in the middle distance. These *cris de cœur* evoked antithetical emotions in her listeners—sympathy because of her obvious anguish, and annoyance because she had breached the magic, transparent wall between performer and audience. But she completed the seven-week engagement, and with such telling effect that she enlarged her already legendary reputation.

Her size and bearing and dress onstage amount to camouflage. She favors dark, diminishing clothes (turtlenecks and pants), and she is no bigger than a coxswain: a shade under five feet two, with a bladelike back and thin, wide shoulders. She keeps her head tilted and her eyes shut— in the hope that when she opens them everybody will be gone. But the fear-quelling momentum she works up for each song makes her a passionate performer, not unlike Judy Garland or Edith Piaf. Her voice is big and surprisingly agile. It is a buoyant soprano, capable of endless colors and timbres: pianissimo phrases capped with delicate vibratos; sudden sustained fortissimos that take on a reedy quality; jubilant middle notes; high clarion tones and low reverential asides. Her dynamics are consummate. Her shouts make us strain to catch the succeeding quiet passage, and her whispers soften her crescendos. Her diction says, These words are important—*listen*. And, caught up immediately by the power and shape of her voice, we are lifted onto the plane she has chosen for the song. When she finishes, her songs don't end; they subside.

In private, she performs constantly and brilliantly. Her speech is an extension of her singing. It is reverse parlando: speech raised to near-song. She will start a sentence slightly above middle C with a "Well" that stretches out and then slopes into an "I could just tell you," which gives way to a sustained "ah" and the substance of the sentence. Her rhythms and inflections and accents change continually, and form boxy, graceful melodies. She buttresses her talk with her hands and arms and head (she once, in talking of the bateleur eagle of Africa, turned her head abruptly to her left and crooked her arms horizontally to resemble huge partly open wings—and she was the eagle), with bird flutters and akimbos and vigorous nods, and with a dazzling quick smile that opens like a lens.

Anita Ellis lives with her husband, the neurologist Mortimer Shapiro, in an apartment on East End Avenue. The apartment seems to swim from its spacious back kitchen past a couple of dark bedrooms, an equally dark foyer, and a pillared, shadowy living room, and surface at a big picture window that looks out on Carl Schurz Park and the East River. This view consoles her, for she is quick to say, "I don't like New York. It is not my way." Her way is nature, and, in particular, wilderness, and when she looks out it cheers her to "check on the squirrels and the weather and the river and whether there are any new birds in town." She and Shapiro both love wilderness, but they approach it from opposite directions. She is an animal conservationist and he is a big-game hunter. It is not, to her distress, a pastime that he keeps to himself, for their apartment is hung from one end to the other with heads and tusks and spears and drums and skins and horns. Al Hirschfeld once likened the living room to the Museum of Natural History—a comparison that delighted the Shapiros, but for different reasons. She had learned to live with this panoply largely by ignoring it, and when they are out in the field (Africa, Alaska, Iran), she sallies off by herself while he hunts. She has great affection for Africa. "I'm home when I'm there," she said, standing in front of the picture window and sipping a glass of clear Japanese tea. "I belong completely. I don't understand what Mort does there—all the killing—even though he says the whole experience fills him with peace. When they go hunting, I go walking. I go down to the water hole at noon and watch the animals gather. They're popularly not supposed to come out in the midday heat, but I know better. The last time we were in Kenya, I found a serene clearing and suddenly there were three elephants. Elephants have miserable eyesight, and they couldn't smell me, because the wind favored me, so they went right by and I could have reached out and touched them. I revere that silence just before sunset, and when the sun suddenly disappears, it's like Toscanini: all the sounds start—birds, insects, and later the hunting animals. Those sounds spread out against the wind. I'm convinced this was where music came from. Man listened to all these creatures and imitated them on flutes and such, and finally wrote the sounds down. The sunsets are sometimes so magnificent they make you want to sing, and I have, for Mort and all the men. I sang in time to it—a lot of blues and made-up songs about what I felt—and I only stopped when the night sounds came up.

"I was in and out of the wilderness all during my childhood—in the woods near Montreal, where I was born, and out on the Coast, where I grew up. I was born Anita Kert, on April 12, 1920, a seven-month baby and the first of four children. My brother Mortimer was next, and then Evelyn, and finally Larry, and we're all very much alive. Mort is on the management side of the Los Angeles *Times*, and he's a painter and a poet and lives on top of a mountain. Evelyn has been married twice, but hasn't liked it much, and now she's a wine expert. Larry wanted to be a gymnast, and, of course, he's an actor and singer. My father's name is Harry. He was the tenth of thirteen children. His father was Isaac Kert, and he built all the railroads and dams in Canada, and was a great humanist and philanthropist. He came from Kiev when he was fifteen, without a word of English, and became a contractor. He married Jane Cameron, the daughter of a Scottish minister. They lived eventually in what is now La Fontaine Park in Montreal, and they had a hundred and fifty horses. During the summers when my father was growing up, Grandfather Isaac would take the oldest children a thousand miles into the Quebec woods and teach them to hunt and track. He taught me when I was little. Around the turn of the century, one of my father's sisters, Aunt Hattie, begged to go, and Grandpa let her. They found a man with a broken leg out there, and his name was Jack London. Aunt Hattie had green eyes and black hair, and she and London fell in love and had an affair, and my grandfather ended up as a character in a book of his. My father's oldest brother— Sonny, or Maxwell—died in 1908, when my father was thirteen, and the family never recovered. Afterward, they turned totally inward. I have never understood what happened to Maxwell, and I've never been able to find out. He was exceptionally strong and a great shot. But they were remarkable children, and all the rest of them were alive until this year. They only started to go at the age of ninety-eight, and suddenly there are just five left, including my father, who's eighty-three. Grandfather Kert told my father when he was little, 'You are going to be a rabbi,' and from the age of four he had training every afternoon at home. This didn't stop him from becoming an exquisite athlete. He is just five-eight and he's never weighed over a hundred and twenty-eight, but he was a sixty-min- ute hockey player and a fine boxer. He's perfectly proportioned and so well coördinated it's a pleasure to watch him walk. He married my mother in 1918. She lived in Montreal, but she was born in Bialystok, on the Russian-Polish border, and was brought over during the pogroms when she was four months old. Her parents were Aaron and Molly Per- etz—which means 'poet'—but she grew up as Lillian Pearson. She was one of eight, four of whom died in infancy. Her father had had a cement business in Bialystok, but in Montreal he ran a little shop for sailors. He was very orthodox, and eventually he became a holy man and left the running of the store to my grandmother, whom we called Bubba. We'd go to the *shul* with Bubba on Friday night and sit in the balcony and look down at the men, dressed in their yarmulkes and silk talliths and singing their beautiful music. I have tried always to put that music in my singing." She sang eight bars of a Hebrew chant, her voice full and low. She maneuvered the difficult intervals easily, and held the long, flat notes without quavering. "Both Bubba and Zayda, which is what we called Grandfather, lived to be very old. I don't think either pair of grandparents ever saw the other after my mother and father were married."

Anita Ellis had finished her tea and was sitting on a broad sill in front of the picture window. It was a good blue-and-white day—white light and a non-stop blue sky. Carl Schurz Park was almost empty, and trucks moved along Vernon Boulevard, on the other side of the river. A big black-and-green Moran tug passed, going down-stream. She laughed—a fast, bouncing descending run—and said, "Once when I was walking along the river near Forty-ninth Street a tugboat went by and tied up at a dock, and I asked them if they were going anywhere, and they said the Bronx, and took me along. I had the *best* time. I asked them about sea chanteys—I always ask about music wherever I go. They left me off at Broadway and Two Hundred and Twenty-fifth Street, and gave me a dime to get home on the subway. That sky is what I think of as a California blue. In 1926 or 1927, Grandmother Jane left my grandfather and moved to Hollywood. Two of my aunts were already there, and had told her about the climate and that the place was practically empty. We followed in 1930, and Aunt Ray Champagne—all my aunts married French Catholics—gave us a great big Hupmobile, which had a top that rolled back. My father joined a semi-professional hockey team right away, and for a while that was mainly what we lived on, until he went to work for the LeRoy Diamond Company as a tax man and an accountant. We had the most wonderful life with him. Oh my, I could tell such . . . Well, he took us on the John Muir trail in the Sierra Nevadas, and skin-diving in San Diego. We swam every day, and we learned to sail and ski, both of which I'm still addicted to. We got to know the mountains and the desert, and we got to know the ocean. My mother—my dear mother, who died in 1978—took care of the other side of our lives, what you might call the domestic and artistic side. She played the piano by ear and sang beautifully. Before she was married, Al Jolson heard her sing and saw her dance at a wedding in Montreal, and for years he tried to get her to take roles in Broadway musicals, but she said no. You didn't sing in public any more than you crossed your legs in public. Even so, she got herself a job singing on the radio once a week in Montreal when I was about one, and when my father found out, he simply updated the taboo—'My wife does not sing on the radio'—and that was that. Mother was dark and had very curly hair. Her eyes were big and brown, and she had Russian cheekbones. She was a quarter of an inch taller than I am, and she had a beautiful figure. I was the ugly duckling of the family, and had slightly crossed eyes until I was fourteen or so. My mother always told me that I wasn't beautiful but that I had a terrific personality. One morning, Mother, who was carrying baby Larry, pulled a Horatio Alger by helping an old man across the street who had a son who was a producer, and soon we were registered at Central Casting. Larry got a baby part right away, and later he and Evelyn were in *Les Misérables*, with Frederic March. I ended up with an M-G-M contract at a hundred and eight dollars a week, and I was in *Babes in Arms*, and *Strike Up the Band*, with Judy Garland and Mickey Rooney. I was literally a born dancer, and I seemed to already know time and double-time steps. Judy and I became quite chummy. We had a language together—fantasy, and all that. She had an exceptional ear, and she never liked to be alone. Mother's ambition all along was for me to be a singer, and when I was sixteen I started studying with Glen Raikes. I graduated from Hollywood High in 1938 and enrolled at U.C.L.A. and I would have been a psychology major except the singing had taken hold, so I switched to the Cincinnati College of Music. I auditioned for Eugene Goossens, and got a scholarship to study opera. I did well in everything—composition, theory—except solfeggio, because I had to perform in class, and that was when my troubles began. In the movies, I had simply been dancing, which was different. You aren't conscious of people staring at you, scrutinizing you, the way they do when you sing. I studied in Cincinnati with Leone Kruse, an old Wagnerian opera star, and she taught me to respect the voice as an instrument, and how the more you do for that instrument the more that instrument will do for you. She taught me that you are limited as a singer only in your range. While I was in Cincinnati, I got a job as a popular singer at WLW, which was the most powerful station in the Midwest. It was a program called *Moon River*, and it was on every midnight. I had already done radio work on the Coast, with Tommy Riggs, the ventriloquist, and had discovered that singing on radio didn't bother me. If there was a studio audience, I'd turn sideways and sing at the control room, which I couldn't see very well anyway, because of my nearsightedness. I stayed in Cincinnati a couple of years, and I met my first husband, Frank Ellis. He was studying drama and he'd gone to the University of Kentucky and he had a beautiful voice. He was Scottish-English-Irish, and tall and handsome. We were married in 1943, and off he went to the Air Force, where he became a colonel. I went home and worked for the Red Cross and got back in U.C.L.A. About this time, I became a friend of Salka Viertel. She had been a famous German actress and was married to the film director Berthold Viertel, who is the principal figure in Christopher Isherwood's *Prater Violet*. Her house was the center of the émigrés on the Coast—the Chaplins, Stravinsky, Schoenberg, Kurt Weill, Huxley, Isherwood, Stephen Spender. Chaplin would tell Salka he wanted So-and-So to dinner, and he'd buy the food and she would cook. One time, I was invited, and I made some remark to Chaplin about how wonderful it was that he had sided with the poor people of the world, how he was one of them. He looked astonished, and he explained that though he had once been poor he had no feeling for the poor, that we would always have poor people no matter what we did, and that he had risen from the poor because he was a genius. I was still at the stage where everything said by father figures like Chaplin was law.

"Then things began to break for me as a singer. I auditioned for William Paley for a fifteen-minute CBS radio program, *Songs Overseas* and got it, over Martha Tilton and I think Peggy Lee and Margaret Whiting. I did it for two years, and then went to New York for my own show on Mutual. Tommy Rockwell, who handled Dinah Shore and Frank Sinatra and Perry Como, took me over, and he wanted to team me up with Como on the show that sent him on his way. But Colonel Ellis came back from overseas and said we were going to the Jackson Army Air Base, in Mississippi, where he was to be a commanding officer. How could I not go, when we'd spent only two weeks together since we'd been married? Tommy Rockwell did everything to talk me out of it, but I went, and it wasn't hard for me. I got into things I'd never imagined—signing up Louis Armstrong and Duke Ellington for dances on the base, organizing lectures for the officers' wives, starting a newspaper, interviewing P.O.W.s. I also began to learn what the real world was like. I discovered the unbelievable life most blacks lead in the South, and I finally got so upset I went to see the governor. He got sore and told me he'd have Frank and me transferred, and the next thing General Curtis LeMay came for a visit and said he'd had complaints. I kept my sanity by learning to fly. When I got my license, Frank and I would go up in a P-38. We'd go up in the sky to play. But pretty soon Frank was relieved and sent to El Paso. El Paso! That did it. I told Frank I was going to resume my singing career. I went back to the Coast, and in 1946 Frank and I were divorced. We were always good friends. He was killed in a plane crash in 1957."

Anita Ellis said it was time to leave for an appointment with Marion Manderen, her voice teacher, who lives in North Tarrytown. Anita was wearing a black turtleneck and black pants. In the cab to Grand Central, she talked with great animation of a trip to China she had taken in the fall of 1976 with her husband and ten economists, doctors, and educators. She found a window seat on the train, and took off her coat. "I've never stopped vocalizing," she said. "It's like meditation for me. It makes me whole and peaceful. My mother and grandmothers had the most influence on me as a singer. Mother sang Romberg and Kern and Gershwin, and Grandma Jane sang Scottish airs, and Bubba sang Jewish and Russian songs. My sister Evelyn had a beautiful coloratura soprano. I also listened to Jolson and Crosby and Sinatra when I was growing up, and to Mel Tormé and Peggy Lee and Margaret Whiting and Jo Stafford. I didn't hear Billie Holiday at all until I did a benefit with her and Duke Ellington and Ivie Anderson in L.A. I couldn't get over how she changed—from that naked, smoking, tough woman in the dressing room to the cool, motionless, vessel-of-life singer onstage. Ivie Anderson was like a little girl in comparison. It didn't take me long in Cincinnati to find out that emotionally I couldn't be an opera singer. I thought of lieder for a while, and when I sing Sondheim and Wilder and Kern, who often write a form of lieder, I approach their songs that way. I always have to have a subtext, a motivation, before I sing a song. I've used my trips to the wilderness I don't know how many times. Sondheim's 'Anyone Can Whistle' is motivated by a big male zebra in Africa. Our guide had told Morty to try for it. Morty fired and it went down and got up and kept going, and they followed it as it fell and got up, fell and got up, and I ended up behind a tree practically having a nervous breakdown. The words 'I can dance the tango' in 'Anyone' mean we're wildly alive and then they try to kill us when we're doing the best we can. That's what that song is about to me. The subtext of 'I Loves You Porgy' is different but related. In the early fifties, I did a weekend at a hotel on Virginia Beach. The first morning, I was having breakfast looking out over the ocean, and a little child of three or four asked the black woman who was waiting on my table if he could go swimming. Well, what he said in his little voice was 'Fimmin'? Fimmin'?' She told him no, he couldn't swim at that beach, and she'd take him to a water hole later. After breakfast, I found that creature and took him down to the water, and the woman came running, and she was furious. She said, 'You can't do that! You can't do that here! You might get him killed later when he gets bigger and they find out he went swimming at this beach.' When I sing 'I Loves You Porgy,' I'm holding that child by the hand. I'm singing to him, and we're looking for a place we can just be. So my feelings come first, and the words come after and express them on different levels. I have to be careful, though. If I get too involved, I'm afraid I'll wander from the melody. You can't let too much emotion in."

Marion Manderen met the train and drove Anita Ellis to her house, which is on a tidal pond near the Hudson. Anita Ellis made a cup of tea to warm her pipes, and Marion Manderen sat down at her piano at one end of her living room. Anita Ellis kicked off her shoes and, standing by the piano in her stocking feet, sipped her tea.

"Marion," she said. "I was thinking on the way up of 1964, when I had the tonsil operation. Do you remember? I couldn't sing a note for six months. Why couldn't I get a note?"

"Your cords weren't coming together," Marion Manderen said. "You couldn't make a singing tone. We worked at least six months. We'd get so absorbed that darkness would fall. Then one day it came. Anita, what I'd like to do first is some humming. I want you to hum until you feel your lip tickle. Do: *me me me may ma moo.*" She sounded middle C several times.

Anita Ellis straightened her back, clasped her hands in front of her, made a triangle with her legs, and looked into the middle distance—or, in this case, into a mirror hanging over a fireplace. She sang the syllables on C as half notes.

"Keep the humming going through it," Marion Manderen said. She sat with her left shoulder to the keyboard, and she mimicked Anita Ellis's mouth motions. "Make it even lighter. Don't press down on the vowels." Marion Manderen moved down two notes. "Make the tones higher in your head, and farther forward. Don't let the energy of your breath lessen. I want it all in one breath." She moved down the keyboard slowly, and stopped at the C below middle C. Anita Ellis was having more trouble the lower she went, and she stopped and laughed.

"I want you to do: *hung me ma may moo*. On the *hung* get right into the vowel, and use the *ng* to resonate. Do it a little faster now. Throw your *hung* out."

Anita Ellis went through the sounds twice. Marion Manderen asked if she was resonating yet, and she said no. Marion Manderen stared at Anita Ellis's mouth as if she could see the tones emerge and were waiting to correct their shape. The two descended an octave and stopped.

Anita Ellis made a face at herself in the mirror. She patted her hair, which was in loose, even curls around her head, and she tweaked her face. "God. I look awful. I better go off to a spa and get refurbished." She laughed and took a sip of tea.

Marion Manderen played an ascending five-note figure. "Let's do: *eeyo eeyo eeyo eeyo eeyo*. I want you to feel it in your cheekbones." Anita Ellis tried the tones twice. "Don't press," Marion Manderen said. "And I want more on the descending line. More, more, more. Keep your throat open, and as you come down let your jaws go."

Anita Ellis's voice had gotten stronger and stronger. Her middle tones boomed a little, and her lower tones weren't scratchy. A half hour had gone by, and during the next ten minutes she worked through a variety of vowels, and rested. Then Marion Manderen said she wanted arpeggios, and Anita Ellis began with the sound *b*, ascended with *ee ee ee ya ya ya*, and descended with four *a* sounds.

"Keep your upper jaw more elvated, Anita. As you come down, you like to make that gutsy sound. But at the same time keep that *aaa* going out. Keep thinking *aaa* on each note. We want to keep that Italian sound. I have an image of a croquet wicket, of an arch of sounds."

"I think of a dolphin," Anita Ellis said.

"Slide down, slide down. If you can, slide on the outermost rim of that arc without pressing."

A couple of double arpeggios followed, and then a cluster of staccato-note exercises, and the lesson ended with more arpeggios. Anita Ellis's voice had grown strong and pure and open. "All right, Anita," Marion Manderen said on the last run-through. "Crescendo that last note. It's a focussed note, and I want a wide sound, which is the hardest to crescendo. I want energy. I want you to resonate. There! You did it!" Marion Manderen stood up and laughed and clapped her hands once. She headed toward her kitchen. "Before you go, I have some basil from my garden to give you."

The sun, hanging over the Palisades, rode with the train, and its water-reflected light shimmied on the ceiling of the car. Anita Ellis's small, neat profile was dark and sharp against the window. She was quiet for a time, and then she said, "I plunged into work after Frank and I were divorced. I did Red Skelton and Jack Carson, and I had my own show. Then Columbia gave me a contract to dub some Rita Hayworth pictures—*Gilda* and *Down to Earth* and *Loves of Carmen* and *Lady from Shanghai*. Orson Welles directed *Lady*, and he was always having vituperative fits. If anybody said they were tired, he'd shout, 'Why do you have to sleep? You don't sleep when you work! You work and work and work, and when the picture is finished you sleep!' I made lots and lots of money and bought a big house in the Hollywood Hills for my father and mother. Everybody had a room and a bath, and we were one big happy family again. Larry and Evelyn were there, too. We had always gotten along very well. We had never felt the need for anyone else. When Grandma Jane was alive, we had Sunday-night dinner at her house, and the whole family came—in Montreal and later on the Coast. We sang and did Highland flings and Russian koza-choks. It was a *freilich*, a happy time. I hung out, too, with Saul and Ethel Chaplin. They had a kind of musical salon, and you'd see Judy Holliday, and Comden and Green, and Gene Kelly, and Nora Kaye, and Shelley Winters. The songwriters came and ran down their new songs. I got to know Arthur Laurents there, and we became bosom friends and gave lit-tle dinners for screenwriters and the Hollywood Ten and such.

"In 1949, I went to Paris for two and a half months to make some recordings, and I thrived. I met Art Buchwald at a money changer's in the old Jewish section. He'd written a play that nobody in the States would read, so he'd gone to Paris on the G.I. Bill and was a student at the Alli-ance Française. He was a very funny man. I also met Harry Kurnitz, the screenwriter, at the money changer's, and one night Kurnitz, who had lots of money, took Buchwald and me to dinner at an incredibly plush French-Russian restaurant. I had had almost nothing to drink in my life, but that night I had a lot of champagne and got excited and festive, in my Ber-nardo sandals and my red silk dress with its pleated skirt. Kurnitz cried and cried and kept asking the musicians in the restaurant to play sad Jew-ish songs, and Buchwald and I laughed and laughed, and finally I got sick and had to be taken home. I also got to know Maxim De Beix, who was with *Variety* and was quite old and was married to a young, pretty woman who worked in a *parfumerie*. When he took me to lunch once, I asked if I could bring Art, because I knew Art wanted somehow to get a job on the Paris *Tribune*. At lunch, De Beix said that he was going to die soon and that when he did Art could take his place with *Variety*. Well, I tell you . . . he looked marvellous and we all laughed, but do you know he *did* die soon and Art *did* take his place, and from there worked his way to the *Trib*.

"When I got back, I went to Hollywood and dubbed for Vera-Ellen in *Three Little Words* and *The Belle of New York*. Fred Astaire was in both of them, and I had to sound like her and phrase like him—not a breath apart. He was a relentless perfectionist. He worked days on a single step. He was interested in the lighting and where the shadows fell. He was interested in how the colors of the sets jibed with the songs and with his dances. Everything had to mesh before you could shoot a foot of film. While I was out there, I went to a party at Danny Kaye's, and Johnny Green *made* me sing 'All the Things You Are' against my every wish, and that was when Max Liebman heard me. After the disaster at the rehearsal, I went to an analyst in New York and at the same time worked with Luther Henderson, the pianist and composer. After six months, the analyst said that if we were to continue, I'd have to get a singing job. I auditioned, and followed Pearl Bailey into La Vie en Rose. I was so scared opening night I broke out in blotches and had to sing the verse of my first song behind the curtain before my brother Larry pushed me onto the stage. Herbert Jacoby and Max Gordon heard me, and I went back and forth between the Angel and the Village Vanguard for the next couple of years, and then into Bon Soir. I stayed with the analyst four or five days a week for three years, but I still had a long way to go. I could have made a lot of money, but my fear made me turn down jobs all over the place. I did understudy Pat Suzuki and Arabella Hong in *Flower Drum Song*, but only because Oscar Hammerstein wanted me to. It was the last big job I took until I went into Michael's Pub.

"On July 31, 1960, I married Mort Shapiro. I'd met him in the fifties, when his first wife was still alive, and I knew I was hooked and tried for years to get over it. Mort doesn't talk about his past much, but things have filtered through, such as his father's having started out as a ragpicker on the Lower East Side and having become extremely wealthy in the cloth business; Mort's being brought up with a silver spoon and going to Columbia when he was fifteen; his father's disinheriting him because Mort's first wife was much older than he was. We were married in an empty room in a house in Turtle Bay that Stephen Sondheim had just bought. He lived on the bottom two floors, and we moved into the top three. I loved being married, and I became a *wife*. I knew almost nothing about cooking, so I read *Larousse Gastronomique*, which lets you go at your own pace, and I took five lessons from Dione Lucas. Now I'm a very good cook. Food has the most beautiful textures and colors and smells, and I love the peace and contentment of preparing it and the pleasure of giving it away. Right after we were married, though, Mort said that we had to have Billy Rose for dinner, and we did, along with Harold Rome and Melanie Kahane. We used to go to Chambord for dinner and I knew the maître d', so I went to him and told him how many we were having, and he fixed duck with olives and cold mussels in lemon sauce. I carried the whole works home myself and fixed some rice and everyone sat on boxes around the table and said they'd never tasted such a meal. I didn't tell Mort what I'd done for years. I had gotten to know a lot of the painters—Stephen Greene and Helen Frankenthaler and Andy Warhol, when he was just starting—and they began coming to dinner, and sometimes a hundred people would eat my paella and mussels in wine. Jasper Johns and Larry Rivers and Frank Stella would come, and Ellis Larkins would play, and sometimes I'd sing. Virgil Thomson also came, and he still does. He loves to talk, and the more shocking he is the better he likes it."

Anita Ellis took a cab from Grand Central to East End Avenue, and it went up Madison Avenue in the yellow evening light. "I never thought to ask for things for myself before," she said, "but maybe I'll sing more now and be less of a housewife. I'm scheduled for a concert at Alice Tully, and Ellis Larkins and I have just made a record. I think I know now that I can sing well."

American Singers

Teddi King

Mary Mayo

Barbara Lea

A certifiable body of classic American songs now exists, and we need an elegant and accurate phrase to describe them. These songs, variously and disconcertingly known as "pop songs," "popular songs," "counter songs," "novelty tunes," or "show tunes," have been composed during the past eighty years for the stage, the movies, and Tin Pan Alley by the likes of Jerome Kern, Irving Berlin, George Gershwin, Cole Porter, Richard Rodgers, Fats Waller, Harold Arlen, Duke Ellington, Willard Robison, Vincent Youmans, Hoagy Carmichael, Alec Wilder, Ann Ronell, Vernon Duke, and Stephen Sondheim. Modern American songs are not lieder. Their harmonies, melodies, rhythms, and forms are altogether different, as are their emotional impetus and effect. They are not art songs—a term that smacks of chapbooks and colloquiums. And they are not just popular songs or non-academic songs or jazz songs or cabaret songs or supper-club songs or theatre songs or movie songs. The belated recognition that they are not ephemeral, that they are the work of melodists directly descended from Tchaikovsky and Puccini and Rachmaninoff, has been brought about by many things, among them Alec Wilder's *American Popular Song;* the Wilder-organized radio shows given over to performance of the best American songs by the best American singers; Mabel Mercer's continued reign as the queen of American singers; the brilliant recitals given at Town Hall and the Ninety-second Street "Y" in New York in the early seventies by the late Johnny Mercer; Bobby Short's sempiternal engagement at the Café Carlyle; and the increasingly frequent appearances by Anita Ellis, Barbara Lea, Marlene VerPlanck, Mary Mayo, Sylvia

115

Syms, Helen Merrill, Johnny Hartman, Helen Humes, Tony Bennett, Nancy Harrow, David Allyn, Blossom Dearie, Hugh Shannon, Mark Murphy, Margaret Whiting, Matt Dennis, Jackie Cain, Dick Haymes, Mel Tormé, Peggy Lee, and Maxine Sullivan.

The singers who have been carrying forward this movement have made the beauty and ingenuity of American songs clear. They are the first to join the two principal strains in American singing: the "popular" kind (pioneered largely by Gene Austin and Ruth Etting and Bing Crosby and traceable to European light-classical music) and jazz singing (pioneered largely by Ethel Waters and Louis Armstrong and Billie Holiday and traceable to blues and gospel and instrumental music). They possess qualities that few of their forebears had fifty years ago, when the first sizable wave of "popular" singers appeared. Those singers worked chiefly with the big bands, and were wholly functional. They were intuitive and homemade, pushing their songs along before them, and praying that they would stay on pitch and finish in the same bar as their accompanists. Most big-band fans considered them unnecessary and boring—interludes to be tolerated until the next "instrumental," with its complement of solos. They were obliged to sing dreadful, of-the-moment material, and to sit on camp chairs at the front of the bandstand throughout the evening. Primitive sound systems, or even the band, made them inaudible to themselves and to those in the audience who *did* want to hear them. Their descendants are more fortunate, and are far better equipped. They are excellent musicians who can sing a song exactly as written (many have had classical training) and then, using their knowledge of Mildred Bailey and Billie Holiday and Mabel Mercer, improvise or enlarge on it. They are at once better schooled and more inventive than their predecessors. They are masters of diction, timing, intonation, and melody. Most are middle-aged, and came up during the last days of the big bands. Surviving the forties, they foundered on rock in the sixties, although a small number worked in studios and in the hotels of Las Vegas and Miami. The dilution of rock and the disappearance of the 10 percent federal entertainment tax have helped their renaissance, but the few big bands left rarely hire singers of their sort, and neither does television. Hospitable night clubs have appeared around the country, but even these are prone to fads or poor judgment. So it is always a joyous occasion when the new singers land jobs.

Three of the most gifted and tenacious of these new singers have been Mary Mayo, Barbara Lea, and the late Teddi King. Teddi King died in November of 1977. She suffered from a debilitating disease, but few knew of her illness, and she never allowed it to affect her demeanor or her singing. She was a miniature person. Her hands and feet were tiny, and her small, pretty face was dominated by lustrous eyes. She was barely five feet tall, but her voice was large and relaxed. When she performed, she invariably wore a hat, which was like adding a mansard roof to a bungalow. She had a rich contralto and a wide vibrato, and a peaceful, spacious way of phrasing. She never hurried a note, even at fast tempos, and she gave each song a serenity that carried it through the noisiest room. The particulars of her style were less important than the harmonious wholes she made of her songs. Traces of Lee Wiley and Mildred Bailey showed up, but her work was her own. She had a Boston accent and a pealing, old-fashioned laugh. She lived in a big apartment on the Upper West Side with her husband, Josh Gerber, who is shy and genial, and is an expert society-band drummer. She had a quick, dancing, half-moon smile. She talked about herself one afternoon in New York not long before she died:

"Josh and I were married in 1949, and by then I was *the* lady singer in Boston. I worked with Nat Pierce's band, and I was on all three of the local musical television shows. George Wein opened his first Storyville Club, in the Buckminster Hotel, and I got to know him and Charlie Bourgeois. Charlie started waving my banner around. Storyville moved to a bigger place, in the Copley Square Hotel, and George Shearing came in with his quintet. I sang for him, and he said my sound fitted the sound of the quintet. I went with him for two years, beginning in the fall of 1952, and the whole association was a joy. Then I went out on my own, and worked places like Mr. Kelly's in Chicago, and the Rendezvous, in Philadelphia. John Carradine was in the show at the Rendezvous, and one night he sat out front and stared at me, and when I finished he said, 'I want to thank you for not shouting at us.' Those were musically happy years, but they ended when George Wein became too busy to handle me, and I took on a New York manager. He didn't know the cloth I was made of. He didn't know the subtleties of my work. All he knew was Las Vegas. So I had an act written and sequinned gowns made, and I went to Vegas. I signed a contract with RCA Victor, and I had a couple of singles that did very well. I worked the big rooms and was on network TV, and the public became aware of my name. But it wasn't me. I was doing pop pap, and I was in musical despair. I didn't have my lovely jazz music and the freedom it gives. Elvis Presley got bigger and bigger, and rock arrived, and I got very depressed and thought of quitting the business. Josh and I had kept a little apartment in Boston, and we went back to it. George Wein had just moved to New York, and he told us we should, too, so we did. I opened the Playboy Club in New York and stayed there off and on through the sixties.

"I took a job on Nantucket the summer of 1970. The first day I went to the beach, I started feeling strange. I could barely maneuver, and I got a

rash on my arms. I was in and out of the hospital on Nantucket all summer, but no one could find out what was wrong until I went to the Pratt
Clinic, in Boston, where they diagnosed what I had as systemic lupus ery-
thematosus. It attacks women more often than men, and it goes after the
connective tissue. Flannery O'Connor eventually died of it. You take cor-
tisone. It makes you very susceptible to infection, so you can't get too
fatigued, and you have to stay out of the sun. I was bedridden quite a
while, and my main concern was whether I'd be able to sing again. Then
I started to mend, and in 1971 I worked at the Columns, in West Dennis,
on Cape Cod, with Dave McKenna. They gave me a room upstairs, and
the whole thing was a terrific tonic. Dave is one of the great accompanists.
Bobby Hackett, who had just moved to the Cape, would sit in, and *he* was
one of the great accompanists, too. I've been working where I could since
then—at festivals and on Alec Wilder's program and for six weeks at the
Café Carlyle last winter.

"I think my illness changed the emphasis in my singing. I've always
been enamored of sound, but I was afraid I might not have the voice I'd
had, and I began concentrating on lyrics. That, and I fell under the influence of Mabel Mercer, who is my goddess now. I'd never dwelt on lyrics:
I sang them and that was all. But I began watching Mabel, to see how she
touched people, and I discovered it was the way she put the lyrics first.
Her lyrics are her magic. Then she told me that, no matter how beautiful
its melody, she selects a new song only after she has gone over its lyrics
to see if they have any meaning for her. When I sing, I'm in a little shell.
I feel as if I'm reciting a poem. If there is a person in the lyrics—in 'It
Never Entered My Mind' or 'Little Girl Blue' or 'I'm in the Market for
You'—I become that person. The lyrics direct my choice of notes. They
take over, and I can just open my mouth and the sound follows. So I don't
think ahead in my phrasing, and every time I do a song it comes out
slightly differently. My singing is also influenced by the external things
of the moment, like the room or the people or the accompanist. A good
accompanist breathes with you. An inferior one forces you back into
yourself.

"My mother had a glorious natural voice, and she and my father, who
was a song-and-dance man in vaudeville, were always singing and listening to music on the radio. I was born Theodora, and I'm a Bostonian,
purebred. My mother lost three other children, so I became an only child.
She has never changed—shy and sweet and childlike. She leaned heavily
on my father for suggestions and interest, and then followed through on
her own. He died about a year ago, but she's kept their big old apartment
in Revere. My dad was self-educated and well read, and he could have
gone into anything. He was handsome and had a little mustache, and he
had such presence that when my parents gave a party everyone sat and

waited in the living room—it was as if they were waiting for Godot—until my father came in. Then the party started. When vaudeville gave out, he got into a printing-and-publishing firm and became a proofreader. My talent surfaced when I was four and sang 'Am I Blue?' in a great deep voice. I took classical piano for a year in the sixth grade, and since I'm a very disciplined person, I went on by myself, using whatever piano books the teacher had given me. It still relaxes me to play Bach and Debussy. Then we moved to Malden, and I finished school there. I was in the glee club, but I was more interested in acting than in singing, and I joined the dramatic club in high school. I minded not being able to afford going to college but the Boston school system was marvellous then, and a high-school diploma was the equivalent of at least a year of college. And I knew that it's not impossible to absorb learning by yourself if you have a mind to. I went into a typing-and-shorthand job after school, but my head was in the arts, and I tried out for a repertory company called the Tributary Theatre of Boston. It was in the New England Mutual Hall, and it played Shakespeare and O'Casey and light American comedy. I did a couple of readings for them, using a lot of accents—they liked it, and I loved doing it, because accents have always seemed to me to reveal the inner cadence of a country. They also discovered I sang, which I'd been doing right along on the side, so they gave me the role of a singing mermaid in a musical *Peter Pan*. I wasn't listed in the program, but Elliot Norton, the Boston critic, wrote in glowing terms about the young lady who played the mermaid and sang, and that triggered something in me: maybe I should think more seriously about singing. I never missed a show at the R.K.O. I'd sit in the front row with my lunch to see Sinatra and Helen Forrest and Helen O'Connell and Jo Stafford. When the R.K.O. had a Dinah Shore sing-alike contest, I entered it and beat out five hundred girls. My singing career began immediately. Winning night, two young gentlemen came backstage and said, 'We caught the show and wonder if you would be interested in singing with a friend who's starting a band.' The friend was George Graham, and he'd just come off Georgie Auld's band. He had a complement of the best musicians in town, and I joined for five dollars a night. They were at the Ritz Ballroom, on Huntington Avenue near Symphony Hall, and I was there for several months. I suppose I sounded like Billie Holiday, because she had influenced me a great deal. Then I took a weekend job with Jack Edwards at the Coral Gables Ballroom in Weymouth, on the South Shore. They were grooming him to be another Vaughn Monroe, and we had a lot of radio remotes. I was paid thirty-five dollars, so I quit my day job as a typist at the Boston Navy Yard. A family club called Cappy's, in Easton, Massachusetts, near Brockton, hired me next. Josh was the drummer, and I got to know him driving back and forth to Boston. This was 1946, and for the next three years I sang around Boston. I also studied voice with Mrs. Chester MacDonald, who had taught at the New England Conservatory. She said I had natural voice placement, and within six months I was singing lyric and coloratura things. She was heartbroken when I left her after a year. I studied a little jazz piano, too, which helped me with chords and changes, with dominant sevenths and flatted fifths. I feel best now when I'm working. The rest of the time, I take it easy and let the silly, petty things roll off my back."

Mary Mayo has an extraordinary range. She has said, "My voice runs from low A below middle C to A-flat above high C. I used to be able to go to C above high C, but it's not something you ever need." She can be compared to Sarah Vaughan, but Vaughan's voice is heavier and less subtle. Her lowest register is cavernous but somewhat harsh, her middle tones are three deep, and her high range is rather piping. Mary Mayo's instrument is of a piece from top to bottom. Her highest register is liquid and effortless, and it pours into her serene middle range. Her lowest register is a silken evening voice. She does not hit her notes dead center but favors the area just a hair above, which gives her singing a light, suspended quality. Of the singers of her generation, she is the most limpid and graceful. Her diction, like Teddi King's and Barbara Lea's, is faultless; she sets each word before the listener. She is of average height, and she has broad shoulders and a heart-shaped face. Her coloring and manner reflect her singing: platinum-blond hair, very white skin, and an after-church smile. She moves little when she performs, but she takes on an intense, almost beseeching look, which, underlined by her broad dynamics, becomes inescapable in a song like "Molly Malone." She is married to Al Ham, an independent record producer, and they have a daughter, Lorri, who is studying acting and who also sings. Mary Mayo lives in a light-filled apartment high over Morningside Park. It is a suitable aerie for her voice. She smiles a great deal when she talks, and her speech is tinted with a Piedmont accent:

"My father, Franklin Riker, was born in Burlington, Vermont, and he came to New York in 1888, when he was twelve. Someone heard him sing in a choir up there and recommended that he move to the city. He lived in Brooklyn with an aunt and was a boy-soprano soloist at Old Trinity Church, downtown. He eventually became a *helden-tenor,* and he sang at the Met when Caruso was there. He studied in Europe with Jean de Reszke, Cotogni, and Stahlschmidt. He returned to America just before the First World War, prepared for *Tristan* and *Siegfried,* but Wagner had been put away for the duration. After the war, he did sing Wagner, in English, and then he went into teaching. My father was a tender, kind man. He had very blue eyes, and his hair was white when he was thirty.

He was robust and had pink cheeks, and his hands were always warm. My mother's name was Lois Long, and she was born in Statesville, North Carolina. She's ninety-three, but she's still a pixie and full of spunk. She used to play softball and ride sidesaddle. She and my father met in New York. She had had an early, unhappy marriage, and had a daughter, and was studying at the Masters School of Music. My father heard her sing in church. She was a lyric coloratura, but he thought she could be a dramatic soprano. He told her, 'You're not using the best part of your voice.' She was furious, but eventually he convinced her, and she became a Flagstad singer, a Traubel singer. Her voice had a certain opulence and was a perfect instrument. There were no breaks in it, and she never had to make adjustments in going up and down the scale. She'd take a high F or G, and it would envelop you. It came at you, and it was globular. I've never heard that sound anywhere else except in Farrell and early Tebaldi. Once after I had sung for her, she said, 'You've got to realize, my darling, that you're just a silver bell.'

"When I came along, my mother went home to Statesville. I was born just after midnight. She had been playing bridge and listening to Galli-Curci records. There always seemed to be at least a half-dozen adults around when I was growing up. They made you insecure and yet you tended to lean on them. We moved to Philadelphia when I was two, and not long after that my father was offered a job at the Cornish School, in Seattle. We lived in the Hotel Sorrento there, and I became addicted to hotels. I was the only child in the hotel, and one Christmas I got sixty-five dolls. One had white silk hair pulled back in a bun and was several feet tall. Then we moved to San Francisco, to another residential hotel, and I learned to love foghorns and the sea. The Met touring company was looking for a second lead to Lily Pons, and my mother auditioned twice and got the job. But something went wrong within my family back in Statesville—some sort of a financial reversal—and Mother had to decide between the job with the Met company and going home, and of course she went home. I'd visited Statesville every summer and Christmas since we'd moved to the Coast, so I knew what it was like, but I missed the sea and the fog so much that I cried for a year.

"I finished high school in Statesville, and did two years of college—one at Mitchell College, at home, and one at Peace College, in Raleigh. When I was eighteen, I came up to Juilliard to study classical singing. I had won the G. Schirmer Award for high musical attainment. I had also won a prize in a singing contest sponsored by the Norge refrigerator people when I was fourteen. The song was 'Ah! Sweet Mystery of Life.' I didn't study singing until after I was fifteen, because my father felt that children sing naturally and correctly, and I'd always had a very easy voice. I studied with my father my first year of college, and continued those studies at Juilliard. But we had a lot of popular music around the house. My father admired Jerome Kern very much, and even knew him, and my grandmother was a Gene Autry fan and was invariably willing to listen when I learned the latest song. So I was ready for what I heard when I got to New York—Woody Herman and Dizzy Gillespie and Coleman Hawkins. Hawkins' 'How Deep is the Ocean?' and 'Body and Soul' sent me on my way. I stayed at Juilliard a year, and in 1946 I won an Arthur Godfrey talent show and worked for him briefly. I spent a summer on the Normandie Roof of the Mount Royal Hotel, in Montreal. They wanted a singer who looked and sang like a lady, and I was paid fifty dollars a week. They gave me room and board, and on Sundays, when I was off, I sat in the room and read magazines and ate bonbons. In the fall, I was with Frankie Carle for three weeks, and then, through a singer named Elise Bretton, whom I met in a choral group, I went with Tex Beneke and the Glenn Miller Orchestra. I became a Moonlight Serenader, and was also given solos. Al Ham played bass in the band and wrote for it, and we fell in love. In Olympia, Washington, we were married secretly, because people in the band weren't supposed to be married to each other, but Walter Winchell broke the news twelve days later. Tex gave us his blessing anyway. After a few months, Al and I came in off the road and starved for a while in New York. We did some club dates and I got some commercials. Then Johnny Mercer heard a test recording of 'Blue Moon' that I had made, and I was signed by Capitol Records. That helped me get a job on the Frank Sinatra show. Someone told me he'd said, 'I don't like girl singers, but I like that one.' It was a hard time for him emotionally and in his career. He was chasing Ava Gardner, and he was out of fashion as a singer. He was also a perfectionist. He'd check my camera shots, he'd check my hair, and we'd have long runthroughs. But nothing went right. Frank opened the show with the verse of 'Bewitched,' and the mike was dead. The stagehands took a long time getting the curtains right, and someone dropped a sandbag that just missed Frank. We had a new director each week. By the fourth week, I was dropped. But the job helped, and I worked steadily until 1956, when Lorri was born, and for ten years I went to mothering. I'm a categorized person, and I couldn't sing and mother at the same time. Anyway, everything has happened to me by luck. I have absolutely no drive. In the sixties, I started in at the studios again, doing commercials and such, and I worked for Al, too. I sang the title song he wrote on the soundtrack of *Harlow*. Last March, I spent two weeks at Michael's Pub. That was the first New York club date I'd had in twenty-five years, and I loved it and am ready for more.

"My specialty at Juilliard was French art songs. I had grown up with Galli-Curci and Lawrence Tibbett and Paul Robeson. If I had studied more, I would have been a lyricospinto, which is a kind of wedding of

Tebaldi and Sills. But I ended up a lyric coloratura. I have always loved the freeness and velvetiness and roundness of the great classical voice. I would like to have those qualities, and I would also like to have the sound Joe Venuti got on his violin, and the sounds of Johnny Hodges and Benny Carter and Ben Webster. I missed Billie Holiday and Mildred Bailey, but I've admired Nat Cole—the Cole of the Trio—and Jo Stafford and Margaret Whiting and Ella Fitzgerald and Peggy Lee and certain things about Doris Day. Margaret Whiting is a terrific example of how to pronounce words. The way she sings 'you're' is so clear. It's not 'your' and not 'you are' but 'you're.' My father believed that you should warm up like a pitcher before you sing, that you shouldn't perform without reaching a certain 'intensity of mood.' To gain this, you should stand very quietly, with a straight back, and sing a soft vowel sound, sustain it, and change the vowel when you move up a tone. You do this for half an hour, eventually locking yourself into the general vocal area you'll be working in that day. When I sing, I feel whatever the song is saying. The lyrics light up the melody—give the melody a tongue. Most melodies are dumb before they have words. I wish to get into the person's head—the listener's head. I don't sing at people, I sing *to* them. Even in a theatre, I pick out one face and sing to it. If I have rehearsed enough, everything becomes spontaneous, and I don't need to worry about melody, or about anything. It isn't fair to the audience to be concerned whether your earring is going to get tangled in your hair or your heel is going to get caught in the hem of your gown. My earlier singing was pretty and melodramatic, but now I'm giving a great deal more of *me*. I'm a different singer now from what I was seven or ten years ago. I've starting improvising. You find yourself eventually. I remember one of the early reviews I got. It said something to the effect that I was a pleasant enough singer but, alas, a not too exciting one. Things like that stay in your head—particularly when they're right. I'm anything but an exhibitionist, but I'm always aware that, whether I like it or not, when I stand there singing I'm on the line."

Barbara Lea is a singers' singer. She has no appreciable style, because style implies self, and when she sings she puts her ego to one side and attempts to make each song exactly what its composer and lyricist intended. She has a deep, dry, forceful voice; her tones resonate. She also has an even vibrato, great rhythmic agility, sharp dynamics, and voice timbres that move from soft to sandpaper. One immediately senses the bell of deliberation she moves under. Offstage, she has a damn-the-torpedoes manner, and she always seems slightly incredulous. Her face is square and handsome, and her chin determined. Her eyes slope at the corners. Her hair is reddish and short. Barbara Lea has a canny ear, and she likes to talk about singers and singing:

"Billie Holiday couldn't sing a song without embellishments. What she did, especially in the early days was terribly honest and direct. She flattened out the melody of her songs. She could swing incredibly. Sweet-and-sour, dill pickles, strong, cutting—she was an absolute. She sprang full grown from the head of Jove. Mabel Mercer ushered in a new era of singing. She ushered in the era of paying attention to each word. Before, sad was sad and happy happy, and they were always the same. She became terrifically specific with lyrics. She is a singing actress, as was Ethel Waters, who was outside the general run of singers. Frank Sinatra was the first big singer who took great care with his phrasing. He was a *purposeful* singer. He paid attention. There is a lot of shtick in Sarah Vaughan. She doesn't value songs. But she has a fine voice and a fine ear. When Mel Tormé sings straight, he sings beautifully. His tone is second to no one's. I wish he didn't have to be a star. I wish he could be a nobody, he's so talented. Bobby Short structures a song beautifully. He gives it such a dramatic lift. When he's got it together, his movements are marvellous—eyes, face, shoulders. And he'll break out those hands. He's not self-indulgent.

"Nor have I ever been. I was born in Detroit, and we moved out to Melvindale, which is near Dearborn, when I was very little. We were always singing and making music around my home. I grew up assuming everyone could sing and play instruments. My brother, who sang, tap-danced, and played harmonica, kept winning amateur contests. It was the age of amateur nights. People still entertained themselves, and it was still possible to be a Hollywood star. I was born Barbara LeCocq, which was changed to Leacock when I was four or five. I started using Lea when I made my first recordings, in the early fifties, and I've also had three married names. My father was an assistant attorney general in Michigan. He could be a brilliant, charming, sparkling man, and other times he could be critical and picky and putting-down. He probably should have been a classical clarinettist. He played in the pit band for Al Jolson's *Sinbad* after the First World War, and he studied with the first clarinettist of the New York Philharmonic. But, with his strict background, it was unthinkable to go into music. My mother is intelligent and fun, and everybody loves her. She wasn't around a lot when I was little. She worked, and my grandmother took care of me. But she's very motherly, my mother. There were hard times when we lived in Melvindale, even though we were comparatively well off. We moved back to Detroit when I was ten. I'd been in a little town where I was the smartest in the class and my father was on the school board, so I was resented. I got in the habit of trying to be inconspicuous. When I was sent to a huge school in Detroit, I waited for them to find out I was good, but they never bothered. It took a long time before I learned to come out of that shell.

"I went to Wellesley. I liked the music department, and the place was physically beautiful. I studied counterpoint and orchestration and composition, but there was no ear training, and my ear deteriorated from lack of use. I spent a lot of time in Boston listening to jazz and singing with groups like the Crimson Stompers, at Harvard. I had started singing in high school and had had some coaching. Summers, I sang a little at an outdoor dance place near a cottage we had in Belle River, Ontario. Father had to ask the leader if I could sing with the band. Billie Holiday was my idol, and I saw Mildred Bailey in Boston. After graduation, I supported myself as a secretary in Boston, at thirty-five dollars a week, and I collected cover charges at the tables for George Wein at his Storyville Club. I sang with Lester Lanin-type groups. Then I went to New York, and through a friend of my parents I found a steady job in a clip joint in Union City. There were four chorus girls, too, and all of us were expected to sit with the customers, but I was bad at that. I was bad at everything. I had no stage presence. I was scared to death. I didn't know what to do with my hands. So I retreated to Boston, and worked in lounges where it was safe and dark. I slowly got tough. I worked with a piano player in Boston who couldn't read, couldn't keep a beat, couldn't transpose, couldn't play the songs of the day, and hated to play the piano. And that gave me a great musical independence—I learned to sing with anyone, anywhere, under any conditions. I made my first record in 1954, and moved to New York for good. Things began to happen. I made a record for Riverside in the spring of 1955. It got great reviews, and John Wilson listed it as one of the albums of the year, along with Marlene Dietrich and Bing Crosby and the *Oklahoma!* soundtrack. I won a *down beat* poll as the best new singer in 1956, and I worked at the Village Vanguard. But I didn't believe any of it. I considered myself a college kid who happened to sing. I didn't accept myself as a grownup. I had gotten married and my husband managed me, but we split up and I was convinced I couldn't go on working without him. So I started at the Lane Theatre Workshop, on West Forty-sixth Street. It was run by a brilliant man named Burt Lane, who, by choice, is now driving a cab. Jean Shepherd sent me there. I began to learn about people: that they didn't always mean what they said, that you didn't have to tell the truth—or, rather, that other people didn't. I learned something about alternatives in life and art. I began to come out of my dream world. I had a twenty-dollar flat in SoHo, which I had to heat myself. I made a movie full of liberal dialogue about Castro called *Rebellion in Cuba,* and I had a substantial part in *Finnegans Wake.* The first was shot in Coral Gables and I was the leading lady and it was terrible, and the second was made in New York and shown maybe twice. I got a job with the Stanley Woolf Players in the Catskills. Tony Curtis came out of them. We stayed in Liberty and went out to a different hotel every night. It was thirty a week and room and board. I did some Off Broadway and a lot of summer stock, and I generally worked enough to get unemployment. During this time, I sang when I got the chance—at a family place called Vinnie's Horseshoe Bar, in Astoria, and on a concert tour with Marian McPartland and Mose Allison. I sang all the time in elevators and supermarkets and on the street. But I didn't work anywhere as a singer after 1964. I had become a housewife and an actress in California, and after that I got my master's in drama at San Fernando Valley State College, and came back East and taught speech at the American Academy of Dramatic Arts and acting at Hofstra College.

"In 1972, I ran into a piano player I'd worked with fifteen years before. He said he was in a little place at Fifteenth Street and Irving Place, and I sat in with him for three hours one night. I began dropping in there, and I started going back to Vinnie's Horseshoe one or two nights a week. Things have multiplied, and it looks as if I'm back singing again. I did Alec Wilder's radio show and had two engagements at Michael's Pub. But I will always keep my hand in the theatre.

"There is nothing as sensual as singing. Acting is quite different. There is the teamwork, and exploring another person and his emotions and responses. In a way, everything is given to you—costumes, script. The words are not your responsibility but the character's. Singing is nothing but *me*, and years ago I was swamped by the responsibility of it. Now my face isn't locked, my back isn't frozen. I can let my face and my body go with what I'm singing about. Phrasing has to do with the meaning of the lyrics and the play of rhythm against rhythm. Even when I'm singing a phrase, I hear two or three other ways of singing it. I like to think the unheard ways are subliminally present. Singing is a very physical act. It's your lips and teeth and mouth. It's your chest, where the sounds are resounding. The meaning and textures of the words you sing roll around in the body before they gather and go into the microphone. It all comes back through your ear, and that's another sensation, as is moving any part of your body while you're singing. I didn't realize how marvellous the textures of the consonants are until I studied speech with Arthur Lessac. He likens the letters of the alphabet to the instruments of the orchestra. 'B's, 'P's, 'D's, 'T's, 'K's, and 'G's are drumbeats. 'Ch's and 'Dg's are cymbals. 'L's are saxophones. 'R's are trombones. When you say a word like 'asks,' you fall in love with English and realize what an extraordinary language it is. Something happens at a good performance. The singer and the audience hold it together. When Teddi King was at the Carlyle, singer and song and audience became one. I'm totally involved when I'm singing, but part of me is always monitoring the rest of me to keep the content and the precision in balance. I want to weave as nearly complete a tapestry as I can. Singing isn't playing an instrument. There are words, and words have their own music. They also have meaning, which should be expressed in your tone, your timbre. The tone you employ is consciously not always the most beautiful. When you sing 'That man of mine ain't comin' home,' in Irving Berlin's 'Supper Time,' you should use a sound that expresses anger and sadness and finality. Some singers sing every song with the same tone, and that is like speaking in a monotone. If you're going to do 'Down in the Depths on the Ninetieth Floor,' you should have some rage and bitterness in your tone. You should not have a beautiful sound. There are many singers who *use* music. I resent that. Music is sacred. The song has to control the performance. Doing anything else—employing this or that trick—to make the audience applaud is an outrage. Then you are making them applaud *you*.

"A good accompanist must know that he and the singer are there to serve the song. He should love songs, and I mean music *and* words. And he should be free of attitudes and prejudices and prejudgments—like if it isn't a so-called jazz tune, it isn't good. The most important quality musically in an accompanist is rhythm, and that means being able to swing and to control the motion of the song. A good accompanist has to know how to go along with your phrasing—whether to play counterpoint or echo you or put in a little resonant harmony. Just one right note from a good accompanist can send you flying. An accompanist like Jimmy Rowles *listens*, and with one like Dave McKenna I can almost *see* the power descending from Heaven and coming out in those hands."

Barbara Lea has worked more and more since those words were written in the late seventies. Here is a postscript on what she sounds like in the late eighties—and on what happened to the great cabaret revival of the seventies:

Singers seemed to be everywhere in New York in the seventies. Mabel Mercer and Bobby Short were enthroned at the St. Regis and at the Carlyle, and Hugh Shannon was at Soerabaja and David K's. Anita Ellis had her famous six-week stint at the Bird Cage. Sylvia Syms turned up fairly regularly, along with Blossom Dearie and Jackie and Roy. Johnny Hartman and David Allyn and Mark Murphy were at Michael's Pub. Matt Dennis, Mel Tormé, Anita O'Day, Peggy Lee, Margaret Whiting, and Johnny Mercer came in from the Coast. Excellent but little-known singers like Barbara Lea and Teddi King and Mary Mayo and Carol Sloane reappeared, and there were new singers like Marlene VerPlanck and Nancy Harrow. Ella Fitzgerald and Sarah Vaughan became fixtures at the Newport Jazz Festival—New York, and Lee Wiley came out of retirement for her final public appearance, at the 1972 festival—with indelible effect. Old Masters like Helen Humes and Alberta Hunter and Joe Turner had long engagements at the Cookery. Tony Bennett and Lena Horne gave a show on Broadway, and so did Bing Crosby. Frank Sinatra started playing Carnegie Hall. Then a lot of these irreplaceable figures died (Johnny Mercer, Shannon, Hartman, King, Humes, Turner, Hunter, Mayo, Wiley, Crosby, and Mabel Mercer), and, what with economic pressures and aging voices, the renaissance flickered and went out. (The odd, synthetic presence of Linda Ronstadt during the past couple of years has not been of much consequence.) So American singers have gone back underground. One is Barbara Lea, who, singing better than she did ten years ago, has no superior among popular singers. She now works three or four times a month at Jan Wallman's Restaurant on West Forty-fourth Street. Accompanied by the excellent pianist West McAfee, she sings the songs she wants to sing in the way she wants to sing them, and the results are often electric. Her voice, always a precise, resounding contralto, has grown. It once had a dryness and rigidity that were particularly noticeable when she was tired or was singing under difficult conditions. She now moves effortlessly from delicate passages to fortes. She croons. She growls. She uses a feather vibrato and a bravura one. She acts, as all good singers should. She even whistles well. For all this, she remains the servant of her songs. She keeps her vowels hollow and her consonants solid, and she brings the lyrics up into the face of the melody. And she has a flawless sense of melody, of how to make a series of disconnected notes come together and move as if they were one magic note. She is passionate about pure singing and about singing itself, as she pointed out in the introduction of her instructional book *How to Sing Jazz*, published by Chappell in 1980: "So here again is that prime rule: SING. Sing all the time. Sing with the radio, with records, with the canned music in grocery stores and elevators. Sing with the piano. . . . Sing without accompaniment. Sing all the time. If singing is not first nature to you, sing and sing until it is second nature."

Here is how one of Barbara Lea's sets went at Jan Wallman's. She warmed up with Alec Wilder's "It's a Fine Day for Walkin' Country Style," decorating it with a passage of whistling. Cole Porter's "Dream Dancing," brought out of obscurity during the past ten years by jazz musicians, followed in a medium tempo. Then she did a *slow* "Limehouse Blues," converting it to an equally slow version of the beautiful "Poor Butterfly." She did some growling and shouting on "Harlem on My Mind," written by Irving Berlin for Ethel Waters, and passed easily through Annie Dinerman's busy "Valentine." She sang Rodgers and

Hart's "I Must Love You," and Kurt Weill's "This Is New," ad lib. She swung Rodgers and Hammerstein's waltz "Hello, Young Lovers," and Rodgers and Hart's "My Funny Valentine," which she did with the verse and partly a cappella. And she put great resonance into Jerome Kern's "Make Believe." She sang two Dave Frishbergs—a blues and the almost heavy "The Green Hills of Earth." She did a very fast rendition of Billie Holiday's "What a Little Moonlight Can Do," forcing that silly song past its limits. She sang all hundred and eight measures of Porter's "Begin the Beguine," doing it a cappella and ad lib and in medium-slow time; the song, usually cardboard and paste, became an elegant, even sinuous, ballad. She closed with a dramatic reading of John Clifton and Ben Tarver's "Come to the Masquerade." It was an almost flawless set—full of first-rate songs, sung with imagination and great care by a singer who sings as easily as she breathes.

A Quality That Lets You In

Tony Bennett

The number and variety of American Singers are astonishing and almost endless. Their names form an American mythology: Russ Columbo, Whispering Jack Smith, Gene Austin, Jeanette MacDonald, Nelson Eddy, Sophie Tucker, Alberta Hunter, Arthur Tracy, Al Jolson, Kate Smith, Rudy Vallée, Bessie Smith, Jelly Roll Morton, Fred Astaire, Louis Armstrong, Mildred Bailey, Red McKenzie, Ivie Anderson, Ethel Waters, Bing Crosby, Ella Fitzgerald, Billie Holiday, Tony Martin, Ethel Merman, Johnny Mercer, Jack Teagarden, Josh White, Joe Turner, Jimmy Rushing, Mabel Mercer, the Boswell Sisters, the Andrews Sisters, the Mills Brothers, the Ink Spots, the Golden Gate Quartette, Helen Humes, Mary Martin, Ray Nance, Leo Watson, Paul Robeson, Maxine Sullivan, Lee Wiley, Dick Haymes, Bob Eberly, Ray Eberle, Helen O'Connell, Louise Tobin, Pha Terrell, Woody Guthrie, Gene Autry, Pete Seeger, Johnny Cash, Eddy Arnold, Noble Sissle, Bon Bon Tunnell, Richard Dyer-Bennett, Helen Ward, Hildegarde, Morton Downey, Martha Tilton, Cleo Brown, Helen Forrest, Frank Sinatra, Georgia Gibbs, Jeri Southern, Nat King Cole, Hoagy Carmichael, Anita O'Day, Kenny Baker, June Christy, David Allyn, Mark Murphy, Eddie Fisher, Julius La Rosa, Frankie Laine, Vaughn Monroe, Frances Langford, Sylvia Syms, Johnny Mathis, Rosemary Clooney, Nellie Lutcher, Leadbelly, Judy Garland, Dinah Shore, Billy Eckstine, Eartha Kitt, Buddy Greco, Peggy Lee, Harry Belafonte, Anita Ellis, Irene Kral, Bo Diddley, Elvis Presley, Lena Horne, Doris Day, Pearl Bailey, Perry Como, Vic Damone, Paul Anka, Margaret Whiting, Mel Tormé, Bobby Troup, Matt Dennis, Hugh Shannon, Jo Stafford, Johnny Hartman,

Tony Bennett, Blossom Dearie, Teddi King, Mary Mayo, Kay Starr, Patti Page, Carmen McRae, Jackie Cain, Roy Kral, Teresa Brewer, Dean Martin, Marlene VerPlanck, Barbara Lea, Sarah Vaughan, Annie Ross, Ray Charles, Mahalia Jackson, Shirley Horn, Bobby Short, Julie Wilson, Helen Merrill, Carol Sloane, Stella Brooks, Dinah Washington, Chris Connor, Andy Williams, Jack Jones, Steve Lawrence, Eydie Gormé, Peter Allen, Dionne Warwick, James Brown, B. B. King, Aretha Franklin, Joan Baez, Barbra Streisand, Bob Dylan, Janis Joplin, Nina Simone, Nancy Harrow, Glen Campbell, Dave Frishberg, Roberta Flack, and Linda Ronstadt. They have, in the past fifty years, become ubiquitous—on the radio, on records, on jukeboxes, in the movies, on the stage, in night clubs, on television, and in concert halls. Indeed, they have created, as a huge, ceaselessly moving and changing body of troubadours, the most pervasive and familiar sounds in American life. Many are famous, and some are among the most famous people of this century. Few adults in the Western world are unaware of Bing Crosby and Frank Sinatra and Judy Garland and Nat King Cole and Tony Bennett and of the anthem status they have, respectively, given such songs as "White Christmas," "I'll Never Smile Again," "Over the Rainbow," "Nature Boy," and "I Left My Heart in San Francisco." One of the reasons for this outpouring of song was the invention of the microphone, which, together with its handmaidens, radio and the recording, made two things possible: omnipresent singing, and a successful singing career without a voice. Another was the appearance in the tens and twenties and thirties of the first great American songwriters; the lives of their countless marvellous songs were wholly dependent on being performed, and so a new and insatiable demand for more and better singers arose. Still another reason was our old habit of letting off excess emotional and romantic steam through singing. (Never has there been more singing in this country than during the Depression and the Second World War.) Consider the minstrel singers, the cowboys, the slaves who first sang blues and spirituals, the young women who performed the latest Stephen Foster in the parlor of an evening, the hillbilly singers, the Irish and Neapolitan tenors, and the light-classical singers such as John McCormack and Lawrence Tibbett. The first microphone singers were the crooners, who, with their patent-leather baritones and oily vibratos, evolved from the basically European singing of the McCormacks and Tibbetts in the twenties. And out of the crooners came Bing Crosby, who, cutting the silver cord to Europe, almost by himself invented American popular singing.

Bing Crosby and Ethel Waters were the first American singers to learn this trick, and they did it in large part by listening to jazz musicians. Crosby in particular listened to Louis Armstrong and Duke Ellington (he recorded "St. Louis Blues" with Ellington in 1932), and he was tutored by

Mildred Bailey when he was one of Paul Whiteman's Rhythm Boys. He hung out in Chicago with Bix Beiderbecke and Jimmy McPartland. He learned to sing legato, to phrase in a "lazy" fashion. He learned rubato and the ornamental, open-glottal notes—the "aaums" and "oowoos"— that made every phrase he sang sound as if it started with a vowel. The great instrumentalists like Beiderbecke "sing" on their horns, and through them he was taught to flow melodically. He learned to make his comfortable, front-porch baritone appear capacious and important. In turn, he taught a generation of popular singers. The best of them was Frank Sinatra. Sinatra had also listened to Armstrong and Mildred Bailey, but he had as well, grown up on Billie Holiday and Mabel Mercer. Sinatra was a more serious singer than Crosby. At the outset of his career, Sinatra sang with Tommy Dorsey's band, and Dorsey, a lyrical player of the first order, taught him—in Dorsey's words—how to "drive a ballad." Sinatra's ballads, freed of Crosby's ornamentation and reverberative effects, took on an almost churchlike dimension. He *believed* the lyrics he sang, and he delivered them with an intense, clean articulation. His voice was smaller and lighter than Crosby's, but his phrasing and immaculate sense of timing gave it a poise and stature Crosby's lacked. Sinatra, in his turn, brought along another generation of popular singers, and one of the best is Tony Bennett, who has become the most widely admired American popular singer. Alec Wilder, who has known Bennett for many years, once wrote, "The list of 'believers' isn't very long. But those who are on it are very special people. Among them, certainly, is Tony Bennett. But first I should say what I mean by a believer. He is one whose sights stay high, who makes as few concessions as he can, whose ideals will not permit him to follow false trails or fashions for notoriety's or security's sake, who takes chances, who seeks to convey, by whatever means, his affections and convictions, and who has faith in the power of beauty to survive, no matter how much squalor and ugliness seek to suppress it. I am close enough to him to know that his insistence on maintaining his musical convictions has been far from easy. His effervescent delight in bringing to his audiences the best songs, the best musicians, the best of his singing and showmanship is apparent to anyone who has the good sense to listen to him in person or on records." Wilder went on to ponder Bennett's singing: "There is a quality about it that lets you in. Frank Sinatra's singing mesmerizes you. In fact, it gets so symbolic sometimes that you can't make the relationship with him as a man, even though you may know him. Bennett's professionalism doesn't block you off. It even suggests that maybe you'll see him later at the beer parlor." For all that, Bennett is an elusive singer. He can be a belter. He drives a ballad as intensely and intimately as Sinatra. He can be a lilting jazz singer. He can be a low-key, searching supper-club performer. But Bennett's voice binds all his vocal selves together. It is pitched slightly higher than Sinatra's (it was once a tenor, but it has deepened over the years), and it has a rich, expanding quality that is immediately identifiable. It has a joyous quality, a pleased, shouting-within quality.

For a time in the early seventies, before he moved to California, Bennett lived in controlled splendor in a high, spacious apartment on the Upper East Side. At home and on the road, he divided his time between his singing, which is his meat and marrow; tennis, which he had taken up not long before and which he believes is essential to his singing well; drawing and painting, which he has practiced off and on since he was in school; and his family, which included Danny and Daegal, who are grown up, his new wife, Sandy, a cool, pearl-blond, pearl-skinned beauty from Leesville, Louisiana, and their four-year-old daughter, a jumping bean named Joanna.

Bennett lived some of his New York days this way:

It was a little after nine in the morning, and Bennett, dressed in a silk robe, a yellow shirt, and modish tan pants, walked through his living room and into his studio-dining room. The living room, a careful orchestration of sharp whites, oyster whites, and pale grays, contained a sofa, overstuffed chairs, heavy glass-topped tables, a wall-to-wall shag rug, and a grand piano. A bookcase beside the window held Blake, Picasso, Klimt, Miró, Eisenstaedt, Rodin, Norman Rockwell, Klee, and songbooks by Cole Porter, Jerome Kern, George Gershwin. The studio-dining room was clubbier. Canvases were stacked with their faces to one wall, and above them, on a cork board, were pinned a map of the United States, the Declaration of Independence, and a reproduction of a Bennett cityscape. A big, U-shaped cabinet, its top covered with paints and brushes, was set against the window, and in front of it, on a slab of Lucite, were a stool and an easel. The longest wall in the room was taken up by a white desk and several shelves of stereo and recording equipment, tapes, albums, books, and framed photographs. A small dining-room table and two chairs were in a corner opposite the kitchen door. Both rooms faced south, and their windows were enormous; standing in the doorway between the rooms, one could pan easily from the Fifty-ninth Street Bridge to the Jersey shore. The sunlight everywhere looked soft and expensive. Bennett turned on an all-music FM station, then stuck his head in the kitchen and asked his cook, Edith, for a mug of coffee. He took a bowl of apples and pears from the coffee table in the living room and put it on a corner of the dining table. A small, new canvas rested on the easel, and after he had squeezed some red, green, and yellow paint onto a palette he started sketching in the outlines of the fruit. The Beatles' "Yesterday" came on the radio, and he hummed along with it. He worked quickly and deftly with his brush, and in a minute or two the outlines of the fruit and bowl were on the canvas. Edith, a trim black woman in a white uniform, put Bennett's coffee on the desk, and he thanked her. He sketched in a vase of long-stemmed red roses on the table just behind the fruit. "I wish I would stop right there," he said, "and just make it a sketch. I always go too far and clutter everything up. It's just recently that I've regimented myself to paint every day. When I'm on the road, I take a sketchbook, and it's a relief, between cities, to sketch everything you see. Later, a lot of those sketches turn into paintings." He put down his brush and riffled through a sketchbook lying on the desk. There were scenes of trees and houses in Hollywood, of Eddie Fisher's garden, of a rain-soaked park in Leeds, England, and of chimney pots in Glasgow. They were graphic and tight and detailed. "I don't understand why, but painting comes to me much easier in England. It's almost like I slip into a different style." He picked up his brush and pointed at the reproduction of the cityscape on the cork board. "I'm really pleased about that. It was done right out this window, and the original is in a celebrity art show in Lincoln Center. Red Skelton is in the show, and Kim Novak and Duke Ellington and Henry Fonda. Skelton's painting is of an Emmett Kelly-type clown, which is really a self-portrait. He sold a painting once to Maurice Chevalier, and Chevalier hung it in his house between a Picasso and a Cézanne. Ellington's painting in the show is of Billy Strayhorn, and it's full of flaming blues. It's as mysterious as his music. Henry Fonda's is in the Wyeth school. But I think maybe Kim Novak is the most talented of everybody. She has a beautiful control of paints and a lot of expression. I like Impressionism and the Old Masters— the way Rembrandt could turn out a drawing that was just as fully realized as any painting. I like doing what they did rather than reaching out for something new. I try and paint in their tradition."

Joanna appeared in the living-room doorway. She was about two feet high and had long dark-blond hair and huge eyes. She was in her underwear and held a pacifier in one hand.

"Hey, Jo. How are you this morning, darlin'?" Bennett said.

"Fine. I lost my pink umbrella. It was hanging on my tricycle." Her voice was birdlike.

"Well, we'll look into that. Do you want to sit here on the stool and watch Daddy paint?" He hoisted her onto the stool, and she looked as if she were sitting in a treetop. She dropped her pacifier on the floor, and Bennett picked up an apple from the bowl and handed it to her. She held it in both hands and took a tiny bite. He laughed. "That won't make that much difference. I'll just paint it out." He blended the apple into the background and scraped the results with a palette knife.

"There you are, Joanna," Sandy Bennett said. She was wearing a blue-and-white patterned dress and a blue blazer. Her hair hung over one eye. "Come and get dressed. We have to go and get you some shoes, and then I have to get back here and interview some new nurses." She sighed and pouted. Joanna put down the apple, which had four dime-size bites in it, and skinnied off the stool. "Then I'm going to call the French Lycée, Tony. It might be tough for her, but she can have a tutor, too. There are lycées in Los Angeles and London and Paris, so if we spend three months in any of those places, she'd have a school. I mean, that's what our life style is."

"Right, San," Bennett said, and put the final strokes on his painting. Joanna ran out of the room and Bennett shouted after her, "Hey, Joanna, do you want to go buy a kite tomorrow morning and fly it in the Park?"

"Yes! Whoopee!" she shrieked, and vanished around the corner.

It was late afternoon on the same day, and Bennett was at a back table on the ground floor of the Amalfi, on East Forty-eighth Street. He had been eating at the Amalfi since the days, twenty and more years before, when it was a one-room place on West Forty-seventh. Phil Rizzuto was a couple of tables away, and Bennett greeted him and sent a drink to his table. Bennett was to sing a couple of songs at ten o'clock at a benefit, and he ordered a light supper of macaroni shells stuffed with ricotta and a bottle of Chianti classico. Bennett has the sort of face that is easily sculptured by light. In broad daytime, he tends to look jagged and awkwardly composed: his generous Roman nose booms and his pale-green eyes become slits. But the subdued lighting in the Amalfi made him handsome and compact. His eyes became melancholy and shone darkly, the deep lines that run past his mouth were stoical, and his nose was regal. His voice, though, never changed. It is a singer's voice—soft, slightly hoarse, and always on the verge of sliding into melody. Rizzuto called over and thanked Bennett for the drink, and Bennett nodded and raised his wineglass in Rizzuto's direction. "I'm not that crazy about singing at big benefits," Bennett said, "but Ed Sullivan, who's running this one, has been good to me and I like him. I like concert halls, and what I do now is pick the best halls here and abroad, and give just one concert on Friday night and one on Saturday. I do that about thirty weekends a year. It's much nicer working concert halls than night clubs. The audience holds on to every inch of intonation and inflection. But night clubs teach performers like me. They teach you spontaneity. They teach you to keep your sense

of humor. They teach you to keep your cool. All of which I needed not
long ago when I gave a concert in Buffalo and decided to experiment by
not using a microphone. The hall isn't that big and they could hear me,
but I guess without the microphone I just didn't sound like *me*. So people
started shouting. But I remembered what Ben Webster—the great, late
Ben Webster—once told me: 'If I had it to do all over again, I'd leave my
anger offstage.' And I did. I went backstage and got a mike, and everything was all right. In addition to my concerts, I do television specials,
like the one Lena Horne and I did—just the two of us, no one else—a
while back. It got very nice notices, which proves you just don't need all
those trappings. I also work in Vegas, and at Bill Harrah's places in Lake
Tahoe and Reno, for six weeks a year. Vegas is great, with all the performers on one strip, like a kind of super-Fifty-second Street. They can
afford anything, and they treat performers marvellously. But Bill Harrah
is fabulous. I think he started out with bingo parlors in Reno thirty-five
years ago, and now he owns these big places in Tahoe and Reno and has
a huge collection of classic cars. He meets you at the airport with a Rolls-
Royce and gives you the keys to the car and a beautiful home with a pool.
At the end of the engagement, he throws a party for you in his own home.
It's like some kind of fantastic vacation.''

Bennett took a forkful of shells and a sip of wine. "It's beautiful not to
compromise in what you sing, and yet I've done business since I had my
first record hit for Columbia, in 1951. I've always tried to do the cream of
the popular repertoire and yet remain commercial. Hanging out with
good songs is the secret. Songs like 'All the Things You Are' and 'East of
the Sun' are just the opposite of singing down. And so are these lyrics,
which Alec Wilder wrote and sent me a few days ago. He said if I liked
them he'd set them to music. I think they're beautiful.'' Bennett pulled a
sheet of onionskin letter paper out of his pocket. The lyrics read:

ME THAT WARM FEELING

Give me that warm feeling
That makes me believe again,
Give me that soft answer,
The kind you gave me way back when.
Give me some true kindness
That brightens the sky again.
Give me the best that's in you
And encouragement now and then.
Dust off those long-lost manners!
Bury ambition and guile!
Unfurl those lovely banners

Of virtue and laughter and style!
Give me that warm feeling,
Take off that impersonal glove.
Remember, remember, we're dealing
With that fair and that rare thing called love!

"I love singing too much to cheat the public. And I can't ever lose that spirit by listening to the money boys, the Broadway wise guys who used to tell me, 'If you don't sing such-and-such, you'll end up with a classy reputation and no bread in the bank.' But if I lost that spirit, my feeling for music would run right out the window. It's this obsolescence thing in America, where cars are made to break down and songs written to last two weeks. But good songs last forever, and I've come to learn that there's a whole group out there in the audience who's studying that with me. There's a greatness in an audience when it gets perfectly still. It becomes a beautiful tribal contact, a delicate, poetic thing. A great song does that. It also works two ways: the performer makes the song work, and the song inspires the performer.

"All kinds of things go through my head when I'm singing. I think of Joanna a lot. I think of things from my past; I even *see* them. If I'm working in a beautiful place like Festival Hall, in London, I think of the great lighting, the great clusters of light, and they inspire me. If a song is truly believable, it becomes a self-hypnosis thing. And when that happens I automatically start thinking a line ahead, like when I serve at tennis and am already thinking of the next shot. My concentration becomes heavy, so that if I forget the words I can do what Harold Arlen told me: 'Just make up new words in the right spirit and don't let anybody know, and you'll be all right.'

"I've always liked the Billie Holiday tradition of allowing the musicians you're working with to take charge and to solo, and my arrangements are always written that way. Jazz musicians create great warmth and feeling. When they play well, they make *you* sing, too. I've worked with Bobby Hackett and Woody Herman and Duke Ellington and Stan Kenton and Count Basie. And I've worked with Harry Edison and Jimmy Rowles and Tommy Flanagan and Zoot Sims and John Bunch and Billy Exiner. You can't beat the perfection of Basie. He even talks the way he plays: one or two words take care of conversation for the month. Like when he saw the distance he'd have to go to reach his piano on this tiny, miserable stage we were working on somewhere out West. 'Man, that's a long walk,' he said."

Bennett laughed, and told the waiter, a diminutive carryover from the old Amalfi, that he didn't have time for espresso but that he would see him soon. He waved to Rizzuto.

It was ten-thirty the next morning, and one of those dancing blue New York days: the shadows had knife-edges, and the sidewalks were full of diamonds. Bennett was standing with Joanna at the curb in front of his apartment house. She was holding on to his right index finger, and she barely topped his knees. They were headed for the East Meadow, in Central Park, where a sequence of a quasi-documentary about Bennett's New York life was to be filmed. One sequence had already been done in his apartment, and another would be filmed tomorrow night at a concert he was giving in Alice Tully Hall. Joanna was in a blue knitted jumper with a matching top, and Bennett had on a gleaming white safari suit and a dark-olive shirt open at the neck.

"Daddy, let's go see if the flowers we planted are still growing," Joanna piped.

Bennett hunkered beside some shrubs next to the building's door and rubbed the dirt with his hand. There was nothing there.

"Whynot? Whynot? Whynot?" Joanna chanted.

Bennett looked sheepish. "I guess we forgot to water it, or something. But we'll try again."

A rented black limousine the length of the one Jelly Roll Morton said he had to take to Central Park to turn around pulled up at the curb, and Bennett and Joanna got in. It had a red shag carpet, and the jump seats were separated by a cabinet containing a bar, a radio, and a tiny television set. Bennett told his driver, a squat, cheerful man named Caesar, to stop at a shop specializing in kites, at Second Avenue and Eighty-fourth Street. Two cameramen and a grip followed the limousine in a cab. Joanna diddled with the television, switching from channel to channel, and Bennett told her to slow down or she wouldn't be able to see anything at all. She paid no attention. At the shop, Bennett and one of the cameramen chose a couple of big, semitransparent German kites that looked like birds. Bennett was all thumbs, but he managed to get one of the kites assembled by the time the limousine pulled up at Fifth Avenue and Ninety-eighth Street. The East Meadow stretches from Ninety-seventh to 101st Street and is vaguely bowl-shaped. Joanna sailed in the south gate ahead of Bennett and, sensing the expanse in front of her, took off up the Meadow, her legs going like a sandpiper's. Bennett, laughing and shouting, caught her at 100th Street. The cameramen stationed themselves on a low rise on one side of the Meadow. A time followed that recalled the mad footage in *A Hard Day's Night* in which the Beatles race wildly and aimlessly back and forth across an immense field. There was almost no wind, but Bennett got the kite twelve feet into the air, and he and Joanna ran up the Meadow. The kite crashed. Joanna picked it up and ran south, Bennett galloping after her. They went up the Meadow, down the Meadow, across the Meadow. Joanna maintained her speed, but Bennett began to puff. The cameramen declared that they had enough film, and Bennett laughed and wiped his brow. He picked up his jacket from the grass and flung it and the kite across one shoulder. Joanna latched on to his index finger and they went back to the car.

Before he showered and changed his clothes at the apartment, Bennett asked Edith to fix a light lunch. Joanna was fed in the kitchen and packed off for a nap. Bennett was due at three o'clock at a studio on Christopher Street, where he was to rehearse with the Ruby Braff-George Barnes Quartet. The quartet was to accompany him at Alice Tully Hall. Edith set the table in the studio and brought in a chicken salad and a large glass of boysenberry juice. "Man, tennis has nothing on that kiteflying," Bennett said. "But all that running around will make me sing better this afternoon. Maybe if I'd known about it a long time ago, it would have gotten my career going a lot faster. The way it was, I didn't become any sort of authoritative singer until I was twenty-seven. For seven years before that, I scuffled. After the war, I used the G.I. Bill to study at the American Theatre Wing, where I worked on bel canto with Peter D'Andrea. And I studied voice with Miriam Speir. It was at her place I first met Alec Wilder. I never passed any auditions, and I worked as an elevator man at the Park Sheraton, in an uncle's grocery store, as a runner for the A.P., and as a singing waiter out in Astoria, where I was born. I was born in August of 1926, as Anthony Dominick Benedetto. I'm using Benedetto again to sign my paintings. We lived in a little two-story house in Astoria which is still there. My father came over from Italy in 1922, but I don't know much about him, because he died when I was nine. He had a grocery store on Fifty-second Street and Sixth Avenue, where the C.B.S. Building is now. I remember he was a beautiful man, who was much loved by his family and friends. He had an open, warm voice, full of love and melody, and he sang beautifully. He'd always get the family out on Sundays to sing and dance. My mother, whose maiden name was Surace, was born down on Mott and Hester Streets, and she lives out in River Edge, New Jersey. After my father died, she went to work in the garment district and put my brother and sister and me through school. She has spirit and that great gift of common sense. Judy Garland went crazy over her when she met her. I went to P.S. 7 and Junior High School of Industrial Arts, which used to be near the Waldorf-Astoria. It was way ahead of its time. I studied music and painting, and they'd work it so that you didn't have to be there every day, so long as you did your work. You could go over to the Park and sketch trees. I had a music teacher named Sonberg, and he'd bring a Victrola into class and play Art Tatum records. Imagine that! It was around then I decided to be a singer. Of course, I'd been singing all my

life and in the shadow of show business. I had an uncle in Astoria who
was a hoofer in vaudeville and worked for the Shuberts. He'd tell me
about Harry Lauder and James Barton and how they were humble people
who had their feet on the ground. He'd tell me about Bill Robinson and
how he had to follow him once and it almost killed him. He'd tell me
how the acts in those days honed their shows all the way across the country and back, so that when they finally got to the Palace in New York
they were sharp and ready. I had my first professional job when I was
thirteen, at one of those Saturday-night get-togethers at a Democratic club
in Astoria, and later I sang at little clubs by myself when they'd let me."
Harry Celentano, a bellman at the Algonquin, who went to school with
Bennett, remembers those days: "He used to sing 'God Bless America'
and 'The Star-Spangled Banner' in assemblies, and when he was a little
older he'd go into places out there like the Horseshoe Bar and the Queen
of Hearts—this quiet, shy little kid—and get up and sing all by himself.
Some of us would go with him, and he'd stand there and sing 'Cottage
for Sale' like a soft Billy Eckstine. We didn't take him seriously, and we'd
shout and throw peanuts at him, but he never batted an eye. But he was
also into art then. He would play hooky and draw these huge, beautiful
murals right on the street, with chalk. Mothers and children would stop
and watch, and they were amazed. Then we'd come along and play football over the mural, and that was that."

Edith asked Bennett if he'd like more chicken salad, and he shook his
head. "My first scrape with any kind of professionalism came at the Shan-
gri-La, in Astoria, where the trombonist Tyree Glenn had a group. He
heard me singing along with the band and asked me to come up and do
a song. I think it was Duke's 'Solitude.' I'll never forget that kindness. I
went into the service late in the war and ended up in the infantry, doing
mopping-up operations in France and Germany. My scuffling years began
to end in 1949, when I auditioned for a revue Pearl Bailey was in at the
old Greenwich Village Inn. It had people like Maurice Rocco, who used
to play the piano standing up. I became a production singer in the show,
which meant I was a combination m.c. and singer. Pearl told me, 'It'll take
you five years before you can handle yourself on a stage, but at least I can
get you started.' Bob Hope heard me in the show and asked me to come
up and sing at the Paramount Theatre with him. It was his closing night,
and before I went on he told me that my stage name, Joe Bari, wasn't any
good, and he asked what my real name was. I told him and he thought a
moment and said, 'We'll call you Tony Bennett,' and went out on the
stage and introduced me. Then he took me on a ten-day tour with him,
and everybody—Les Brown and Marilyn Maxwell were in the troupe,
too—showed me how to get on and off the stage without falling down,
and things like that. Maybe a year later, Mitch Miller auditioned me at

Columbia. I sang 'Boulevard of Broken Dreams,' and it became a semi-hit. This gave me the strength to go out on the road and work clubs in places like Philadelphia and Boston and Cleveland and Buffalo. So I'd started this crazy adventure that has lasted twenty years. Then I had hits like 'Because of You' and 'Just in Time,' and I became international in 1962, when I recorded 'I Left My Heart in San Francisco.'"

Edith came in from the kitchen and said, "The doorman called, Mr. Bennett. The car's downstairs."

The concert at Alice Tully the next evening was billed as "An Evening with Rodgers and Hart," and it was a smooth and engaging success. The hall was sold out, and the audience was hip. Bennett sang the verses of most of the songs, and by the time he got a note or two into the chorus there was the applause of recognition. He was in a dinner jacket, and his stage manner was startlingly old-fashioned: he used a hand mike, and he whipped the cord around as though it were a lariat; he half danced, half fell across the stage during rhythm numbers; he saluted the audience and pointed at it. He was clumsy and at the same time delightful. He sang twenty-one Rodgers-and-Hart tunes, and many were memorable. He sang a soft, husky "Blue Moon," and then came a marvellous, muted Ruby Braff solo. "There's a Small Hotel" was even softer, and Braff and George Barnes reacted with pianissimo statements. During Braff's solo in "The Most Beautiful Girl in the World," Bennett sat on a stool to the musician's right, and near the end of "I Wish I Were in Love Again" he forgot his lyrics and soared over the wreckage with some good mumbo-jumbo and a fine crescendo. "Lover" was ingenious. Bennett sang it softly, at a medium tempo (it is usually done at top speed), then briefly took the tempo up, and went out sotto voce. He did "I Left My Heart in San Francisco" as an encore. The ovation was long and standing.

After a small backstage party, Bennett got into his limousine and was driven home. He settled deep into a corner of the car. "It's what I used to dream of—a concert in a big hall like Alice Tully. But it hasn't all been smoothness since I started doing business. When I had my first record hits, in the early fifties, I suddenly found myself with an entourage, most of them takers. And I didn't like it. Maurice Chevalier was doing a one-man show here around then, and all he had was a piano and a hat, and that made me realize I was off on the wrong foot. Since then I've been through a divorce and done a little time on the psychiatrist's couch. But I don't think I need that. Most of the people who go to psychiatrists, their hearts and minds have never caught on to any one desire. I never had that problem. But I had a different one when Frank Sinatra came out in *Life* and said I was the greatest singer around. Sophie Tucker once told me, 'Make sure that helium doesn't hit your brain,' but it did, and for several years, to match up to his praise, I overblew, I oversang. But I've found my groove now. I'm solidifying everything, and working toward my own company. You learn how to hang on to money after a while. I like to live well, but I'm not interested in yachts and fancy cars. There are things I'm searching for, but they won't take a day. I'd like to attain a good, keen intellect. Alec Wilder set one of William Blake's poems to music for me, and I was reading Blake last night. Imagine being that talented and feeling so much at the same time! I'd like to make more movies. I played a press agent in *The Oscar*, and I loved the whole make-believe about it. I'd like my own regular TV show, which would be devoted to good *music*. None of that stuff with the musicians off camera and the shots full of dancers. I like the funny things in this life that could only happen to me now. Once, when I was singing Kurt Weill's 'Lost in the Stars' in the Hollywood Bowl with Basie's band and Buddy Rich on drums, a shooting star went falling through the sky right over my head, and everyone was talking about it, and the next morning the phone rang and it was Ray Charles, who I'd never met, calling from New York. He said 'Hey, Tony, how'd you do that, man?' and hung up."

A Vast Minority

Mel Tormé

At fifty-five, Mel Tormé has been a professional singer for fifty years. He knows more than five thousand songs, and has yet to forget one, no matter how long it has stayed on ice. He has written nearly three hundred songs, at least one of which is a standard ("The Christmas Song"). He is a good modern pianist and a good arranger. Tommy Dorsey, Gene Krupa, and Stan Kenton wanted him as a drummer. He has written three books, and is twelve chapters into his autobiography. The first book, a Western called *Dollarhide*, was published in 1955 under the nom de plume of Wesley Butler Wyatt. In 1970, he published *The Other Side of the Rainbow*, a sad, probing, sharp-eared recollection of what it was like to work on a weekly prime-time television show with Judy Garland. Three years ago, he brought out an old-fashioned, disarmingly transparent novel about a popular singer. He called it *Wynner*, and it had a first printing of fifty thousand. He recently sold a large collection of Colt revolvers, and he is an aficionado of First World War aircraft, of American movies, and of the composers Percy Grainger and Frederick Delius. He has had five children by three wives, whose years in residence were 1949–55, 1956–66, and 1966–78. He has said, "California is strewn with houses I almost owned."

In the past three or four years, he has given half a dozen superior New York concerts, backed by a revolving host of first-class jazz musicians. But until his recent appearances at Marty's, a club on the East Side, he had not worked in a New York night club since 1976. During one of his stays at Marty's, he talked of his life—in a tiny dressing room on Marty's second floor, in a yacht-sized gray limousine sailing between the club and

143

his midtown hotel, and in his hotel suite. He is a small man, with a Romanesque face that leans toward Charles Laughton one moment and Mickey Rooney the next. He has a full, pliant ego, but it hasn't troubled his manners or his morals. He loves to talk, and he talks very fast, in a strong, smooth, husky voice. He thrives on overwork and loves to complain about how tired he is. He doesn't drink, smoke, or take pills, and he calls telephone operators "sweetheart."

"I was born in Chicago on September 13, 1925," Tormé said. "I'm four years older than my sister, and there were just the two of us. My parents were movie maniacs, so my sister was named after Myrna Loy and I was named after Melvyn Douglas. My father, William, came over from Brest Litovsk in the early nineteen-hundreds and settled in New York. An immigration agent on Ellis Island mistakenly changed his name from Torma to Torme, and I added the accent in high school. My father remembers dodging Cossacks one night in Brest Litovsk and running smack into a huge white figure that he thought was a ghost but turned out to be a goat—'I ran so breathlessly home I thought my lungs would burst.' Immigrants had to learn to do everything. He had a drygoods store in Chicago. He worked in a dress factory and sold dresses retail. He was a jewelry craftsman. During the Depression, he drove his gray-green two-door Model A Ford out into the Illinois countryside and bought eggs and milk from farmers and sold them to shops in small cities. He and my Uncle Art—my father had two sisters and two brothers—invented a popup book. They took the invention to the same company that published Big Little Books, and—myth of American myths—they never made a penny. My father was also a hell of a Charleston dancer, and his sister Fay danced at Liberty Bond rallies. He's a gentle, loving, sympathetic, supportive human being—but a dreamer. My mother's the strong one, the one who managed the purse and held the family together. She was born Sarah Sopkin, but she changed her name to Betty a long time ago. She's pretty and short—slightly taller than my daddy. She has soft, roundish features, and I look more like her than like Father. He's eighty-two and she's seventy-nine, and they've been married fifty-seven years. They live near me in Beverly Hills and are very active socially.

"It's got to be a fairy tale, but my mother swears I sang a complete song by the time I was ten months old. I did know a lot of songs when I was four. I learned them from my mother, who demonstrated the new sheet music at Woolworth's during the Depression, and from the radio, which I was addicted to. I also learned from Alberta, a three-hundred-pound woman who practically raised me. She played superb barrelhouse piano, and on weekends she was in an all-girl band at the Savoy, right near us in Chicago. When I was four, my father and mother took me to the Blackhawk restaurant to hear the Coon-Sanders band. I sang along at the table, and during an intermission Carlton Coon came over and said something about what a droll little fellow I was and asked if I would like to sing a number with the band. It was the time in this country when kids were stepping from the cradle into show business. Carlton Coon was the drummer, and I sat on his knee while he played and I sang 'You're Driving Me Crazy.' I remember the *boom-boom-boom* of the bass drum, which was one of those huge, twenty-eight-inch models. I became a Monday-night feature with the band, at fifteen dollars a session. After that, I sang with Louis Panico and Frankie Masters, and when I was six I went into a kid review run by the bandleader Paul Ash. We played once a week in those big, luxurious Balaban and Katz neighborhood theatres. In 1933, I won the children's division of a radio audition contest at the Chicago World's Fair. I sang a Jolson song and did a dramatic recitation. Ireene Wicker, who was 'The Singing Lady,' was one of the judges. I went right into a new soap opera, 'Song of the City,' as Jimmy the newsboy. During the next six or seven years, before my voice changed, I was one of the busiest child radio actors in Chicago. I was in 'The Romance of Helen Trent,' 'Mary Marlin,' 'Mary Noble, Backstage Wife,' 'Jack Armstrong, the All-American Boy,' 'Little Orphan Annie,' and a show of Edgar A. Guest's called 'It Can Be Done.' I also did Arch Oboler's spook program, 'Lights Out,' at eleven-thirty at night. It was broadcast from an empty studio, and a minute or so before air time the cast gathered in a silent circle on the stage while an organist played. It was supposed to get our wind up, and it did. I discovered by the time I was in my teens that I had a fantastic ear for accents." In rapid succession. Tormé did Robert Newton, a Scottish accent, Cary Grant, Gary Cooper, and Robert Walker.

"I had a tough time in school, partly because of my size and partly because I was always a little cocky. There was no money for a professional kids' school, so I went to Shakespeare Grammar. I got beaten up regularly—usually by an Irish kid named Steve. My dad would tell me, 'Melvin, don't get scarred up if you want to be in show business.' One day, he came home from his butter-and-egg route and found me bleeding and dirty, and—gentle man that he was—lost his temper and whacked me hard because I had gotten mauled again. That did it. I waited for Steve the next morning. He was very strongly made, a really staunch kid. I broke his nose and knocked him downstairs, and I was suspended from school a week. I don't know why those heroics work, but they do, and after that he left me alone. But Steve had an older brother, and not long after that he and two other kids jumped me from behind when I was leaving drum-and-bugle practice—I had begun to pick up on the drums. They straddled my chest and made me eat tobacco. Which is the reason I have never smoked. The next year, I went to Hyde Park High, on the South Side. I had begun to write songs, and my voice had changed. When I was fifteen, I got an audition through my Uncle Art with Harry James. I sang one of my own songs, 'Lament to Love,' and I played a drum solo for him. Harry kept saying, 'That's nifty! That's nifty!' Finally, he said, 'How about coming with the band? We'll write to you.' I loved the big bands—they were an elixir to me—and I went home six feet off the ground. But I made the mistake of telling my best friend, a rich kid named John Poister. He was editor of the school paper, and the following week there was a headline: 'HYDE PARK PRODIGY TO JOIN NAME BAND.' I heard regularly from Harry James' manager, but months went by and nothing happened. Then Harry wrote and said he was sorry but for me to go on the road with the band at my age meant that I would have to have a full-time tutor, and the whole thing was too complicated and expensive. Kids at school were already calling me a liar and 'Harry James' ex-drummer.' But I refused to show anybody the twenty or so letters I had from James. Then, in June of 1941, a new Harry James recording came out with the 'Dodger Fan Dance' on one side and my 'Lament to Love' on the other. It was also recorded by Les Brown and Sonny Dunham and Lanny Ross, and it made 'The Hit Parade,' and stayed there for weeks. Everything turned around, but the whole experience gave me a little chip on the shoulder that I had for a year or two after I left school.

"About this time, the drummer Ben Pollack came through town and heard me sing some of my songs. He was putting together a band for Chico Marx, and said he could use me. He said *he* would write. I waited and waited, and nothing. Then I had a dream—and my dreams almost invariably predict the reverse of what is to happen. I dreamed that a guy pulled up in a bakery truck and gave me a telegram from Ben Pollack: 'SORRY, WE CAN'T USE YOU.' The next day, a telegram came from Pollack to the effect that he was sending a hundred and thirty dollars and for me to take the El Capitan to the Coast. I joined the band as a singer and vocal arranger in August of 1942, just before I turned seventeen. It was a wonderfully musical group, and I stayed until it broke up, a year later. Chico would do his thing once or twice a night and leave the rest to us. We had Marty Napoleon on piano, Marty Marsala on trumpet, Barney Kessel on guitar, and George Wettling on drums. Paul Weston and Fred Norman did the arrangements. I was a little rough-cut at first. One night, at the Lakeside Park Ballroom, in Denver, four of the toughest-looking kids I ever saw turned up in front of the bandstand and asked for 'Sweet Eloise.' I was supposed to sing 'Abraham,' from 'Holiday Inn,' and when I started it one of the kids grabbed my leg and pinched me real hard. My reflex—if that's what it was—was a kick that removed all his front teeth. They had to put together a flying wedge to get me back onto the bus safely. After I had been with the band six months, I asked Chico if I could get billing on marquees and such, and he said, 'Sure, kid.' I was singing a lot more, and I figured I deserved it. A day or two later, when we arrived in Steubenville, Ohio, for a one-nighter, I looked up at the marquee and there in big letters was: 'CHICO MARX AND HIS ORCHESTRA WITH VOCALIST MEL TROME.' I settled down after that. George Wettling left, I took over on drums, and the band broke up at the Golden Gate Hotel, in San Francisco. I made my first movie, *Higher and Higher,* with Frank Sinatra and Jack Haley. That was enough for my mother and dad. They had always wanted to live in California, so they threw out my Big Little Books, which would be worth a fortune now, and moved to the Coast. Things began to happen for me. I took over a vocal group out of Los Angeles City College called the School Kids, and it became Mel Tormé and his Mel-Tones. I did the arrangements and sang most of the solos, and Ben Pollack managed us. We recorded for Decca and became a working Hollywood group. We were together three or four years. I also made three more films and signed with Albert Marx's Musicraft label. I recorded some vocals with Artie Shaw and appeared on the Fitch Bandwagon radio show. I sat in on drums all over the place. Gene Krupa offered me a job as assistant drummer and Stan Kenton offered me three hundred a week for two weeks. I got to know Buddy Rich who was with Tommy Dorsey.'' Tormé switched into his Buddy Rich, and did an uncanny imitation: "'Hey, kid. I heard you play. You sing better.' We've been friends ever since, although it's taken me thirty years to learn how to handle him, to josh him out of his occasional uglies. When I first met him, he wanted to leave Dorsey and start his own band, but Dorsey wouldn't let him go until he found a good enough replacement, which, Buddy Rich being Buddy Rich, wasn't easy. So, unbeknownst to me, Buddy cooked up a situation where I was asked to sit in for two numbers with Dorsey. They happened to be 'Sunny Side of the Street' and 'Opus No. 1,' and I knew both of them backward. Dorsey liked what I did so much he asked me to join him. I said O.K. if he would take my vocal group, too, but he had the Sentimentalists, so it fizzled. Buddy and I work together a lot nowadays, and we like to keep the gags running. When he had a small group seven or eight years ago in Buddy's Place, on Second Avenue in the Sixties, I called him up and said, 'Hey, Traps, I'm coming in tonight, although I don't know why anyone wants to waste his time listening to a ninety-one-year-old drummer.' I get there and am seated at ringside, and at the end of the set Buddy introduces me: 'Ladies and gentlemen, I'd like you to meet the greatest singer in the world, a man with a golden voice and a heart to match,' and on and on. He finally finishes and I stand up and they put a spot on me. Silence. Not a sound. A packed room sitting on its hands and staring at me. For an instant, I admit it, I was shook. Then it dawned: he had set the whole thing up with the audience.

"Woody Herman and Les Brown had heard me, and they persuaded the manager Carlos Gastel to take me on. I went into the Bocage, on the Coast, with the Page Cavanaugh trio, and it went very well. Arthur Freed signed me to do 'Good News,' and in 1947 I came East to play the Copacabana. I came on a wave of bobby-socks adulation which had been created mostly by the New York disk jockey Fred Robbins. 'Robbins' Nest' was *the* New York d.j. show. I think Fred Robbins spent all his time making up names for me—'Mr. Butterscotch' and 'The Kid with the Gauze in His Jaws' and 'The Velvet Fog.' I was twenty-one and full of ants. At the Copa, I sang Harold Arlen's 'Ill Wind' and a lot of other high-class material. I thought I was going to kill those people, and I was greeted with ennui. On opening night, this big dame in a red-and-white dress turned her back on me at the beginning of my show and stayed that way until the end. It was Sophie Tucker. The reviews were a repeat of high school in Chicago. George Frazier put me down, and Dorothy Kilgallen said I was 'an egotistical little amateur.' The only thing that kept me there was the kids. They'd pile in for the last show on Saturday. It was a hurtful time, and after it was over I had to recoup. Carlos Gastel never lost faith an instant. He was astonishing. He saw something in me that didn't really take its proper shape for many years. He said to me then, 'You will never be the mass star you want to be, Torment'—which is what he called me. 'but there is a vast minority of people out there who will always support your work.'"

At a midweek show at Marty's, which was full and quiet, Tormé, in a tuxedo and working with a trio sang a medium-slow version of the Gershwins' "Isn't It a Pity?," and Noël Coward's "Chase Me, Charlie." Then he did Nellie Lutcher's "Hurry On Down" in a slow drag that was almost recitative. He did a very fast "Mountain Greenery" built around an ad-lib interlude, and he returned to Rodgers and Hart for "Isn't It Romantic?," on which he carved *"beautiful slow ballad."* "Pick Yourself Up," complete with a chorus of voice-and-piano Bach counterpoint, gave way to Gerry Mulligan's "The Real Thing," for which Tormé had written the lyrics. He sang *all* the choruses of Cole Porter's "It's De-Lovely," closing with a yammering string of mock-Yiddish words that brought the house down. Billy Joel's "New York State of Mind" was his first encore, and he finished the set with a fast "Love for Sale" decorated with a full (sixty-four bars) chorus of scatting. The show lasted just under an hour. It didn't parade its scholarship and originality; there was none of the Sumerian delving that some New York cabaret singers indulge in to prove how original they are. He never missed a note, a vibrato, a difficult lyric. His words were bold and distinct, and his melodies were graceful and commanding. Tormé has a light, effortless baritone. His songs seem to overflow, to surge out of him uncontrollably, as if singing were the easiest thing in the world for him. His songs have no joints or dead spaces. Each is as reasoned and organic and complete as a good sonnet. He can belt a song, filling a concert hall with ten-pound tones, and he can sing a whispery "Memories of You." He can do pillowy ballads and fast patter songs. He can do nonense songs and slow blues. He can build Harold Arlen's "Blues in the Night" into a four-story Stanford White cottage. He has the presence and suppleness and humor of Ethel Waters. He makes his face into rubber, using an endless series of grimaces and winks and smiles.

"Performing is very tricky," Tormé said after the set. "It is a good idea to allow some small piece of unhappiness from your life to be a part of your work every night. It gives your singing depth. Standing ovations don't impress me. I can sing badly and get one. When that happens, I can walk offstage in a deep depression that may last several days. Other times, I get apathetic reactions when I *know* I have been great. Once in a while, though, that strange silver cord that goes between me and the audience grows taut, and it's—well, exhilarating. You learn in time that each performance is *not* the end of the world, that things can go awry because of—what? A faulty digestive tract, a moon tide, a drunk in the house.

"I'm a great eclectic. Of course, I admire Bing Crosby and Sinatra and Billie Holiday and Ella and Joe Williams and Ethel Waters. But I also admire Bessie Smith and Leo Watson and Bon Bon Tunnell and Connee Boswell. And Harold Mills, of the Mills Brothers, and Patti Andrews, of the Andrews Sisters. Also, people you don't ordinarily think of as singers, like Buddy Rich and Johnny Mercer and Bobby Sherwood and Woody Herman and Ray Nance. I love Ivie Anderson and June Richmond, who was with Andy Kirk. Helen Forrest may have been the best big-band singer. And I love Ray Charles and Joe Turner and Helen Humes. And Trummy Young and every horn player who turns to singing. They just never miss. I can't say I was crazy about Mildred Bailey. That little voice never seemed to fit such a big woman. And Jack Teagarden's singing bothered me. He had a loose-lipped, going-to-sleep quality. And the later Louis hurt my ears.

"I love singing in a small room with people on top of me. I have a constant need to communicate. Once, in a small room in San Francisco, I noticed this beautiful young couple in front of me. They had their heads together, they were holding hands, they were *listening*. I caught their eye, and it became a private three-way performance, and before it was over tears had spilled out of my eyes. I *see* lyrics when I sing—flowers and Central Park and autumn leaves and blue skies and Garbo's face. I sing from my diaphragm now. When I was the Velvet Fog, everything was head tones." Tormé sang "All the Things You Are" in a high husky voice, slipping immediately back to the forties. "Now it all comes from down here, and when I go from my low register to my highest, I'm not singing falsetto. Those are pure tones, just as Buddy Rich's double-stroke roll is pure. I never sing anything the same way twice. This led to my being crossed off Richard Rodgers' list, and I idolize his music. He heard me sing 'Blue Moon' in a rehearsal, and I phrased it a bit differently, and he said to me 'No, that is not the way to sing my song. You do it this way— one, two, three, four.' I told him I was simply trying to make the lyrics sound conversational. Later, when David Frost did a tribute to Rodgers on his television show, Rodgers dinged Sinatra and Peggy Lee and Ella and me as guest singers because all of us had taken liberties with his songs.

"I spent most of the fifties getting over the Velvet Fog image. I wanted to be a jazz-oriented singer—I don't know what a jazz singer is, since all good popular singers are jazz-influenced. It took some running to do it. I recorded for Capitol and Coral and Bethlehem, and I had a daytime talk show on television. It was the first of its kind. When rock hit, in the sixties, the intake of money fluctuated, but I kept going. I could see by then that I had a growing following of the kind of people I *wanted* to follow my work. I like people I admire to admire me. I signed with Atlantic and then with Columbia, and both were disasters of a different kind. In the mid-seventies, when I hit fifty, something happened that I don't quite understand yet. I seemed to enter the years Carlos Gastel foresaw. I'm singing better than I ever have, and everyone seems to agree. My personal life has straightened out. All my wives have been beautiful, but I am bad at picking women who are good for me. Out of those relationships, however, have come five great children. I'm a dogged perfectionist with a desperate desire to be super-professional. Do I dare say I finally am?"

Bob's Your Uncle

George Shearing

The brilliant blind pianist and singer George Shearing doesn't like his listeners to get too close. During the first part of his career—in England, where he was born, in 1919—he hid behind the styles of other pianists. He was considered England's Meade Lux Lewis, England's Art Tatum, England's Teddy Wilson. In the second part of his career, which began in the late forties, just after he settled in this country, he disappeared inside his smooth, famous quintet (vibraphone, guitar, piano, bass, and drums), emerging occasionally for a solo chorus but in general restricting himself to sixteen or twenty-four bars. The disguises he has used in the third part of his career, which started in the late seventies, when he gave up his quintet, are his most refined. He now works in a duo with a bassist, but he is no more accessible than he ever was. He has long been thought of as a jazz pianist, but he is apt these days to play Kurt Weill's "Mack the Knife" at a very slow tempo, clothing it with thick Bartók chords. Or he will play the "Moonlight" Sonata straight for sixteen or twenty bars (he is an excellent classical pianist), and then, in the same tempo and using Beethoven harmonies, slip seamlessly into Cole Porter's "Night and Day," staying with it à la Beethoven for a chorus or so before easing back into the sonata. He will play Porter's "Do I Love You" in Mozart fashion, and his own indestructible "Lullaby of Birdland" as a Bach fugue. Or he will do a sorrowing, almost chanting rendition of Jobim's "How Insensitive," and give Alec Wilder's "While We're Young" a full-scale ballad treatment, filling it with substitute chords and Art Tatum decorations. What is always present, though impishly concealed, is a superlative pia-

nist, who can play Mozart with a feathery correctness, then improvise
with swinging abandon. Shearing has a beautiful touch, which falls somewhere between the sparkle of Nat Cole and the buoyancy of Art Tatum.
His jazzlike playing is colored by Teddy Wilson and Hank Jones and
Erroll Garner and Bud Powell, but he does not have a style in the conventional sense. He has perfected a unique *sound,* a kind of handsome
aural presence, made up of his airborne tone and his pleasant, slightly
foggy tenor voice; his extraordinary harmonic sense; and his refusal to use
pianistic clichés. Shearing talked about his playing:

"When I sit down at the piano, I make sure my stool is in front of middle C," he said. "Then I know I have three Cs on my left and four on my
right. I have my seven octaves, and I know just where I am and where I
can go. I've heard too many players slog the piano. I feel sorry for an
instrument that is brutally treated. I love tone production—connecting
my notes so that they sing, instead of coming out clump-clump-clump.
When you improvise, in addition to your tone production you must have
a musical atmosphere in your head—a musical climate. You must have
compounds of scales and arpeggios to fit the chords you improvise on.
Sometimes as I improvise I hear a horn in my head, or an alto or a tenor
saxophone, or a flugelhorn. On a slow ballad, I hear Hank Jones, who is
so good he should be deported. The gift of improvisation is being able to
weave from one chord to another. It's a question of immediately getting
what's in your mind into your fingers. If you could explain it, which I
can't, all the surprise and spontaneity and unexpectedness would
disappear.

"I don't know when I first exposed an audience to my singing, but I
started singing some twenty years ago. I can't help the instrument I don't
have, but I love to sing, and I hope that my love for it will reach the
audience. There is a happiness that goes through my mind when I sing,
a joy in being able to put words and music together. I suppose my favorite
lyricists are Porter and Mercer and Lorenz Hart—and certainly Charles
de Forest, whom nobody seems to have heard of and who is very much
alive. I have a hellbent attitude to elocute—if there is such a word—the
lyrics to the best of my ability. I always hold Sinatra and Tormé and Nat
Cole in my head when I sing.

"I no longer wish to work all the time. My ears get tired. I want to play
bridge with my wife, Ellie. I want to work on my VersaBraille computer.
I want to build up my compact-disk library. I want to do more disk-jock-
eying. I want to ride my tandem bike. Eventually, I probably won't play
in public anymore, but I'll certainly play here."

During the past eight or nine years, Shearing and his bassist have frequently joined forces with the singer-composer-instrumentalist Mel

Tormé and his drummer, Donny Osborne, and they have developed an effortless and engaging act. Shearing accompanies Tormé's singing, Tormé plays piano with Shearing, Shearing sings by himself and with Tormé, Tormé plays drums with Shearing. Tormé has said this about Shearing:

"I call George the Master. He is a blissful, constant surprise musically. When we do two performances in an evening of songs like 'Star Dust' and 'Dream Dancing,' each version George plays is a spontaneous and exquisite work of art. He's got a marvellous facility for inventing substitute chords in great songs. A lot of pianists use substitute chords simply to call attention to themselves, but George does it to enhance and embellish the song. Add to that the incredible warehouse in his brain of classical music and of popular songs that no one else has ever heard of. He's a lovely man, and the only time I have seen him irascible is when people around him don't do their job right. The last time we worked together, he played a solo number in which he got softer and softer, creating a hypnotic delicacy and quietude. When he was almost beneath hearing, the sound man suddenly turned up the volume, wrecking everything. George made his feelings plain after the show."

And Shearing has said this about Tormé: "We practically breathe together. We're two bodies with a single musical mind. We have a mutual love for the tone-poem writer, Frederick Delius. I throw Delius quotes at Mel all the time when I accompany him, and he recognizes them straight off. If I change a note in a chord he will answer with an altered note—his ears are that finely tuned. So is his voice, which is invariable in tune. In fact, it is in as good shape at sixty as it has ever been in his life. Mel is literarily oriented, and his reading of lyrics when he sings is marvellous. I know just where a phrase is going to stop, where he's going to take a breath. We're a marriage, Mel and I."

Shearing has also worked often with Marian McPartland, his old friend and compatriot. She said the other day, "I first heard George in 1948 or 1949, at a club called the Silhouette, in Evanston, Illinois. He had his original quintet, with Denzil Best on drums and Marjorie Hyams on vibes and Chuck Wayne on guitar and John Levy on bass. It was, of course, a mixed group, and whenever George was asked about it he'd say, 'I don't know what color they are, I'm blind.' Without question, he's a genius. Every time I hear him or play with him, I rediscover how much music of all kinds he's absorbed. And he writes wonderful music—tunes like 'Lullaby of Birdland' and 'Conception,' which has a bebop melodic line as good as any Charlie Parker wrote. And there's 'Changin' with the Times,' and 'Bop's Your Uncle,' which is a play on old English expression 'Bob's your uncle,' which means everything is O.K. He loves to joke around and laugh. I've played with him, and he'll put you on the spot by suddenly changing keys or going into a different style. And his puns are famous. It's hard to think of him as blind, because he constantly challenges himself. Sometimes I'm embarrassed to be around him and hear him talk about all the things he's doing outside of music. We've confided in each other at different times. George knows things about me that no one else does, and I probably know secrets about him.''

Shearing lives with his wife Ellie in a comfortable, modern apartment in the East Eighties. It has a sunken living room with yellow walls, an oatmeal wall-to-wall carpet, a fireplace, a Bösendorfer grand piano, an Eames chair, a wall of Braille books, and a marble head of Shearing by Ben Deane. Shearing's workroom, just off the foyer, contains two side-by-side upright pianos, his Braille word processor, all kinds of sound equipment, and a reclining chair that vibrates, massages your back, and plays tapes of birds singing in a ruined English abbey. Ellie Shearing is an excellent cook, and her sit-in kitchen has a six-burner electric stove and a plate warmer built into a wall. Shearing has a portable floor-to-ceiling temperature-controlled wine celler in one corner, and in it are Château Lafite-Rothschild, Acacia Chardonnay, Fetzer Zinfandel, and Beaulieu Vineyard's Georges de Latour Private Reserve. (Shearing still marvels at the time he invited the jazz producer and oenophile George Wein to dinner and gave him, as a test, a decanted bottle of the Georges de Latour, vintage 1970. Wein took two sips and named the vineyard, the wine, and the year.) The apartment also has a stately dining room and a bedroom. Shearing moves around a lot, and when Ellie Shearing rings the lunch bell he travels the fifty feet or so from the living room to the kitchen in about three seconds. He also likes to lie flat in his Eames chair and talk, his hands crossed on his stomach. This is what he said one afternoon:
"Blindness is more of a nuisance than a handicap. People say they forget I'm blind, and that's the best compliment they can pay me. I have no desire to live a single day in an undignified way. I was born blind, and when I was a kid in London I used to go everywhere by myself. I went on the road with my quintet for ten years with guide dogs. It was one of the most enlightening experiences of my life. Maybe I'm a devout coward on the road, but I like my hotel rooms if possible to have a bathroom to the left, two chairs with table between them, and a closet and bureau on the right. I can distinguish light and dark, and I like the window to be in front of me when I enter. An empty room is full of acoustics. In a full room, like this, sound dies. I have to snap my fingers in a full room that I don't know to find out when I'm approaching a wall or a bookcase. This is called facial vision. The movement of air is important. I can tell where people are around me simply by the way they displace the air. I think of sound as the vibration of air, and I think of color—I really don't know

what color looks like—as the vibration of light. I used to travel by myself in New York taxis, but I don't much anymore, because you never know where you will end up. In general, getting around New York is wonderful, because of the grid pattern and the sharp corners. It's harder to lose your sight during your life than to be born blind. If you nurse the impairment, though, you'll be a pathetic blind man rather than a productive one. A sense of humor never hurts. Once, Ellie and I were waiting for a table in a local restaurant. It was very crowded, and a waitress carrying a huge tray of empty dishes tried to squeeze between Ellie and me. I didn't know what was happening, and I had my arm through Ellie's. The waitress said, 'Hey, what's the matter with you? Are you blind? I said, 'As a matter of fact, I am.' Ellie said she will never forget the expression on the woman's face."

Shearing laughs a lot, and it loosens his imposing looks. He has a beaky nose, a high forehead, and grayish hair. He tilts his head up slightly when he is listening. Shearing stopped talking, sat up, stood, and, turning, went quickly up the living-room steps, across the foyer, and into his workroom. He talked as he went. "I've started writing some memoirs," he said, "and I'd like to read aloud what I've done. I've finished the first chapter and begun the second." He sat down at his VersaBraille machine and began to read, his fingers moving over a Braille tape. Here is some of what he read:

"It appears that at the age of three I made gallant but improper attempts at producing music. I used to hit the piano with a hammer. The Shillington Street School, where I went, was in Battersea, in southwest London. The area was known as the Latchmere, so called because of a well-known pub, which benefitted from the same handle. This was just one of many pubs dotted around the neighborhood in case the inhabitants got thirsty. And, regrettably, they did. On numerous occasions, children would be heard crying outside pubs while adults inside were doing their level best to get to be the way I was born. It is with sadness that I relate the fact that my mother was a serious contestant. My mother, however, did her very best to keep these miseries at a minimum after I was born. Almost everything was purchased by the Y.P. method (Yours Perhaps). The installment collector was known as the tally-man. He would appear every week to collect his money. More often than not, he would be greeted with a friendly 'I'll see you next week.' This rather unpleasant task was often foisted upon one of us kids. In which case, it would be 'Mum will see you next week.' Purchases would be made far in excess of what would seem necessary, so that we could have collateral to borrow money to buy more, to have collateral to borrow, and so on.

"Dad was a coal man. This meant that his job was to carry as heavy a load as possible from his horse and cart to a private home or a place of business. He would leave home at about 6 a.m. and return about the same hour p.m. He worked for the same firm for three months short of fifty years and received the equivalent of twelve dollars a week. He got to retire on a handsome pension of a dollar a week. Like all working-class Englishmen, he was very proud. In my teens, when I thought of changing jobs, my dad would say, 'Why do you want to do that, son? The boss has been good to you.' I could never understand why paying me my hard-earned salary was being good to me. But through all this seeming consideration of management Dad was a strong Labour man. He used to take me to the park on Sunday afternoons to hear some guy speaking in favor of Labour and, at times, for or against Communism. When no such oratory was to be found, we would witness part of a cricket match. Of course, we were never late home for afternoon tea, which would consist of watercress sandwiches and wonderful cake made by my mother.

"Were I more adept at putting things in their proper order, I would have saved some of the sweetness of the foregoing lines to lessen the depression of some of those to come. I remember the sound of rats scampering across the linoleum floor and the sound of my dad's boot trying to hit and kill them. I remember women begging their husbands not to get in a fight outside a pub when they had had too much to drink.

"Let's take a brief glimpse at my mother's life. Dad was earning a poverty-line salary. Mother had nine kids to raise, so she took care of the family during the day and cleaned railway trains at night. It's no wonder she tried to abort me—the youngest of the family. And no wonder I became blind in the process. Although she tried drowning her sorrows in drink, I feel that she really had a guilty conscience about my position and did her very best to repent.

"To this day, I am grateful that blind children were required to spend four years in residential school between the ages of twelve and sixteen. Linden Lodge was the name of the school I attended. Although it could not be counted among the twenty most beautiful residences in England, we had wonderful grounds, with a lawn, flowers, tennis courts for the staff, football and cricket fields, and all the things a little boy from Battersea didn't know existed. Cricket and football were played in the open air only by the partly sighted children. We blind kids played handball by using a football with a bell on it. Cricket was played inside by using a fair-sized balloon with a bell on it."

Shearing got up and went back into the living room and sat in his Eames chair. "That's all I've written so far," he said. He crossed his hands on his stomach. "I learned my Bach and Liszt and studied music theory at the Lodge. When I graduated, I went straight to work in a pub. A year or so later, I joined Claude Bampton's all-Blind Band. It was sponsored by the Royal National Institute for the Blind, and had been put together under the aegis of the bandleader Jack Hylton. There were fifteen of us, and we played Jimmie Lunceford and Benny Carter and Duke Ellington. We carried our own rostrum, and six grand pianos for the finale. Our suits were from Hawes & Curtis, on Savile Row. None of the bands of top condition would have dreamed of surrounding themselves with such glamour. Our leader was sighted, and he used a huge baton, which went swish, swish and told us what was what. Our music had been transcribed into Braille. We played all the major theaters in England and Scotland, and the tour lasted almost a year. I had my first contact with jazz in that band. Someone would pick up the new Armstrong or Berigan or Tatum record and say, 'Here's the new sender'—a good musician being known at the time as a solid sender. Through the band, I met Leonard Feather, who lived in London, and he helped me get recording dates and radio broadcasts. In 1941, I married my first wife, Trixie. I'd met her in an air-raid shelter where I used to play four-handed piano with the song plugger I was rooming with. Trixie and I had a daughter, Wendy, who now lives in North Hollywood. I had three or four jobs at once during the war—in theatres, supper clubs, jazz clubs. I had my own little band, and I also worked for the bandleader Ambrose. I toured a lot with Stéphane Grappelli, who spent the war in London. My mother was bombed out three times. We were Cockneys, and Cockneys tell jokes all the time. I remember one: This bloke says to his wife, 'Come on, Liza, the siren just went off.' She says, 'Hold it, Alf. I'm looking for my teeth.' And he says, 'Never mind that. They're dropping bombs, not sandwiches.' Around this time, I heard a recording of me speaking, and that told me I should do something about my Cockney accent. One time, I came home from school and my mother asked me what I had studied and I said, 'Six pieces of suet,' Or that's what she thought I had said. When she saw the teacher next, she asked her why we had been studying suet, and the teacher said the subject was 'Seek peace and pursue it.' Ellie tells me that when we visit London I revert to my old accent, and that if we stayed long enough she wouldn't understand a word I said. And when I see Grappelli I start talking like him: 'Stéphane, we go eat now.' I saved some money during the war, and in 1946 I visited New York. American musicians like Mel Powell and Glenn Miller had told me in England that I would kill them over here. I wasn't sure. Why would they want England's Teddy Wilson when they had the genuine article? But I liked New York so much I came back for good the next year.

"My first job was at the Onyx Club, on Fifty-second Street. I was the intermission pianist for Sarah Vaughan. I would be announced—'Ladies and gentlemen, from England the new and exciting pianist George Shearing'—and somebody would yell, 'Where's Sarah?' Then I spelled Ella Fitzgerald at the Three Deuces. She had Hank Jones and Ray Brown and Charlie Smith with her. When Hank took a night off, I played for Ella. I began to be asked to sit in on the Street, and Charlie Parker took me for walks between shows. Leonard Feather had moved to New York, and he introduced me to people and arranged gigs for me. In 1948, I played the old Clique Club, at Forty-ninth Street and Broadway, with Buddy De Franco on clarinet and John Levy and Denzil Best on bass and drums. We broke up after the engagement, and Leonard suggested I keep Best and Levy and add Marjorie Hyams on vibraphone and Chuck Wayne on guitar. I did some arrangements. Marjorie did some. We used a unison-octave voicing, like Glenn Miller's reed section. Our first New York gig was at Café Society Downtown, for six hundred and ninety-five dollars a week. We did the Blue Note in Chicago, and then the Embers and Birdland in New York—and the quintet took off. It lasted twenty-nine years, and a lot of wonderful musicians passed through—Cal Tjader and Gary Burton on vibes, Joe Pass and Toots Thielemans on guitar, Ralph Pena and Al McKibbon on bass, Charli Persip on drums. Toward the end, we travelled in a twenty-six-foot motor home with nine airplane seats and a couch and a refrigerator. On our last big tour, in the seventies, we did fifty-six concerts in sixty-three days, and I think that's what finally did me in."

Ellie Shearing brought in a tea tray and sat down. "Is that tea, Ellie?" Shearing asked. She said yes, and he made appreciative noises and said he would like a sugar and a half and enough milk to color his tea. "When I first came to this country," he said, "I couldn't believe what you got in a restaurant when you ordered tea. A cup of water that had never come to a boil and a tea bag sitting in the saucer. I'd tell the waitress, 'The water was good for my indigestion, now please bring me some tea.'" Shearing drank his tea quickly and excused himself, saying he wanted to get on with the next chapter of his memoirs. Ellie Shearing reminded him that they were supposed to have dinner at the Harvard Club with an old friend. She is trim and pretty and full of laughter. She has a long face, a wide smile, and auburn hair, tightly swept back. Her voice is big and carries easily around the apartment's corners. She is a quick, energetic talker.

"I marvel at the differences between George's and my background—at the fact that we ever came together," she said. "I was born in Harvey, Illinois, on August 22, 1932. My father was a Lutheran minister who had the same church—the first church he was given—for fifty-two years. His name was Rudolf Geffert, and he was born in Reed City, Michigan, the oldest of nine children. His father and his father's father were Lutheran ministers. He was short and dark and quiet, with a dry sense of humor. He did the Chicago *Tribune* crossword puzzle at breakfast, and he liked to translate Hebrew and Greek into English just for fun. I had three older brothers, and my mother did most of the raising of the children. Her name was Meta Hackbarth. She was little and always overweight, and she was a good plain cook. I was grown before I learned that all food wasn't fried and gray. She was well liked by the congregation, even though she had no patience for small-mindedness. She was born in Wausau, Wisconsin, and raised on a farm, and she hated it. To get away, she went to a normal school and became a teacher. After high school, I spent two years at Thornton Junior College and three at DePauw University. I was a piano major and a voice minor. I graduated in 1955, and my first job was writing radio commercials at WSBT, in South Bend. My second job was running a radio talk show in Niles, Michigan. Then I taught choir at a junior high school in East Grand Rapids. The next summer, I got into summer stock in New England through my old high-school speech teacher, Mae Sexauer. My mother was livid when she found out: her only daughter going on the wicked stage. She told me that I would bring shame on the family, that she'd disown me. But she eventually came to see me. After summer stock, I got a little apartment in New York, on Thirteenth Street between Avenue A and B, and I taught music in a high school out in Levittown. I worked one summer in 'Around the World in Eighty Days' at Jones Beach, and I was in 'To Broadway with Love,' a spectacle that ran at the Texas Pavilion during the 1964 World's Fair. I had been doing choral work around town, and I auditioned for Norman Luboff and was his alto soloist for three years. In 1967, Norman told me I should go to Hollywood and work in the studios, and I did that for four years. I kept body and soul together by teaching remedial reading in the Hollywood public schools. One of my students was a ten-year-old who had lived in communes all over the West. He could shoot, skin a deer, and make deerskin clothes, but he couldn't tell an 'A' from a 'B.' Within six months, he was reading at third-grade level. I told him I looked forward to teaching him the next year, and he said, 'I'm sorry, Miss Geffert, but my parents are moving again, and I don't know where I'll be.'

"I met George in 1971, at a Christmas party at his place in San Francisco. He was married, and I was dating someone regularly. We didn't see each other again for two years. By that time, George was divorced from Trixie, and we began housekeeping. We were married in 1984, in my dad's church. One of my brothers, who's a minister, performed the ceremony. When George and I started living together, I had been alone for a long time. I had to learn not to leave doors half open, not to kick my boots off in the middle of the room, not to not put things back after I had used them. George is very independent. He does not expect to be waited on. He's very sensitive, both emotionally and physically. His fingers are so delicate that he can feel dust on a table. Living with George can be difficult—sometimes on the road we're together twenty-four hours a day—but he's my best friend, and he's great fun."

The Man Who Lost His Humility

Julius La Rosa

Some of the American singers who have emerged from the shade cast during the past forty years by Frank Sinatra are Tony Bennett, Steve Lawrence, Buddy Greco, Paul Anka, Dick Haymes, Vic Damone, Peter Allen, Mel Tormé, David Allyn, Merv Griffin, Vaughn Monroe, Matt Dennis, Pat Boone, Andy Williams, Glen Campbell, Mark Murphy, Eddie Fisher, Jack Jones, Frankie Avalon, Robert Goulet, Bobby Troup, Neil Sedaka, Johnathan Schwartz, Johnny Hartman, Tony Martin, and Julius La Rosa. Among the most highly regarded by singers are Vic Damone, Jack Jones, and Julius La Rosa. La Rosa's career, though, has tended to move sideways, and even downward, more than it has upward. It reached bottom very soon after it began—in 1953, when he was twenty-three years old. For two years, he had been a member of the oppressed band of entertainers that the radio-and-television personality Arthur Godfrey had gathered about him. They appeared on Godfrey's daily radio show and on his weekly television program, and were often referred to by him as his "family." Most of them were mediocre, and all of them had a basic purpose—to feed and pamper Godfrey's ravenous ego. (In their gentle but devastating way, the comedians Bob and Ray used to needle Godfrey by satirizing conversations between Godfrey and his basso-profundo announcer Tony Marvin. Ray would do Marvin, reducing his words to obsequious and largely unintelligible booms, and Bob would do an uncanny Godfrey—homey, drawling, glutinous, sinister.) La Rosa talked about his days with Godfrey. He was in the tiny book-lined study of a split-level house he lives in in Irvington, New York, with his wife, Rory (née Rosemary

Meyer), whom he has been married to for thirty-one years and who came from a German-Czech family in Manitowoc, Wisconsin; his nineteen-year-old son, Chris; his twenty-six-year-old daughter, Maria, a Fordham graduate; and his huge black Lab, Mischief, whom he describes as "your basic old dog—faithful, friendly, getting deaf and blind." Although La Rosa is a delicate and tightly controlled performer, he talks in bursts and shouts. He sounds like surf on rocks, like thunder in flat country. Sometimes he shouts the opening syllable of a word and whispers the rest, and sometimes it is the other way around. Sometimes whole sentences explode.

"I had joined the Navy in 1947 and had become an electronics technician, and I had been using my voice to get myself out of various kinds of boring duty," La Rosa said. "I had sung at the enlisted men's club and the Officers' Club. In 1950, I was stationed in Pensacola, and Arthur Godfrey visited on some sort of Navy business. People forget now how big he was. He had his daily radio show and his weekly television show. CBS had a special vice-president at his beck and call, and even William Paley deferred to him. Somebody put a note under his door where he was staying in Pensacola telling him he should hear this kid Julius La Rosa from Brooklyn sing. So he did. I sang for him at the enlisted men's club—'The Song Is You' and 'Don't Take Your Love from Me.' He asked me to come up and sing on his radio show. I got leave and went to New York, and sang on the radio show, and then on the television show, and he said on the air that when I was discharged from the Navy I was to come back and I'd have a job. I think he recognized that this unprofessional, unshow-businesslike, totally unfinished product—with the natural manner and the innate shyness—was a perfect foil to his personality. Ten days after I got out, I started on the radio show. It was November 19, 1951. Six months later, I started doing the television show, too. Everything went well until the fall of 1953. A notice had been put on our bulletin board to the effect that the cast of the TV show was to take some sort of dancing lessons. I had a family emergency, and I asked to be excused, and was. When I got back, I discovered I would be punished for missing the lessons. Perhaps I had become a little smart-ass. I was getting six or seven thousand fan letters a week, and I was only twenty-three. But it was a red flag to me to be treated arbitrarily, so I got myself an agent—which was strictly against the Godfrey house rules. He was Tommy Rockwell, of General Artists, and he wrote Godfrey a letter. I knew something would happen, and it did—on October 4, 1953. I had been waiting an hour and fifteen minutes to do my song on the television show—it was 'Manhattan'—and after I did it Godfrey said, 'That was Julie's swan song with us. He goes out on his own now, as his own star, soon to be seen on his own program, and I know you wish him Godspeed, the same as I do.' Somebody recently sent me a kinescope, and I think those are Godfrey's words. He projected a kind of Peck's-bad-boy image, and had turned malicious, because I—the little boy next door who happens to sing—had supposedly lost my humility. There were headlines, and the press came down hard on Godfrey, and what did I do but go and apologize to him for what was happening—guilty because I had done what Daddy didn't want me to do! I now understand that he was an imperfect man, not a nice man. He had that fever of the successful which makes you become the inflated thing you think you are. The Godfrey experience was central to my life. It still follows me. I'm the man Arthur Godfrey fired, the man who lost his humility.

"After I left Godfrey, I worked in theatres where they still had live shows, and in clubs and on television. I learned my job in public—how to walk onstage, how to control an audience, what materials to use, what taste was. It took me fifteen years to learn these basics. I had my one big hit record, 'E Cumpare.' It was a Sicilian song that I sang as a kid. It's a kind of 'Old MacDonald Had a Farm' with instruments instead of animals. I did some acting in summer stock. In the mid-sixties, I studied myself. I decided what I couldn't do and what I could, and I put together a show called 'An Evening with Julius La Rosa,' and I took it on the road. It was not a success. In 1968, I hired a manager and got some new arrangements and opened in one of the lounges in Las Vegas. When I was about to sign on for twelve weeks, we got a call from WNEW, in New York. Would I like to do a disk-jockey show, from one to four in the afternoon—what they call housewife time? I took it, and here I was learning on the job again, doing another apprenticeship, letting personality bail me out. If I made a mistake, I blamed myself on the air, and the listeners loved that, and in time I became comfortable at what I was doing. The ratings went crazy at first, then settled to a very respectable level. I was making a hundred thousand a year, and I stayed until 1977, when they had a change in management and I was not renewed. So it was back to the saloons and summer stock, but in a different way. I have two shows now—a big, commerical one, in which I use a big band and everything has an exclamation point and I sing 'E Cumpare' and 'Sorrento.' And I have small, hip show, like the Oscar Hammerstein one I did at Michael's Pub."

LaRosa is a handsome, stocky, medium-sized man. He has widely spaced eyes, and he often pops them when he is emphasizing a word or phrase. He has double parentheses on each side of this mouth. His fingers are thick and powerful, his teeth are small, and he has a firm, rocky chin. When he sings, his expression flickers between bemusement and outright smiling. His work bears little resemblance now to Frank Sinatra's. La

Rosa's phrasing is built closely around the meaning of his lyrics. No singer has clearer diction. His voice, a pleasing baritone, has a slightly mystifying quality. This quality is not in its timbre or its texture; it seems to encase his voice. It gives it a cheerfulness, a hello-sunshine sound. La Rosa's gentleness is reflected in long connective single notes and in a self-effacing vibrato. His sense of dynamics is unsurpassed. He can shiver the timbers and buzz like a bee. He uses his acting abilities cautiously and well: he likes to lift an eyebrow, dip his head and close his eyes, and be regal with his hands, in the manner of Mabel Mercer, whom he first saw in the fifties.

La Rosa made himself a fresh cup of coffee in the kitchen, and Mischief followed him into the study and crashed to the floor. He looked like a Welsh mountain range. La Rosa sat on a stool in a corner, but he didn't stay there long. He talked about singing and about accompanists, and as he did he slid off the stool and walked quickly to the window, to his desk, to one of his bookshelves. "I'm an honest singer, who never tries for anything stylistic," he said. "I'm not a dynamic performer. The lyrics are more important to me than the melody. I try to tell the story of the song in a way that no one has heard before. I try to sing as if I were just talking casually with someone. I've always loved to sing, and was pushed forward whenever there was an occasion. I didn't have any serious training until I was in my early twenties, when I started lessons with Carlo Menotti—not Gian Carlo, just Carlo. I had sung in the All-City Chorus, which was made up of the cream of the city's high-school glee clubs. It was directed by Peter J. Wilhousky, who was amazing. He could sing in about four octaves. If he wanted to correct the sopranos, he'd sing them what he wanted in a pure soprano, and it was the same with the baritones and bass-baritones. One time, we were doing 'Begin the Beguine' and the baritones were messing up, so he made each of us sing the passage solo. After I'd done my version, he shouted, 'That's it! That's the way it should be done! Listen to La Rosa!' It was the first time I can remember that I was truly pleased with myself. I used to think of the melody all the time. It was part of the honest-singer thing—to sing the notes as they were written. Maybe it was also part of trying not to sound like Frank Sinatra, who took liberties with songs, and who was a big influence on me and a lot of other singers This was the Sinatra of the mid-fifties, who learned from Fred Astaire, who learned how to dance with his voice, to chop off his word endings. Now I'm secure enough to take chances with the melody—to do a little jazzing here and there. My phrasing was controlled at first by my breathing. When my breath ran out, the phrase ended. I was on the swimming team in high school, and I could swim fifty yards underwater and hold my breath almost a minute. I've been blessed with a good ear and good intonation, and I've gradually got all the technical things under control—phrasing, dynamics, concentration, fitting yourself to your audience and to the room you're in, not being rattled by bad accompanists. An accompanist shouldn't tell a singer how to say what he has to say. He shouldn't make him wait for the resolution of a phrase. He shouldn't play things that are so beautiful that the singer forgets what he is doing and starts listening to the piano. An accompanist should put a nice pad under the singer. He should play what we call footballs—those nice, big round whole notes, and not strings of eighth or sixteenth notes that serve to let you know he is there. Dave McKenna is a marvellous accompanist. He knows the lyrics, and he pays attention to them. So does Tony Monte. Mike Abene doesn't get in your way, and neither does Tex Arnold. I like Loonis McGlohon very much. The best accompanist I ever heard was Joe Massimino. He used to work with Mike Douglas, but he's out of the business now, running an Italian gourmet market in Tustin, California. When I'm singing, my mind goes wherever it wants. I think of someone in my family, of an old flame, that I better not forget the paper on my way home. In a strange way, this gets me to the juices of the song—particularly if I'm tired and it's one o'clock and there are only six people in the room and one more show to do."

La Rosa asked Mischief to go lie someplace else. The dog raised his huge head and looked in La Rosa's direction, then got to his feet like a whale surfacing. He rocked out of the room, filling the doorway, and collapsed in the hall. "I come from a demonstrative background," La Rosa said. "Not long ago, I had an argument with my mother, and I told her that if she was going to treat me like a twelve-year-old I was going to act like a twelve-year-old. We've worked it out since, just as my father and I have worked things out. He came over from Palermo in 1922, when he was sixteen. He taught himself how to build and repair radios, and he did that until he retired. He's about five feet seven. He's a benevolent man with a ruddy complexion and a small mustache—he'd shave the mustache off when he got mad at my mother. It's physically impossible for him not to tell the truth and it's physically impossible for him not to shout when he's angry. He's a strong-minded man, and about ten years ago things got very cold between us. I had been going through some therapy. I had got very impatient with him—I was picking fights with him. I was in my early forties, and he was in his sixties. So one day I went to his house in New Jersey, resolved to get everything on the table. I said, 'I know you love me, and you know I love you.' My mother was in the kitchen, and she shouted to my father, 'What's he saying?' My father shouted back, 'He's come to tell us he's seen the light!' So for the next couple of hours we fought and screamed and yelled and got it all out. We both retained our honesty, and we reached a kind of peace.

"My father's name is Salvatore, and my mother's is Lucia. She came over in the early twenties from Castel Buono, which is outside Palermo. She was fifteen and a half when she married my father, and she had had three children by the time she was eighteen. She had four in all, but two died, leaving my older sister, Sadie, and me. Sadie is a widow with two daughters, and lives near my parents. My mother is a soft, quiet, unassuming woman. People say she's too good. She has simple needs and simple wants, and what makes her happy is to see her children and grandchildren happy. Both my parents have long since lost what I call their *baciagaluppo* accents—that Italian immigrant way of speaking English where you add an 'a' to everything. My parents still lived at a Hundred and Ninth Street and Second Avenue when I was born, but I grew up in the Ridgewood-Bushwick section of Brooklyn. It's part Brooklyn, part Queens, and not far from Astoria, where Tony Bennett came from. Our neighbors were Italian, Jewish, and a smattering of Germans. I remember swastikas hanging outside German-American Bund meetings. We were poor, but we had everything we needed, and some of the extras. When they put steam heat in our building, they raised the rent from fifteen dollars a month to twenty, and my parents had a fight about whether or not it was exorbitant. We had a four-room railroad flat on the third floor. My sister and I slept in the front room on fold-up beds, and my parents had the bedroom. The kitchen was the center of the house, and food was the center of the kitchen. We never scrimped at the table. Part of keeping up appearances was that there was enough to eat. If you had six people for dinner, you didn't have six lamb chops—you had a dozen or sixteen. I went to P.S. 123, then to Grover Cleveland High School. I graduated in 1947. I had no real confidence in anything. I loved singing. I was a pretty good baseball player. I was a good Friday-night dancer. So I joined the Navy. It was partly an act of defiance and partly to learn about electronics, so that I could go into business with my father—a typical two-edged teenage act."

For many years, La Rosa and Gene Lees, the West Coast lyricist, singer, and jazz writer, have carried on a voluminous correspondence. They met for the first time several years ago. Lees has this to say about his friend: "Popular singing in America used to be dominated by the Irish, but since the arrival of Sinatra it's been Italians. I think Julius La Rosa is the most brilliant member of the Sinatra school. He is a born naturalist. He always sang well, but he is singing far better now. His voice has a woody, Italian quality—you hear it in Aldo Ray and Brenda Vaccaro. It's a quality of voice comedians try to get when they're doing gangsters. Julie shares the inferiority complex of New York Italians. They have a self-effacing way that often makes them pretend to be dumb. I heard Tony Bennett suddenly break off a discourse on Picasso one night, and say, 'But what do I know about Picasso?' I've heard Julie do it. But he's a very intelligent man, who writes well and knows far more than he lets on. His confidence as a singer has become solid and stable only in recent years. I've watched it grow with great pleasure, and I suspect that at last he's on his way."

A Queenly Aura

Mabel Mercer

There have been five consummate cabaret singers in this country: Mabel Mercer (Staffordshire, England; 1900), Bobby Short (Danville, Illinois; 1924), Julie Wilson (Omaha, Nebraska; 1924), Blossom Dearie (East Durham, New York; 1926), and Hugh Shannon (De Soto, Missouri; 1921). Their bearing, style, voice, and attack are totally dissimilar, but their repertoires overlap, and they are in the same line of work—singing superior songs, some of them largely unknown, to small audiences in intimate rooms in such a way that song, singer, listener, and room become one. Mabel Mercer is their doyenne. There is no gifted American singer who has not learned from her. She came up through English vaudeville and the Paris boîtes—in particular, Bricktop's—and settled here in 1941. She studied singing for a time, and she approaches each song as if she were introducing it: here are its lyrics, my dears, here is its melody, and here is the beautiful whole they make. She sits almost motionless in an armchair when she sings (or singtalks, depending on her powers that evening), her head tipped back, her hands occasionally sketching air, her eyes fixed on the middle distance. Her regal bearing goes Queen Elizabeth one better: Mabel Mercer has humor. Sometimes Bobby Short's elegance appears brittle and baked-on, but it is not, for his taste—clothes, songs, witticisms—is infallible. He declaims his songs, and he occasionally ends them with an arms-wide, lights-out, bass-drum-thump theatricality. His diction peals, and he has enormous energy. Like Mabel Mercer, he is black, and his accent, a fastidious drawl, both mocks and celebrates his listeners. His piano playing tends to race around, upsetting tempos and dynamics, but he knows the right chords, and once in a while he achieves an Art Tatum fleetness. He grew up close to jazz. So did Blossom Dearie, who is short and blond and has a buttermilk attractiveness. Her little, high voice suggests thimbles and Limoges. Her diction is crystalline, and she is a precisionist; once she has a song set, she never changes a note or a nuance. She also demands silence when she performs. Of these five singers, she is the only one who writes songs. They are funny, light, and highly melodic. She plays the piano like Nat Cole, and she swings. Hugh Shannon is perhaps the least well known of the five. He has spent much of his career in Capri and Paris and Rome and the Virgin Islands. His admirers include some of the wealthiest people in the world, but he considers himself a "saloon" singer. He has a hoarse, rangy baritone, and he flings his songs out. His singing is full of bonhomie, and he gathers his listeners to him. His diction is good but loose, and he addresses the piano as if it were sliding past him; he sits ajar, his left foot banging the floor and his hands making fast, pawing motions. He talks to his songs. He will finish a ruminative "Poor Butterfly" and say softly, in a sort of coda, "Poor girl, poor girl." Julie Wilson is very thin and almost ferociously elegant. She seems to sing most of the time with her profile to the audience, probably because it is of classic proportions. Her cheekbones are high, and she has wide, sad gray eyes. She wears sumptuous gowns, and she has two stylish signatures—she pulls her hair back severely into a bun, and she wears a sizable gardenia over her left ear. She tilts her head when she sings, but it is more a defiant motion than a relaxed one. She has a heavy, bare voice. Her vibrato tends to flutter, but she never lets it out of sight. She is an annunciatory singer, who sometimes ends her numbers with a polite shout. She shakes her listeners until she finds the way in.

Alec Wilder, who was quick to damn and slow to praise, once set down his thoughts about Mabel Mercer: "She transmutes popular song to the extent that by means of her taste, phrasing, and intensity it becomes an integral part of legitimate music. When she sings a song, it is instantly ageless. It might have been composed the day before, but, once given the musical dignity of her interpretation, it is no longer a swatch of this season's fashion but a permanent part of vocal literature. She has never made the slightest attempt to sing in the manner one expects of popular singers. As a result, those who assume that a 'swinging' style is a prerequisite of a singer of such songs are sometimes thrown off or baffled by her constant dignification (if I may risk such a word) of otherwise casual songs. It is not that she is unaware of the rhythmic looseness of an up-tempo song or of a slow blues. It is rather that her purpose is to present a musical point of view which has more to do with the intimate concert hall than with a casual night spot. That impalpable quality known as showmanship is, in her case, inapplicable. Rather [she exhibits] graciousness, magnetism, profound calm, and, most of all, complete authority."

More by accident than by design, Mabel Mercer has spent most of her career singing in supper clubs, and so she is, in the best sense, a miniaturist, who sings to small audiences in small rooms about seemingly small things—a remembered spring, a broken romance, a new lover, a lost childhood. But the supper club—that royal relative of the night club—has almost been obliterated by television, and its patrons have dwindled and grown old. Few of the sort of special, witty, poetic songs Mabel Mercer sings are written anymore, partly because they would seem hopelessly archaic and mannered and partly because the insouciant musical theatre that bred so many of them no longer exists. Moreover, of all performing artists, singers grow old most quickly, and within the past decade Mabel Mercer's voice has shrunk, and it has become difficult for her to sustain a note with any effect. Instead, she has perfected what Wilder called a "graceful parlando"—a way of melodiously talking her songs. Her phrasing and choice of tones and insuperable diction—her style, in short—remains not only intact but inspired; it is simply that rests have supplanted the flow of melody between tones. Her singing in her prime was unique. It lay somewhere between the concert hall and jazz. She had a rich, low mezzo-soprano and a considerable range, and her best tones had the elastic, power-in-reserve sound of formal singers. Her phrasing was jazzlike in that she often placed her notes in surprising places and often used jazz timbres. She was able, in an uncanny way, to make her voice encompass not only many moods but their attendant colors—the purples of love, the blues of sorrow, the yellows of humor, the black of despondency. She was a superb dramatic singer who could handle with equal ease the *Sturm und Drang* of Kurt Weill's "Trouble Man" and the bittersweet feeling of Wilder's "Did You Ever Cross Over to Sneden's?" Every song she sang seemed to be fashioned out of the fabric of her own experience, and to be an individual offering to each one of her listeners. And she still is a marvellous comic singer, who, by surrounding the right word with silence or by dipping it in a growl, invariably provokes laughter. Above all was her easy, alabaster technique—the ingenious phrasing, the almost elocutionary diction, the dynamics (she never shouted and she never relied on the staginess of the near-whisper), the graceful melodic push, the quick rhythmic sense, and, always, the utter authority.

Mabel Mercer was, and is, just as irresistible visually. Seeing her is not a fleeting experience; it recalls the brief, stunning sequence on television during the mid-fifties in which Queen Elizabeth, in New York, was passing in review of some worthy body. The cameras, on closeup, studied her face as she stopped and spoke to people. She looked drawn and tired, but she was unfailingly gracious and gentle. It was an unforgettably attractive human display. Mabel Mercer has precisely that queenly aura. Indeed, she is now of Victorian proportions—short, quite round, and with fine, luminous eyes and a shy child's smile. Her ramrod posture, swan neck, and high cheekbones make her seem taller than she is. And so do her high forehead, which supports a cloud of dark, short hair, and the long, sumptuous, often low-necked gowns she wears. When she sings, she invariably wears a bright silk shawl tossed loosely over her shoulders. She is a study in composure. She sings with her eyes half closed, and she moves her head only to emphasize a phrase or word. (She has not used a microphone until recent years, but, placed casually to one side of her chair, it is unobtrusive.) At the close of each set, she gets up quickly and ducks out of the room. In a minute or two, she resumes her chair and sings two or three encores (she will sometimes sing upward of thirty songs in a sitting), and she is done. Her audiences, released, tend to surface slowly; she recalls times when she has finished singing and there has been no applause at all—presumably because of a surfeit of emotion among her listeners.

When Mabel Mercer came to New York, the city was garlanded with supper clubs, and she worked without pause for twenty years. The fervency of her following was such that between 1941 and 1957 she sang in only two clubs—Tony's and the Byline Room—and when the Byline burned down a new one was immediately built for her. But work has not been plentiful of late. She has appeared at the Café Carlyle and Downstairs at the Upstairs, and she has given several S.R.O. concerts with Bobby Short. Twilights, though, are often the capstone of the day, and for a couple of seasons Mabel Mercer held forth brilliantly at the St. Regis Room. She lived in the St. Regis during her engagements, and when, during one of them, a reporter called to find out if he could visit her there, he was told, a few days later, that she was dubious. She wondered what they would talk about, and she said that there really wasn't much to her life; she had been in show business since she was fourteen, and that was it. Mabel Mercer pursues privacy, she treasures it, she embraces it. Despite constant requests, she refuses to write an autobiography. But after she had conferred with Harry Beard, her manager and amanuensis, she set a day for the meeting. The reporter arrived at the hotel and called her room, but there was no answer, and there was no message at the desk. He turned around, and a short, stocky figure in a brown tweed coat and a long woollen scarf was emerging from the elevator.

"Oh, my," she said, putting a hand up to her mouth. Her voice was low and her accent elegant, "I forgot all about you. I have to go out and pick up a couple of gowns for the Dick Cavett show, which I'm supposed to tape tomorrow. I've done very few TV talk shows, and I'm rather nervous about it."

The reporter asked if he could go with her.

"Oh, certainly not," she said. "But come to the Cavett show with me. They're sending a limousine at one. Harry Beard will be with us, and Jimmy Lyon, my accompanist. But while you're here, come and look at the room." She moved slowly through the lobby, rocking slightly from side to side and threading her way between small mountains of luggage. She stopped just short of the King Cole Bar, at a pair of open glass doors. The St. Regis Room seated perhaps seventy-five. The floor was carpeted, the ceiling was blue, and there were love seats and leather chairs and small tables. Mirrors and gold paper covered the walls. To the right of the doors was a tiny, almond-shaped stand, with a grand piano, a micro-phone, and a French Provincial armchair. The room was full of lunching women.

"It's nice, isn't it?" she asked. She opened her coat and put her hands on her hips. "I do two shows on Tuesdays, Wednesdays, and Thursdays, and three on Fridays and Saturdays. Then I have my two days off, so that I can get up to my house in Chatham, New York, and have a nice rest. They wanted me to start my first show at nine or nine-thirty, and I told them that was too early. Much too early for my people. So I started around ten, and then what did they do at first but close the doors of the room at ten sharp and keep the people waiting outside until the second show began! 'Here, what's this?' I told them. 'You can't do that. These people rush away from their coffee to get here on time and find the doors shut in their faces.' So we've changed all that. They still close the doors, but they bring the late-comers in by a back way. Well, I must go. I'm sorry about today, but you be here at one sharp tomorrow."

The reporter was, and a few minutes later Mabel Mercer came out of the elevator. She was greeted by a tall, stooped man with short gray hair and thick glasses. He was Harry Beard. She was carrying a clothesbag over one arm, and she handed it to Beard. "I've brought two gowns, one black and one white."

"They'll tell you which one they want you to wear, Mabel," he said. "They have their own ideas about these things." He spoke in a concerned, measured way, a nanny clucking over a charge.

A young, good-looking priest rushed up, expectantly smiling.

"Oh, Peter. It's you. How nice," Mabel Mercer said. Peter O'Brien, a Jesuit, spends most of his waking hours shepherding the jazz pianist Mary Lou Williams. He and Mabel Mercer embraced.

"I just stopped by to give you a cheer and see how you are," he said. "I've been moved to another church, at Eighty-third and Park, but I'll still have plenty of time to be with Mary."

"Park Avenue," Beard said. "Well, Peter, you've moved that much closer to Heaven."

O'Brien laughed, and said he'd stop by one evening next week. A short, thin gray-haired man in a black raincoat and a dinner jacket appeared— Jimmy Lyon.

"I'll go and see where the limousine is," Beard said.

"The Cavett people changed the time of the taping from six in the evening to now," Mabel Mercer said. "I told them it's practically impossible for a singer to sing so early. I don't get upstairs from the St. Regis Room until almost three, and I can't just pop out of bed and start performing."

Beard reappeared with the driver. "I put the gowns in the trunk," he said. Everyone got into the car and headed for Cavett's studio, which is on Fifty-eighth, between Seventh and Broadway.

"I can't very well practice in my room at the hotel, either," Mabel Mercer said. "The neighbors would say, 'What's that crazy woman doing singing in her room?' I did get a reaction like that once in the country, when I was learning a new song. I tried a high note and the cat, Valachi, jumped right up from the floor and landed on my bosom. So now I warm up with a recorder. I breathe through it, and I play higgledy-piggledy music on it. Every night before bed in the country, I go to the head of the cellar stairs and play, and Valachi comes bounding up. In addition to the cat, I always have dogs. Just nondescript dogs that come and go. I love animals. Deer come within a hundred feet of the house and stand there with their heads in the air. And there are foxes and raccoons. I have some neighbors who had a bunch of raccoons last summer who'd come to their screen door in the kitchen every evening after dinner and pry it open and then let it bang. They'd keep doing it until they were fed with graham crackers and leftovers. You become aware of so many things in the country that city people simply don't know about. Like the crickets chirp-chirp-chirping. To me, they have always sounded like sleigh bells, and it's a pity there aren't more around at Christmastime. One autumn evening a while ago, I was driving by a big field, and it looked totally black, as if some farmer had burned it off. Then a strip of the black suddenly moved up into the air against the evening sky, formed into a flock of birds, and flew away after a lead bird. There was a pause, and a second formation took off, again with a leader. And so it went, a magic, secret ritual. I sat there fifteen minutes watching, until the field was empty. My house is surrounded by cow farms, and I love to see the cows standing on hillsides. I've had the house many years. My family came from North

Wales, and I used to go there for holidays as a child. I remember endless fields of poppies and wheat and blue cornflowers and how we'd return from long walks decked out with bracelets and necklaces of daisies and buttercups, and I knew that one day I had to have a place in the country. Of course, I never could have bought it now. I got it for nothing, and bit by bit through the years, when I've had a few extra dollars, I've fixed it up. I can't garden much anymore, so I'd like to have the place planted with flowering trees—cherry and crabapple and dogwood and wisteria. Then I'd have a thing of glory. I have a huge bird population. I buy sunflower seeds by the fifty-pound bag. The birds take all my pocket money. When I come down in the morning in winter, they're all sitting and waiting on the telegraph line for me to put out some food, and when I do it's as if they were saying, 'All right, boys. The restaurant is open. Let's go.'"

The car pulled up at the stage door, and Mabel Mercer walked to the greenroom, backstage. It was furnished with comfortable chairs, a color television set, and fifty or sixty photographs of Cavett's guests in action on his show. Beard helped Mabel Mercer out of her coat. "There goes my stomach," she said. "I've been in this business nearly sixty years, and I still get butterflies at times like this."

"It's the adrenalin working, Mabel," Beard said. He felt the clothesbag. "Uh-oh! The gowns have fallen down in the bottom!"

Mabel Mercer felt the bag. "No, they haven't, Harry. They're folded over hangers. Those are shoes in the bottom."

"I hope you're right," Beard said.

The stage manager took Mabel Mercer onstage, and she sat down in a large yellow armchair. She ran through the two songs she would do—"Too Long at the Fair," by Billy Barnes, and Lerner and Lane's "Wait 'Til We're Sixty-five." They went well. She was told her black gown would be better, and she went off to a dressing room. Beard ordered tea with honey for her. "It's taken seventy-two hours to prepare her for this," he said. "She's like a child who has to go to the hospital. I finally told her if she wasn't careful she'd be all right. But she's so natural and offhanded-seeming she can't go wrong. Mabel has walked alone. She has never deviated from what she knew had to be done. It has never been a question of money or vogue."

Mabel Mercer reappeared, in a resplendent black gown threaded with silver. She had a red shawl around her shoulders. She sat down and sipped her tea. One of Cavett's assistants told her she would be on first and that Cavett would like to talk with her on camera before she sang. The greenroom was filling up. Shirley Temple Black, in a red dress, sat down near Mabel Mercer and took out a cigarette. "Do you mind if I smoke?" she asked.

"Of course not, dear," Mabel Mercer replied. "It only bothers me when I'm singing. Years ago, in Paris, when anyone started to smoke a cigar in a place where I was working, he would be asked to put it out, and of course he did. It's not that way anymore." A Cavett assistant asked her if she would like more tea, and she said. "Yes. Sweeten the kitty, if you would."

Cavett came in and shook hands with everyone. He left, and the greenroom settled down to watch her on the television set. After Cavett's monologue, Mabel Mercer went onstage. She looked relaxed and elegant, and she spoke easily and with surprising freeness. She told Cavett that her father, whom she had never known, was an American Negro and that her mother was white. She had been born in Staffordshire into a bohemian household full of painters and people in show business. She said that when she was twelve she told her grandmother, who took care of her while her mother was on the road, that she wanted to be an engineer, and was informed that this was not suitable for young ladies. She was put in a convent boarding school when she was seven, and it was there she realized that there was something different about her. Her schoolmates thought that perhaps she was an African princess, but, if she was, why did she speak English so well? In time, she became a sort of mascot at the school, and was given the nickname Golliwog. She said that the only thing that bothered her was that she had short hair and all the other girls had long plaits, so she tied a couple of pieces of string to a headband and let them hang down like pigtails. Cavett asked her about her years in Paris in the twenties and thirties, and she told him about singing at Bricktop's, and about meeting Cole Porter and Vincent Youmans and Gertrude Stein and Ernest Hemingway. But, she said, none of them made a very deep impression, because they were all young together. Then Mabel Mercer, seated in the yellow chair, her hands in her lap, her shawl about her shoulders, her composure complete, sang her two songs, with great effect. Her diction was glass, and her voice sure and strong. And she got several good laughs in just the right places in "Wait 'Til We're Sixty-five," a song that has to do with maturing bonds and Social Security, and "Tampa, Fla." She came back to the greenroom, somewhat breathless, and there was a heavy round of applause. A stagehand said Cavett would like her onstage for the rest of the show, and she went back. One of Cavett's assistants said that it was the first time she had ever heard applause in the greenroom.

After Mabel Mercer had changed into her street clothes, she went out through the stage door. It was four o'clock. There was a crowd of autograph seekers on the sidewalk, and she was immediately surrounded. She wrote slowly, but she did sign almost a dozen times. All the while, a huge

A.B.C. policeman with a Brendan Behan face and a matching brogue tow-
ered over her. He kept saying, "All right, Mabel. You don't have to do so
many. . . . One more, Mabel, and I'll take you to the car. . . . Now, that's
it. You'll catch your death."

She got into the car. "Well, that's the first time that's happened to me
in all these years—all those autographs," she said.

"You're a living legend, Mabel," Beard said.

"Don't say that, Harry," she replied. "It makes me very nervous. Let's
have some lunch."

"All right," he said, and told the driver to go to Michael's Pub, on East
Fifty-fifth Street. It was nearly empty. Mabel Mercer ordered a Bloody
Mary ("I'm going to break my rule and celebrate"), soup, and a spinach
salad. "My life has come in three parts—England, France, and America,"
she said, after she had finished her Bloody Mary. "My mother was short
and my stepfather was tall and skinny, and they called their act, which
was vaudeville, of course, Ling and Long. I'll never forget one part of it.
They'd all put on white tennis clothes and step out on a simulated court
and the lights would go down and they'd throw luminous clubs back and
forth across the net. My stepfather had invented the luminous clubs, and
you'd see these squashy balls of light drifting back and forth through the
dark, and it was a beautiful spectacle. In those days, vaudeville was full
of jugglers and acrobats and tumblers. The circus is about the only place
you find them now. My mother and stepfather had come over to America
on tour in 1912 and were stranded by the war, and when I got out of
school, in 1914, I went into my aunt's act. It was a family singing-and-
dancing act, and I started as a dancer. We went all over England on the
vaudeville circuit, and we always travelled on Sundays. We'd hire our
own railroad coach, and there would be a sign in the window saying who
we were. When we'd get to a new town, there'd be the excitement of
seeing old friends and of finding out where you'd be on the bill. The closing act was tops, and I think we made it as the next-to-last act a couple
of times. In 1919, another girl and I formed a dancing act and took it to
Brussels, and several years later I joined Lew Leslie's 'Black-Birds,' in
London, with Florence Mills. After that, I became part of a vocal trio—
two men and myself. We sang everything, a cappella and with piano
accompaniment—lieder, Negro spirituals, French songs, 'Yes, We Have
No Bananas,' 'Carolina in the Morning.' One of the men had been a choir-
master, and it was he who caused me to start studying singing. I studied
in Paris and London, and I had aspirations to be a concert singer. But it
just didn't work out that way. I paid for my lessons by working in shows
and singing in night clubs, and that's no way to become a classical singer.
I worked in a variety of shows, travelling all over Europe. One was a circus, where we sang between the acts, and another was *The Chocolate Kid-*

dies. It played in Vienna and in Cairo and Alexandria. I'd go out to the Pyramids every day. It was when they were excavating the Sphinx, and I remember the workers passing pails of sand along and singing chants, like the American gandy dancers. By the thirties, I had settled pretty much into Bricktop's, and it was a lovely era. Bricktop's was very chic, and money was plentiful. There were banquettes around the walls, lit from behind, and an orchestra and a small dance floor. I'd sit right at people's tables and sing to them. That sort of intimate singing is tricky, you know. You can't *look* at the people you are singing to. They get embarrassed. So you look at the ceiling or the far corner of the room, and then they can stare at you and know that you won't look down and catch them. Sometimes we'd sing all night, and once I remember stopping in a café on the way home and listening to Louis Armstrong and Django Reinhardt, the gypsy guitarist, playing duets together. They were still there at noon, playing, just the two of them. In 1938, I came over here to work in the Ruban Bleu. It was run by Herbert Jacoby, whom I'd worked for in Paris, and Cy Walter was my accompanist. Then I worked for a while in the Bahamas, where I got to know the Duke and Duchess of Windsor. And in 1941 I went back in the Ruban Bleu and then opened at Tony's, on Fifty-second Street. Billie Holiday was working across the street, and she came in so much that her boss got mad and told her she wasn't being paid to listen to me."

Mabel Mercer had finished her salad, and she looked tired. She said she was going back to the hotel to take a nap. "I don't remember when I last got eight straight hours of sleep. I suppose it's age. I wake up every couple of hours all night and I read or take a hot bath and sometimes that helps."

The St. Regis Room was already full at nine-thirty, and Mabel Mercer, again in her black gown, was seated at a corner table with several priests. At ten minutes of ten, she arranged herself in her chair, a green shawl around her shoulders. A wineglass of hot water with honey and lemon and slices of orange in it sat beside her on the piano. She said something to Jimmy Lyon, gazed serenely over the heads of her listeners, and started George Gershwin's "'S Wonderful." Bart Howard's "My Love Is a Wanderer" came next, and then another Gershwin, "Isn't It a Pity?" After "Season's Greetings," by Rod Warren, she rearranged her shawl around her waist and tied it loosely. Portia Nelson's "Sunday in New York" and Rodgers and Hart's "Falling in Love with Love" were followed by Cy Coleman's "Sweet Talk." Then came Bob Merrill's "Mira," Joe Raposo's "Bein' Green," and Jerome Kern's "Remind Me." The Kern was highlighted by beautifully rolled "r"s. She paused for a moment, and then she gave Cole Porter's "Down in the Depths on the Ninetieth Floor" a beautiful rendition, and ended with the songs she had done on the Cavett show. She bowed her way out of the room, and when she came back she did Cy Coleman and Dorothy Fields' "Baby, Dream Your Dream" as an encore.

She sat down with Harry Beard and the reporter and ordered tea and honey. Beard said the Cavett show would be on in twenty minutes, and that he wanted to go and find a television set. The reporter asked her how many songs she knows.

"I guess I know roughly a thousand," she answered. "I can sing three or four hundred of them without too much brushing up. I learned a long time ago that you have to keep your mind exactly on what you're doing when you sing. If stray thoughts suddenly pop into your head, you're apt to forget the words. It's happened to me more than once. When it does, I either repeat what I've just sung or sing a line or two of nonsense until the right words come back. They're always there, stored safely away somewhere in the back of my head. I think constantly about the lyrics and what they mean, and I try and make my listeners feel the vision of what the words are saying. All of us know about sorrow and tears and laughter, so it's not my job to sing *my* emotions but to sing my *listeners'* emotions. Then they can take them home with them. In a way, my singing is like putting on certain sets of clothes every night. I'd be a total wreck if I lived all the emotions I sing about. It happened to me just once. I was sitting at a table with some people and singing 'The Last Time I Saw Paris,' and so many things started going through the back of my mind about Brick's and my little apartment in Paris and so forth that I had to stop and excuse myself. At first, I found this sort of intimate singing a terrible wear and tear. I'd get so nervous my lip would tremble and my legs wobble. I'd pray I could walk across the stage and not let it show. I'd sense unfriendly people in the audience or I'd hear a man leave in the middle of a set and say to the maître d., 'Who told *her* she could sing?' Then I understood that you simply cannot please everybody and that there will always be two or three people out front who understand, and it is to *them* that you should sing. I don't know where my sense of diction came from. Perhaps I got it in school. Perhaps it came from my mother. Before she came over here, she'd take me into an empty theatre where she was working, and she'd go up to the top gallery and make me stand down on the stage and sing. I was a very shy child, even with her, but she'd say, 'All right, sing! And I want to understand every word!' I just don't know, I've never had any wish to be famous, and I've always wondered: How can those people sit out there and listen to *me?* If I ever have it to do all over again, I'd like to be a painter, like my grandfather. Or a writer. Something permanent. Look at Mme. Curie. Maybe I'd write children's books about sitting on the beach and the sunbeams coming down and people coming down the beams and talking to me. Fantasies. But I don't suppose I'll ever have the chance."

Mabel Mercer has had a fine decade. Her years of singing in the St. Regis Room were brought to a climax by a seventy-fifty-birthday party in the St. Regis Roof, at which Jimmie Daniels, Sylvia Syms, Mary Lou Williams, Bobby Short, Ruth Warwick, and Hugh Shannon performed. In 1977, suddenly full-voiced, she gave a brilliant concert at Carnegie Hall. The same year, she appeared in London (for the first time in over forty years), at the Playboy Club, and starred in a five-part BBC television film "Miss Mercer in Mayfair." The next year, she spent nine stirring weeks at the Macombo, in San Francisco, and she gave a concert in the Dorothy Chandler Pavilion, in Los Angeles. In 1981, the Whitney Museum held an evening called "American Cabaret," in which she was celebrated by eighteen performers and composers. Frank Sinatra wrote her a letter that reads, in part, "I love you dearly. You are a great friend, a gifted and talented woman, and the best music teacher in the world. Everyone who has ever raised his voice in song has learned from you, but I am the luckiest one of all because I learned the most of all." In 1982, she worked twice at the Kool Jazz Festival in New York. At a concert of Alec Wilder's music, she sang "Did You Ever Cross Over to Sneden's," and the next evening, at Alice Tully Hall, she gave a program with Eileen Farrell. Dressed in a handsome black gown (which she had made) and a light-blue stole, she did ten solos, among them "The Kerry Dance," "While We're Young," "Once Upon a Summertime," "Try to Remember," and "Wait 'Til We're Sixty-five." She closed with dramatic readings of A. A. Milne's "Vespers" (which she had first heard Gracie Fields do) and Edna St. Vincent Millay's "The Ballad of the Harp-Weaver." Anita Ellis was one of the countless singers in the audience. "The joie de vivre, the sweetness, the lesson in how to love!" she later said of the concert. "It was one of the events of my life."

Between these appearances, Mabel Mercer invariably fled to the small eighteenth-century farmhouse in the foothills of the Berkshires, where she has spent every spare minute during the past thirty years. The house lies in a wild, hilly, wooded area between Chatham, New York, and Lenox, Massachusetts. Charlie Briggs, a retired postmaster, farmer, and storekeeper and a still active woodcutter, caretaker, and maple-syrup maker, sold the house to Mabel Mercer. He is a slender, easy, articulate man with a small mustache and weather-narrowed eyes. "I was born in 1912 in Mabel's house," he has said. "We had an outdoor pump and an outhouse. The road that the house faces wasn't electrified until 1947. I

don't know that it will ever be paved. I'm not sure who built the house
or when, but my father bought it from a short, smart businessman named
Thomas Buckley, who owned a good part of Chatham. Chatham was an
important rail center in those days, and I used to ship plums and eggs
down to Pleasantville on the express. The shipping fee for thirty dozen
eggs was twenty-five cents. I've seen this valley change from farms, with
every side field planted or grazed, to residences, and I don't believe you
can buy a dozen eggs or a quart of milk up and down its whole length.
Sometimes Mabel's house wasn't accessible. Sometimes it still isn't. In
heavy snow, the only way to get food to the house was to hand-pull it up
the hill on a sled—a full mile, it was. And in the spring, when the thaw
came, you couldn't get through at all. A horse would sink to his knees in
the mud, and a car was even more useless. I consider myself a lucky man
to have been able to live my whole life in this beautiful area." Briggs
paused, then went on, "Some people around here were upset when I sold
Mabel the house. But many of those people are now her best friends—
which shows you something about her and about human nature."

The house sits close to the ground at the end of a short driveway. It
now comes in three parts. On the right is the original, full Cape Cod-style
house with its center door flanked on both sides by two matching windows. The door is closed and blind-looking, and is rarely used. To the left
of the old house is an ell, probably added in the nineteenth century. It is
set back a few feet and has had a glassed-in porch added at the front. The
porch leads to the kitchen door, which is now the front door. A small
wing, set back a few more feet and added to the ell a year or two ago,
forms the third part of the house. At the back of the ell, a cement terrace,
separated from the kitchen by a narrow sun porch, looks out over a beautiful field, which flows downhill from left to right and is covered by tall
grass. A solitary apple tree stands in the main part of the field. A thirty-
year-old maple shades the terrace and the foundations of two Briggs
barns, now gone, and just to the right of the terrace are a white toolhouse
and a small hickory-nut tree. Alec Wilder gave the hickory tree to Mabel
Mercer for her seventy-fifth birthday, mistakenly believing it to be a wal-
nut tree. "That was our special joke, that tree," Mabel Mercer says. Wilder
loved to visit her house, and he once said, "I've gone up to visit her in
the country a perfect wreck and in two days felt marvellous. It isn't that
she *does* anything—that there is any laying on of hands or such. She just
putters around her house, and cooks, and feeds her animals. But there is
some quality, some corrective force, in her very presence." The uphill side
of the field has half a dozen Christmas-tree evergreens, and between
them are woodchuck holes and four-foot basins of flattened grass—deer
beds. The field is bordered on one side by the road and on three sides by
woods. A stream runs past the field through the bottom of a steep ravine,

and a hundred or so yards to the left of the house there is a small water-fall. There is no other house in sight, and the sky over the field and woods is low and sheltering.

Mabel Mercer loves to laugh. She calls her house Tobacco Road Mansion, and when she moves through it she often mentions the Collyer brothers. What was once lawn around the house is filled with long grass, cinder blocks, saplings, sheets of plywood, low bushes, bricks, gardening tools, flats, flowerpots, and lengths of hose. A rusting power mower rests under an eave of the new wing, and near it is a child's broken wagon. Beside a chair on the terrace, a telephone-cable-spool table with a marble top is propped up by an elaborate arrangement of logs and cinder blocks. The top is covered with vases and jars of wild flowers, most of them expired. An empty metal clothes-drying rack sits nearby, and has a short four-by-four stuck through its legs as ballast. Inside the house, the down-stairs rooms are crowded with furniture, bric-a-brac, pictures, and cartons full of books, magazines, and newspapers. The empty center of each room suggests a clearing in the woods. Every surface is in use. In the living room—or Fire Room, as Mabel Mercer calls it—a mantel is covered with part of her owl collection: a wooden owl, a lead owl, a glass owl, a tin owl, a brass owl, and a ceramic owl. ("I dust them once a month.") On the top of a sideboard in the kitchen are a stuffed rabbit, a stuffed cat, a wicker breadbasket in the shape of a goose with raised wings joined to form a handle, a silver candlestick, three silver wine coasters with glass bottoms, and a metal angel with transparent wings, its feet in a bed of plastic holly leaves and berries.

Late one afternoon, in the summer of 1982, Mabel Mercer sat on her terrace with her old friend Muriel Finch and with Cynthia and Donald Elwood, New York admirers who had stopped in for tea on their way to Tanglewood. (Muriel Finch, who lives fifteen miles away, and Adelaide Wallin, a neighbor of Mabel Mercer's, keep watch over her. Adelaide Wallin calls her at noon, when Mabel Mercer generally gets up—she is a poor sleeper, and often stays awake until dawn—and Muriel Finch calls her in the evening. She also comes by almost every day to look in on her.) Mabel Mercer had just given the Elwoods a house tour, pointing out a sofa in the Piano Room (two pianos, a sofa, and a chair) on which Alec Wilder used to nap ("Every time Alec saw the sofa, he'd say, 'This is deadly,' and lie down and go instantly to sleep"); a handsome iron bedstead in an upstairs bedroom which had come with the house; and Bear, an immense neighborhood Newfoundland who filled the Fire Room floor and was waiting for his daily combing and cosseting. She had then made a pot of Earl Grey tea and served it on the terrace with oatmeal cookies. When Cynthia Elwood asked Mabel if she could pour everyone a second cup of tea, Mabel Mercer said, "There's an English saying that two people should never pour tea at once, because one will have a baby." A heat wave had ended the day before, and the half-dozen different shades of green around the house looked cool and silvery. A sharp breeze blew the talk about.

Donald Elwood asked Mabel how long she had had her house, and she said, "For years I read the 'Farms and Acreage' ads in the *Times,* and when there was something promising I'd get in my car Sunday with a few friends and take a look. I first saw this place on a February day in the early fifties, and it immediately reminded me of Wales, where I went summers as a child. There was snow on the ground, and I had on high heels, but I walked across the field and down to the stream and up to the waterfall. The place was owned by a farmer named Charlie Briggs. His mother, who was beautiful, still lived here. Charlie's a lovely man. He cuts the field, and when I'm away he takes care of the place. He gives me firewood and his maple syrup. I've fixed the house up little by little. I'd tell whoever was working on the improvements, 'When your bill gets to six hundred dollars, stop work, and when I've paid you, start again,' That way, things never got out of hand. There's a new well—a hundred and eighty feet deep. There are three bathrooms. I put dormers on the two front bedrooms upstairs to lighten them and give them more air. I fixed up one of the rooms just for Alec, but he never saw it before he died. I put a round worktable in front of the window, so that he could look out over the field. I hoped the view would inspire him to compose when he was blocked—which he often was when he came to visit. I put down the brick floor in the kitchen, and added the sun porch. I put in this terrace, and added the new wing, which isn't quite finished. I've slowed down so much that everything in the house has slowed down. It seems I can hardly even lift a pail of water anymore. I've had some dizzy spells, and I've stopped driving. I loved to get the car out and let it go. I've never been able to stay away from this house. I'd finish work in New York at three or four in the morning, and once in a while in the middle of the week I'd get in my car and drive up, arriving for breakfast. I'd spend a glorious day, and drive back at six or so in the evening, since I didn't do my first show until ten. And, of course, I came up every weekend—from three or four Sunday morning until Monday evening. I stopped driving because I had a silly accident and lost my nerve. I was coming back from the vet with one of my cats, and the cat was getting feisty in her box, so I reached in to quiet her and a front wheel went off the road. When I got the wheel back on, I went over too far to the other side, and here was this car coming at me very fast. It didn't look as if it was going to slow down or swerve, so I went straight off the road into a field, and hit a fence. I have a 1967 Plymouth, and they told me at the garage that it would cost a thousand dollars to repair, but I haven't done anything. I had just built a little garage, too, and there it sits—full of Plymouth.

"These days, I only have one thought at a time. I can't get out and weed, and it looks like unkempt hair everywhere outside. I sew, I knit. There's housework, and I watch TV, and sometimes I read a historical novel. The days go quickly. Muriel and I get in her car and go to Albany for the day, or over to the theatre in Williamstown. Albany is quite wonderful now, with its new mall. Or we get in the car and just drive, have dinner somewhere, and come home. But what I like to do best of all is sit and dream. I have more here in the country than royalty has."

The conversation was full of summer-afternoon holes, and apropos of nothing, after a silence, Mabel Mercer would launch a new subject, and fall quiet again. Here is some of what she said:

"I still have my apartment on a Hundred and Tenth Street. When I first moved in, in the forties, each window had its own awning and its own window box. Friends would say that they could tell my apartment by the kind of flowers I had in my window boxes. We had night and day doormen, and when I'd drive home from Tony's, on Fifty-second Street, at four in the morning, I'd put the car in the garage around the corner and walk home. But the awnings and window boxes and doormen are gone, and no one wants to drive up there at four in the morning anymore. I don't know why I keep the place. It's a drain, and I haven't stayed there in years. I suppose I'm afraid of the fuss it would take to empty it out."

During the First World War in England, we'd travel from vaudeville job to vaudeville job on Sunday, and we'd hold hands on our way home from work at night, because the streets were so black. Another girl and I had an act, and we went to Ostend right after the war. We worked in hotels and cabarets. My friend would do impersonations of Mistinguett, and we'd sing duets. I'd do a ballad alone—an Irving Berlin song or an American rhythm song. We'd tap-dance, and I even tried acrobatics, but I was as acrobatic as an elephant. It was in Belgium that I learned to eat fried garlic—little pieces cooked quickly in a pan. I loved it so much that my boss had to tell me to stop—that I was ruining the act.

"I arrived in Paris in 1920, and Bricktop arrived in 1924. I went to work for her around 1930, and stayed until I left for America, after the Second World War had broken out. Wars seem to have directed my life. My mother was touring America with a vaudeville group when the first war started, and couldn't get back to England until it was over, and the second war drove me out of Paris to this country, which I had only the remotest thought of coming to. The British and American élite patronized Bricktop's, and there was an elegance and beauty about it all that doesn't exist anymore. People left their gold-and-diamond cigarette cases on their tables when they danced, knowing very well that they would be there when they returned. It was a champagne world. The Duke and Duchess of Windsor used to come in, and I got to know them. And later, when the Duke was the Governor of the Bahamas and I was passing through on my way to America, I sang at Government House. The Duke and Duchess of Kent came into Brick's, too, and the Duke and Duchess of York. The Duke of Kent was my favorite of the brothers—a very gentle man. And I loved the Duchess of York—Elizabeth, now the Queen Mother. She was a doll. I knew Edith Piaf in Montmartre when she was a street singer. She had tiny legs. They were like fingers, and so were her wrists. But what a powerful voice!"

That birdhouse just beyond the maple tree is a condominium, and all twelve apartments are occupied. My cats came to me out of the wilderness. They're named Helter and Skelter, but I call them both Minnie. I speak to them in different tones, so that they know which one I'm speaking to. The mother brought the kitten in her mouth, and I took the kitten in and fed her. The mother Minnie stayed outside a month, waiting for little Minnie and refusing to eat the food I put out for her. She just sat there fifty feet away. Finally, she got so hungry she gave in and ate, and they've both stayed."

As if on cue, mother Minnie, a small, short-haired gray-and-white cat, jumped up on the terrace, a squeaking chipmunk in her mouth, and disappeared into a kitchen window always left open for the cats (and sometimes used by raccoons, too). Mabel Mercer gasped and said "Did you see that? What a naughty cat!" and got to her feet with astonishing speed and went into the house. Five minutes later, Minnie ran out empty-mouthed, stopped at a corner of the terrace to lick her front paws, and abruptly lay down. Mabel Mercer reappeared, a broom in hand. "It's under the sofa in the Fire Room, the poor thing. But it's alive. It probably won't move for hours. We'll look for it this evening." She leaned the broom against the wall by the kitchen door and, back in her customary low gear, walked slowly to her chair on the terrace and sat down. She reached for an oatmeal cookie, and said to herself, "Have another biscuit, Mabel—don't mind if I do."

"When I was little, my mother would never take a walk without a pair of garden shears. She'd snip things from our garden and she'd snip things hanging over our garden wall or any garden wall. She considered such strays legitimate picking, and she'd put them in water to root, and plant them. So I went out one morning and dug up some of our neighbor's flowers and brought them back in my apron, pleased as Punch that I had them roots and all. My grandmother was leaning out a window watching me, and she came right out and took down my panties and spanked me—and, my goodness, the embarrassment! My face was as red as the flowers I'd taken.

"I was left-handed when I was young—gammy-handed, they called it. For a long time, I didn't know my left from my right, and the way I'd tell would be to make the sign of the cross, which you always do with your right hand. That would show me which was my right, and which was my right foot, so that I could start a dance step correctly.

"I've loved to paint as long as I can remember, and was surrounded by painters when I was a child—three uncles and a grandfather are in the Royal Academy. I did a lot of painting in Paris, but the pictures were lost when I moved to this country. I do have several acrylics on paper that I did in the Bahamas, and they're in a box somewhere in the house. Muriel gave me some paints to try and get me started again, but I don't seem to have enough time. It takes a whole day to do a painting, and there are too many other things. But there are pictures I want to paint. When it snows and I look out a kitchen window, I see a house in the formation of the snow and the bare maple-tree branches. It's my imagination, seeing that house, but it's always the same, and if I go out of the room and come back it's still there, as if it was just waiting to be painted."

The sun, almost below the hem of the maple, was on Mabel Mercer's face, and she looked exhilarated, lit from within. She asked if anyone wanted more tea, and the Elwoods stood and said they had to get on to Lenox and their motel. Mabel Mercer, leaning on Muriel Finch's arm, walked them to their car, and when the women got back to the house Muriel Finch brought in the tea things, and Mabel Mercer washed them and left them on the drainboard. The she said, "We've still got yesterday's heat in this kitchen, Muriel. Let's go to Fire Hill Inn and have fried shrimp and garlic bread. I hope they have the little shrimp, like the prawns we used to get in England. It'll be a nice cool drive over and back."

The Human Sound

Bobby Short

Bobby Short's achievements as a performer are all the more remarkable when one considers his equipment. He has a baritone that is frequently plagued by laryngitis, and he has a rapid, almost querulous vibrato. His piano playing is so unfettered it is usually accelerando—a tendency that is beautifully disguised by his accompanists, Beverly Peer (bass) and Robbie Scott (drums), who invariably keep in perfect rhythmic step. But everything in Short's style miraculously balances out. His free sense of time gives his numbers a surprised, bounding quality, his vibrato makes his phrase endings ripple like flags, and his laryngitis lends his voice a searching, down sound. His appearance is deceptive as well. He is slight—five feet nine, with a thirty-inch waist and small, demure feet. He has an oval face, a button nose, and vaguely apprehensive eyes, all of which ride over a hedgelike mustache. But three attributes work for him. He is a faultless and inventive dresser (he is a regular on the best-dressed lists), he has a warm, princely bearing, and he has a stunning smile. The resulting impression, as one meets him, is of a tall, poised, and irresistibly attractive man.

Short lived for a long time on the eighth floor of Carnegie Hall in the apartment once occupied by Thomas Scherman, the conductor. It was the sort of place old New Yorkers covet—a small, reasonable, soundproof triplex. No sound came from outside nor did any sound escape, so Short could sit before the baby grand in his living room at three in the morning and pound and shout with propriety. The small foyer on the first floor contained a desk, a big Queen Anne armchair, a bicycle, and a staircase.

A turnaround kitchen opened off it. The living room, at the top of the stairs, was two stories high, with a vaulted ceiling and a row of high windows facing north. At one end were a small bar, a bathroom, and a second set of stairs. The stairs led to a spacious balcony, which served as Short's bedroom. A bedroom window faced a small roof, where his cats, Rufus and Miss Brown, were aired. The furnishings were high-class Camp. A heavy glass-topped coffee table rested on a zebra-skin rug, and on the rug, beneath the table, were two metal lizards—one gilt, one brass. A pair of big daybeds, which were covered with bright African-looking material and leopard-skin pillows, flanked the table. Near the foyer stairs were a huge wooden lion, a stolid eighteenth-century Italian refectory table, and one of those roofed-in wicker wing chairs that still haunt old summer cottages on Naushon Island. An antler chandelier hung in the living room, and it was echoed by a Teddy Roosevelt leather chair with tusks as arms. Pictures of every description jammed the walls, and the window side of the room was lined with books and bric-a-brac.

Short occasionally models, and one afternoon he posed for a *Harper's Bazaar* sketch. He was wearing an orange-and-white cashmere turtleneck, tan slacks, and low, buckled boots, and for the drawing he had added a square-cut puma-skin coat with an otter collar, designed by Donald Brooks for Jacques Kaplan. And he had on a cowboy hat. He was leaning against a support of the balcony, his hands in the coat pockets, and he looked melancholy and distant.

The diminutive Chinese girl who was sketching him said something. "It *is* a fantastic apartment," Short said. His voice was light, melodic, yet husky. "I was away when they decided to tear down Carnegie Hall, and I guess I didn't really realize what was going on, so I didn't panic. A lot of people who lived here did, and they moved out, and when the building was saved they had a hell of a time getting back in." He cleared his throat unavailingly. "I've had *this* bout of laryngitis for weeks. Every morning, I get on my bike and pedal over to my doctor, on the East Side. He sprays me and makes bad jokes and I pedal back, but it doesn't get any better. But then it doesn't get much of a chance. At the Café Carlyle, it's three shows a night, five nights a week. And I can't just lay off for a week or two. My responsibility is to the Carlyle. I have to be on time and I have to do everything with grace, even when I feel like saying to hell with it, when it's like pulling teeth to get myself up from my early-evening nap and shower and shave and dress and get downstairs and into a cab. The romance of being a supper-club singer! I still do private parties as well. It's extra money for Robbie Scott and Beverly Peer, and I find myself asking a lot of money. Sometimes I'm whisked down to '21' between shows to play for someone's birthday, and I've been flown to Hobe Sound and the Caribbean. And not long ago I was invited to perform at the White

House. It cost me a thousand dollars, what with new clothes and trans-
portation and all, but I was delighted I could *afford* to go. I would have
been a very upset boy had I been invited and not had the money. But the
Carlyle is the middle of my life. In fact, I'm hopelessly associated with it.
Bobby Short of the Carlyle, despite there still being people in New York
who prefer to think of me as their secret, their discovery. I started there
in 1968, and in a peculiar way. George Feyer, the pianist, had been in
residence for twelve years. He took off two weeks that summer, and Peter
Sharp, who owns the Carlyle, asked Ahmet and Nesuhi Ertegun, of
Atlantic Records, who to get as a replacement. They said, 'Get Bobby
Short.' I did my best to make those two weeks as successful as anything
I'd done, and when Feyer's contract ran out they offered me half a year.
For a time, I worked there eight months of the year but now I do two
three-month stints. It's physically impossible to work more than that, and
anyway it doesn't make sense for me to be so available that I lose my
attraction value."

He shed the fur coat and, leaning back on one of the daybeds, struck a
new pose, his hands clasped behind his head and his feet on the coffee
table. A tall, thin, lugubrious-looking man in blue denim work clothes
came in.

"How was your weekend, Wendell?" Short asked him.

"I'm not feeling so well. A cold."

"Are you congested? Well, I've got just the pill for you. Take one now
and one tonight." Wendell went upstairs, put leashes on the cats, and
took them out on the roof. Wendell cleans and cooks and does odd jobs
for Short three days a week.

"I think the Carlyle is probably one of the last places in the world
where you can drink tea with your pinkie comfortably out. It attracts royalty. It's not unusual to have a baroness or a princess around, as well as
Mrs. Palm Beach Gardner, Mrs. Winston Frost, and Bunny Mellon. You
can come into the Carlyle wearing practically anything. It is big enough
and elegant enough and grand enough not to be affected by unusual attire
among its patrons. I'd been to the hotel several times before I worked
there, and I was always treated beautifully. I must deal with the people
who come solely to see Bobby Short. They make all sorts of complaints,
written and verbal. 'Mr. Short didn't sing at all during his first show last
night,' or 'Mr. Short finished his second set ten minutes early.' My God!
And if I sing too many Negro songs, the Negro patrons get self-conscious
and the whites think I'm being militant. Imagine Bessie Smith's 'Gimme
a Pigfoot' being considered militant! Everyone who sings in a café has to
have something about him that says, 'Come close but not too close.' But
people often get too close, too pully on you. Beverly and Robbie and I
have been together for a long while, and we have accumulated a lot of

friends. But we must think of ourselves as caterers at a party. After all, the waiters and bartenders can't get drunk, and I can't sit down with friends between shows and have a quart of champagne or six whiskeys. It takes some stuff to remember your place so long as you're earning a living, and I'll always have to earn a living. If I get overly friendly, the audience thinks, 'Oh, it doesn't matter. We know him so well that we don't have to listen!'

"The people who come to hear me are a mixed bag, and they range in age from eighteen to seventy-five. A lot of them are rich, but I have lived among the wealthy and bizarre so long that their ways don't bother me. I also get professional football players, and Leontyne Price, who is a great friend. Craig Claiborne was there a while ago with a lady from Texas who's a billionairess. The clergy come in, and so do neighborhood ladies, who can walk safely home together. The whole clutch from Elaine's comes in, including Jack Richardson and Norman Mailer. Norman even wrote a poem about me once. But musicians come into the Carlyle, too—people like Miles Davis and Cy Coleman and Joe Williams and Marian McPartland. And a lot of fashion people, but they have followed me all my career—the designers and the models, the manufacturers. There are a lot of French people, and I speak French to them, of course. And there have been a good many young people, including rock groups. They give one hope. People say that graciousness is finished, but it isn't. My people respect graciousness. They are ready to be gracious and they respond to graciousness."

The girl finished her sketches. She and Short packed the fur coat in a box, and she staggered out with it under one arm and her drawings under the other. Wendell shouted up the stairs that a bottle of champagne had exploded in the freezer. Short slapped his forehead. "Oh dear! That's terrible. That's the worst thing I've *ever* done. I put that in there last night before some friends came, but they drank something else and I forgot about it. Is it bad, Wendell?"

"Yes, it's in little pieces. After I clean up, do you want me to go out and get a roast or something?"

"All right, and some Boston lettuce and orange juice."

Short went over to the bar and poured a ginger ale. "I only eat once a day, at lunch," he said. "I can't eat before I work. If I do, I can't breathe when I sing, or else all the wine and cheese come up. Sometimes I go somewhere fancy for lunch—that's my treat for the day—or I cook something here. When I'm not working, I can put together a decent bœuf bourguignon for six or eight people. After they leave, I strip off all my clothes and go down to the kitchen and wash up. It takes me a couple of hours, but it's the best therapy in the world."

A radio, which had been playing, began a Duke Ellington tune.

"I got to know the Ellington band-pack in the early forties when I was living in Los Angeles and was more or less adopted by Harold Brown, a pianist and the brother of Lawrence Brown, Ellington's trombonist. The band would come to the Coast—and those parties! They went on until eight or nine in the morning. All the liquor you could drink and all the available girls in town and Art Tatum playing the piano in a corner. I've been unswerving since then—a lifelong devotee. Some of those things Duke wrote in the late thirties and early forties—they're mind-bending.

Short looked at his watch. "I have to go down to the photography department at Macy's to get an old picture of my mother restored." He picked up a dark oval photograph, torn and faded, of a pretty woman with long hair and deep, faintly smiling eyes. "My mother is remarkable. She lives with my oldest sister, Naomi, in Danville, Illinois, where I was born. Mother was tiny, never weighing more than a hundred and fifteen pounds, and, as you can see, very pretty. When I was a kid, she worked all day, and when she wasn't at her job she was at church or in a P.T.A. meeting or trying to keep her house in order. She was a domestic, as most of her friends were, and she worked from seven-thirty in the morning until early evening. She was ambivalent. Her pride drove her out to work all day, using every avenue of strength she had, but then when I was ten she'd let me go and play the piano and sing in the local roadhouses— provided she knew the mother of someone in the band. She let me do this when she wouldn't allow a jazz record or a blues record in the house and when she thought it unthinkable to go into show business, which was considered a one-way road straight to Hell, thanks to the Puritanical non- sense the Negroes borrowed from the whites. But it was the Depression and things were very rough, and I know that the three or four dollars I brought home on Saturday nights were used to pay the gas bill or buy clothes and books for us children. Mother never cracked more than ten dollars a week as a domestic, and here I could make almost half that in one night's work. I think she respected me for it.

"I was born the ninth of ten children. There were never more than seven of us alive at once. My mother and father came from Kentucky, but they met in Danville. It's about a hundred and twenty-five miles south of Chicago, and it hovers close to the Indiana line. It was the best of all pos- sible places to be poor in the Depression—in a small town where there were no racial pressures. There was a small colored population and an old colored section, but the town was at least superficially integrated. We lived in a newer section, where there were whites. Very often I was the only Negro in my class. I never knew Father terribly well. He was slender and had a marvellous mustache, which was balanced by a tonsure that I inherited. He went through eight years of school, and then his father sent him to four more at Frankfort College, which was more like a high school then. His father was not wealthy, but he owned farms here and there. He'd been born at the end of slavery, and he was a freedman. My father had a talent for mathematics, and he was brilliant at speedwriting. He had gifts that could have made him a much greater man than he was. He held a number of white-collar jobs, civil-service jobs. He ran for justice of the peace in Danville, and he won. But he liked the coal mines. When the Depression hit, he went back to Kentucky to the mines. He sent us money and came to see us twice a year. But the mines were his Waterloo. I was about nine or ten when he died."

Miss Brown shot down the stairs from the bedroom, leaped up on the pillows on the daybed, and lay there, watching Rufus, who was creeping along the base of the bookcase. "Rufus!" Short shouted. "Stop it!" Rufus slid across the floor on his belly, his eyes on Miss Brown. "Go on! Enough! Scat!" Rufus catapulted up the stairs and disappeared under the bed. Short picked up a handful of pistachio nuts from a bowl.

"There was a piano in our house, as there was in every house then, and I taught myself to play and sing. I listened to Ivie Anderson and to Bing Crosby, and once in a while I'd get a good hot radio program from Chicago, and bands like Fess Williams' and Walter Barnes' came through town. I left Danville for the first time when I was eleven and a half. A couple of booking agents came through and heard me sing and play, and they took me off to Chicago—with my mother's permission, of course. I lived on the West Side with a Catholic family from New Orleans, which appealed to my mother, and I went to a Catholic school. When I left Danville, I had no idea what image I projected. There I was, a child sitting in tails at the piano and singing 'Sophisticated Lady' and 'In My Solitude' in a high, squeaky voice in astonishing keys. The lyrics meant nothing to me, and they must have sounded strange to other people coming out of a child's mouth. So I changed and sang things like 'Shoe Shine Boy' and 'It's a Sin To Tell a Lie.' But I could not find it within me to believe that I *was* a child. And I didn't like being a child, because I couldn't stand the patronization connected with childhood. Moreover, it was never in me to be the best colored singer or the best colored student. I simply wanted to be the best singer and the best student. But I have a respect for my race that might surprise some of the people who discovered just six months ago that they are black. I was brought up in such a way that doesn't allow any head-hanging. There is nothing about me that can be called non-white, but I consider myself fortunate because I'm not so well known that people accept me only for my fame. A long time ago, I discovered that the best advertisement for a minority is that member who, without being Uncle Tom, takes the time to mesh with whatever exists socially. He makes it that much easier for the next member who comes along.

"That winter, I worked mostly around Chicago, I did some broadcast-
ing over N.B.C., and a lot of so-called 'club' dates at places like the Sheraton Hotel. I'd be part of one-night shows that included an orchestra, tap-
dancers, and other singers. I became the colored counterpart of Bobby
Breen. I got thirty or thirty-five dollars for each club date, but of course I
had to buy clothes and pay tuition and give something to the family I
lived with. When I finished school, in June of 1937, I was twelve and a
half. But I didn't go home. I went East. New York wasn't easy, because I
started there from scratch, performing all times of day and night for bookers. But I worked at the Frolic Café, over the Winter Garden Theatre, at
La Grande Pomme, and at the Apollo, in Harlem. The audiences at the
Apollo were used to Pigmeat Markham and Butter Beans and Susie and
Moms Mabley, and I was obviously a downtown act. They didn't care
about my white tie and tails. All they wanted was to be turned on. They
probably all had kids my age at home who danced and sang anyway.

"The New York thing came to an abrupt end early in 1938. I suddenly
realized that there I was—a kid with two years of show biz and all the
mannerisims of an adult—and I didn't like it, so I went back to Danville
and stayed there four years, until I finished high school. It was a funny
adjustment to make at first. I had come off what was regarded as the big
time. My mother said I couldn't work for tacky people in tacky places after
working in grand hotels and grand theatres for grand people. So I didn't
work for the first year, but I began to feel the economic pressures and I
went back to work in earnest. I had more pizzazz by then, and I was a
professional. I sought out the best hotels and taprooms around Danville,
and after a while I became solvent and could dress myself properly and
even indulge myself. I finished high school in 1942, and a month later I
opened at the Capitol Lounge, in Chicago. The rage was boogie-woogie.
I thought it was cheap. I made up my mind there was something better.
I had heard Hildegarde on records, and of course she was the queen then.
She had the slickest night-club act of all time. It was produced down to
the last sigh. Even down to a blue spotlight that brought out the color in
the red roses that invariably stood by her piano. She would record whole
Broadway scores, and she sang Vernon Duke and Cole Porter and the
Gershwins and Noël Coward, and through her I became aware of the
Broadway kind of score, of the mystique of the Broadway musical.
"In 1943, I went to the Beachcomber, in Omaha, where I worked for a
week opposite Jimmy Noone, the New Orleans clarinettist, and for a
week opposite Nat Cole. Nat and I became friends and remained friends
until he died. He was a sly, funny man, and he'd sit in the back room and
watch me—a smart-aleck nineteen-year-old—performing out front, and
he'd laugh and say, when I came off, 'What are you *doing* to these peo-

ple?' I got a job in Los Angeles with Mike Reilly—'The Music Goes Around and Around and It Comes Out Here' Reilly—in the Radio Room. He had a comedy band, and they threw flounders at the audience, and that sort of thing. I first heard there about Mabel Mercer and Cy Walter, and I became deeply immersed in Rodgers and Hart. And Don McCrae, who is really Don Redman and who wrote 'Practice Makes Perfect,' came to my house with a huge stack of out-of-the-way songs and told me to learn them. My job at the Radio Room ended a couple of months later. Another comedy band had come in, and the act involved smoke pouring out of the top hat the leader wore. The smoke was flour, and it spewed out all over me, and I was in black tie. After the first show, I refused to go back on, and I was dismissed. I worked around, mostly at private parties for fifty dollars a night, and at the old Trocadero Ballroom, filling in for Dorothy Donegan. Then I got a gig in Milwaukee, where I appeared opposite the Art Tatum trio, with Tiny Grimes on guitar and Slam Stewart on bass. Tatum will always be my idol, and it was marvellous to get to know him. He had the same sort of sly humor that Nat Cole had. He enjoyed pretty ladies and he drank a *lot* of beer. There was no condescension, and in a strange way I think he even admired me, even though he never talked about music. But it always astonished me that for the most part the people who came to hear him didn't really know what they were hearing."

Short jumped up. "Macy's awaits me." He reappeared ten minutes later. He was wearing a perfectly tailored Glen-plaid suit. His shoes were dark, his shirt was a pale blue, and his modestly wide tie was navy with white polka dots. He got a cab on Seventh Avenue. He conducted his business at Macy's in a sparkling way, as if *he* were waiting on the saleslady. In the cab, he had said that he had gone from Milwaukee to the Chase Hotel, in St. Louis, where Hildegarde was the main attraction. It was the first time he had seen her work. Her manager heard him and called Herbert Jacoby, who, along with Max Gordon, owned the Blue Angel, in New York. Jacoby went out to St. Louis and asked Short to come to the Blue Angel the following spring. "Eddie Mayehoff was on the bill," Short said on the escalator. "And Irene Bordoni and Mildred Bailey, and of course I was just the opener. For a long time, I thought my engagement at the Blue Angel was not successful, but I learned later that Jacoby and Gordon often cancelled new acts after the first night. I stayed for a full four weeks. I shared a dressing room with Mildred Bailey, and I got some interesting insights into her. Despite that enormous *poitrine* and her barrel shape and those toothpick legs, she was very vain. She had a lovely face and beautiful skin, and she'd sit at her dressing table in front of the mirror the whole time between shows, fixing her face and staring at herself. We talked constantly, but she never once took her eyes off herself and looked at me."

Short walked from Macy's to Brooks Brothers, where he wanted to look at some dress shirts and pumps. "I met Mabel Mercer, too, for the first time, and Bart Howard, who gave me a lot of his songs. I longed to belong to Mabel's intimate circle, and I knew I had to come back to New York one day on a more permanent basis. Mabel worked as viciously hard as I have. She always sang in small places without microphones, and she considered microphones abominable. Mabel was much more fragile than I. She was, as we know it in America, the outstanding personage of our kind of art. When I first met her, the thing that struck me was her repertoire. I was involved in the same pursuit, and it was true serendipity. Even when she sang a song I knew, it came to be totally fresh. I can't think of any singer who is true to himself who has avoided being influenced by Mabel Mercer. People have accused me of stealing from other performers, but that's nonsense. What one does is absorb the *feeling* generated by a great *singer* like Mabel. She was an enormously private person, and I'm flattered that we had a friendship.

"After the Blue Angel, I went back to California and worked off and on on Monday nights for three or four months at the Haig, a kind of a shack on Wilshire Boulevard, across from the Ambassador Hotel. It was run by a show-biz nut named Johnny Bernstein, and he kept bringing me obscure show tunes. Between him and Don McCrae, my repertoire became sizable. The periods in between my stints at the Haig were very poor. I lived with Harold Brown and his wife. They fed me and slept me and even gave me pocket money, or I wouldn't be here today. Then I got a job at the Café Gala. It was in a big house on Sunset Boulevard which had been bought by the Baroness d'Erlanger for Johnny Walsh to sing in. He was a tall, fantastically handsome Irishman with white hair and beautifully tailored clothes, and he had the largest repertoire I'd ever heard. The Gala was the most chic club in California, or the West, for that matter. It was always filled with ex-New Yorkers, and you'd see Lena Horne and Lennie Hayton and Monty Woolley and Cole Porter. Walsh sold the Gala to a man named Jim Dolan. He gave me a one-week contract, but I stayed from July of 1948 to the fall of 1951. I became the mainstay, announcing shows and playing interim piano. Felicia Sanders worked there, and Bobby Troup and Dorothy Dandridge and Stella Brooks and Sheila Barrett. Eventually, a neon sign appeared on the roof: 'Jim Dolan Presents Bobby Short,' I acquired a new apartment and met all sorts of people high up in the movie business, and international people. I fell into a velvet-lined rut. In fact, one night Olga San Juan turned to Leonard Spigelgass at the Gala and said, 'Who is this Bobby Short? Why isn't he in films, why isn't he making a lot of records?' Spigelgass replied, 'He's too chic.' And that was the truth. I had become the young colored boy who was all chic and who dined at the Café Jay, which sat just twenty, fifteen of them invariably the biggest Hollywood stars, and that was as far as I could go. People kept telling me, 'Go to New York, Bobby. Get out of here and go to New York.' I knew I wasn't ready for New York, but I did go to Paris, first class, by plane."

At Brooks, Short tried on some pumps. "That lady sitting over there is Erika Lund," he said, "and she worked at the Gala when I was there. I still sing one of her songs." They greeted each other warmly, and he told her to stop by the Café Carlyle. Old Home Week continued at the shirt counter, where the dapper, middle-aged salesman told Short he had once been with Young & Rubicam and that he used to go to the Beverly Club, at Lexington and Fiftieth, to hear him. Short looked pleased, bought six shirts, and told *him* to stop by the Carlyle.

Short walked over to the Algonquin and ordered a beer. "I just love this place," he said. "It's an oasis in this mad city. Well, the rest of that year in Paris was insane. I worked for Victoria Spivy and I worked at the Embassy Club, in London, several times. I had an atelier in the most fashionable *arrondissement* in Paris. I had a maid, a private French tutor, I ate well, and when I was in London I bought all the clothes I could. Then it was back to L.A. and the Gala, and in the beginning of 1954 I met Phil Moore, the arranger and composer, and he became my manager. He figured out how my act could be enlarged, controlled, polished. The first thing he did was to put me in a room in Los Angeles with Larry Bunker, the drummer, and Rollie Bundock, the bassist. We made a tape and Phil sold it to Nesuhi and Ahmet Ertegun. Then I was flown to New York by Dorothy Kilgallen, as a birthday present for her husband, Dick Kollmar. The record came out, Dorothy paved the way in her column, and I got the job at the Beverly Club. I went on to the Red Carpet, Le Cupidon, and back to the Blue Angel, where I had top billing and made a thousand dollars a week. I worked the Living Room, the Weylin Hotel, and the Arpeggio. During the summers, I went back to California for short stints, and to Florida, for the first time, and Chicago. Early in the sixties, after I'd been here at the Sheraton-East, the old Ambassador Hotel, Herbert Jacoby and a rich friend and myself took over a room on East Fifty-fourth Street and called it Le Caprice. Herbert had always coveted an *haute-cuisine* French resturant, which Caprice was, and my trying to cater to an eating clientele instead of a drinking one didn't make it. We lasted a year and three months. Then came the heavy time for Mr. Short. I hadn't taken any salary at all for the last three months at the Caprice, and I had gone through all my savings. I was on my uppers. During the summer of 1965, I didn't work in New York at all, except for occasional weekends, and I ended up in Provincetown and Cleveland. But that winter I was lucky

enough to have a standup part in the 'New Cole Porter Revue,' down at
Square East, in the Village. A while after that, I got a job in the upstairs
room at L'Intrigue, over on West Fifty-sixth Street. I handled my own
lights, I seated guests. It fed my cats, paid the rent, and kept me alive. For
the next few years, I subsisted in Boston at Paul's Mall, at the Living
Room here, and at places like the Playboy Club in London. The night-
club business was not what it had been."

The Café Carlyle is a small, oblong room (it seats under two hundred) on
one side of the Madison Avenue entrance of the Hotel Carlyle. A tiny sit-
down bar is concealed behind pillars, and against the opposite wall, on a
low dais, is a grand piano. There are banquettes around the other walls,
which are covered by murals, and the center of the room is taken up by
a dozen tables. It is a dowdy, comfortable place. Short appeared at ten
o'clock, resplendent in a dinner jacket and pleated white shirt, and sat
down in semi-darkness at the piano, flanked on one side by Robbie Scott
and on the other by Beverly Peer. No lights went on; he simply started to
play. He looked solemn and detached and private, as if he were playing
for himself late at night in his living room. It was a graceful, flowing display. He did a Gershwin medley, "Perdido," the theme from "Exodus,"
a blues, and several other tunes. His style bears a loose, enthusiastic
resemblance to Art Tatum's—it is florid and arpeggioed and slurred—and
by the time he had played ten or so tunes a considerable head of steam
had been built up. The lights went on, and he began to sing Cole Porter's
"Let's Fly Away." It was immediately clear that it would be a difficult
night. His laryngitis was compounded by a faulty microphone, and the
crowd was noisy. During his third song, he stopped abruptly when new
arrivals began loudly "*Comment-ça-va*"ing the people at the next table.
Looking over their heads with a slight smile, his hands resting on the
raised keyboard cover, he waited until the room subsided, and then began
where he had left off.
    After the last number, he greeted several people, then sat down at a
table. He mopped his face and ordered a glass of ice water and hot tea
with honey. The headwaiter apologized for the microphone; the repair-
man had promised to come but had not. Short smiled and croaked, "I
know. I know. Phil Moore once told me that it really doesn't matter what
a performer does. It's a question of how many dishes the busboys drop
and of whether or not the microphones work. And it's up to the audience,
too. When you get a bad one, you work harder and harder and sing louder
and louder to compensate, and *they* talk louder and louder to compensate
for you. But a bad microphone is like playing with a drunken drummer.
If I were on a stage, removed, it would be different, but I'm practically
within touching distance of everyone here. On top of that, I know most

of them. Those are Shaker Heights people over there, and the group that came in and made all the noise includes Liza Minelli's estranged husband, and back against the wall is Geraldine Stutz and her husband. Of course, one night you come in and the piano is in tune, the boys feel wonderful, I feel wonderful, and the audience is rotten. Another night, I feel perfectly rotten and the audience sits there as though they were in church. You must never be angry or uptight in the gut; you have to be free and loose. Singing itself is such pure expression. The human sound is the most touching in the world; it's exemplified by someone like Ray Charles. He has that kind of getting inside a song and finding something that the composer himself didn't know was there. And a good performer can't be carrying on emotionally when he sings. You simply can't sing well with a lump in your throat. Take 'I Still Believe in You.' It has one of my favorite lyrics of all time. It's by Rodgers and Hart, and was dropped from a 1930 show called '*Simple Simon*' before the show opened. I first heard Charlotte Rae sing it, and I've known it for a year, but for a long time I could not bring myself to sing it without breaking up. Finally, I absorbed the song, and now I can do it."

Geraldine Stutz went by, and Short stood up and spoke to her, then poured more honey in his tea.

"I guess I have several hundred songs in my repertoire, and when I'm requested to sing a song I've never sung in my life I find that I suddenly know all the words, and we figure out a key and we're off. I can sing songs I haven't sung in ten years, and the only ones I ever have to brush up on are things I sang as a child. Actually, I wish I *could* push some of the lyrics I've got in my head out and replace them with newer material, but that's an occupational hazard; you become a kind of singing Smithsonian. I'm interested in all kinds of *good* songs. Sometimes the lyrics grab me, sometimes the song itself. It's not often that the marriage is perfect. But the Gershwins can be counted on, and Cole Porter made both ends work. Rodgers and Hart were brilliant. Vernon Duke wasn't always fortunate enough to find good lyricists. Yip Harburg was good with him, and so was Ira Gershwin. But I don't think Vernon was easy to work with. I love Harold Arlen and Johnny Mercer, and when they collaborated on the score of 'St. Louis Woman' it was almost too much of a good thing. Johnny Mercer displayed a homespun façade in his work, but he was capable of turning out a truly sensational lyric. I worship Fats Waller, but I feel inadequate with his material. But I do all the Ellington and Strayhorn I can pick up. I get into Noël Coward and Ivor Novello, among the English songwriters. My thinking English friends bring them over to me. I prefer Coward to Novello; his songs hold up beautifully. I feel almost intellectual when I sing one. It's just like reading a Huxley novel. I like some of the things that Charles Trenet and Jean Sablon sang in the thirties and forties in France. English songs tend to be sentimental, but French songs are unique—tough, and the thirty-two-bar form be damned. But it is the Americans who excel at writing popular songs. You can go anywhere in the world and hear American songs."

For his second show, he sang a dozen songs, among them a fascinating, meditative "I Can't Get Started." Then came a couple of Burt Bacharach songs, a swinging "Nashville Nightingale," a slow Stella Brooks blues, the Bessie Smith "Cake Walkin' Babies," and a long, intense reading of "Bye Bye Blackbird." In the fast numbers, his tempos raced in all directions, his face took on a strained, almost diabolical look, he reared back and shouted, and he often ended a song by flinging his right hand out, leaping to his feet, and standing statue-still, his eyes fixed high on the back wall of the room. For slow ballads, the lights were lowered and he sang quietly, his voice husky and small, his accompaniment full of soft tremolos and runs. The audience came around quickly, and by the time he had finished "Blackbird" there wasn't a murmur in the room.

He sat down and ordered more tea with honey, and talked about the songs he'd just sung, a couple of which were unfamiliar. "'You Better Love Me' is from *High Spirits*, which was based on *Blithe Spirit*, and 'Sand in My Shoes' is from *Kiss the Boys Goodbye*, the 1940 Loesser-Schertzinger thing. It was never a terribly successful song, but it's the most requested thing I do. That 'Can't Get Started' I love. Ira Gershwin wrote lots of stanzas, and he's a nifty one for going back and rewriting his lyrics years later. Did I do 'By Straus'? That was from a 1936 revue, and it was by the Gershwins. Bert Lahr and Beatrice Lillie were in it, and Vernon Duke wrote his 'Now' for it. It was, I believe, first recorded by George Byron, the tenor who married Eva Kern, Jerome's widow. It was on the General label, and Byron's pianist on the date was Bobby Tucker. A voice coach who took a shine to me in Hollywood in the early forties introduced it to me. Then I did a couple of Bacharachs. 'Nashville Nightingale' was a Gershwin number, written in the late twenties. Vernon Duke gave me it, too. He never pushed any of his own songs, but he would sit with me for hours and push everybody else's. He came to New York once with fourteen unknown Gershwin tunes and wanted me to record them immediately, but unfortunately nothing came of it. 'It Never Entered My Mind' was from *Higher and Higher*, a 1940 Rodgers and Hart effort, and I think I first heard Shirley Ross sing it on an old Blue Seal Decca. The 'Bye Bye Blackbird' is a little different, because I interpolate part of 'I'm a Little Blackbird Looking for a Bluebird.'"

Short looked up. The room was packed, and the lobby outside the glass entrance door was filled with people waiting for tables. He smiled. "I better get up to my dressing room and change again."

According to Where I Go

Hugh Shannon

Hugh Shannon is a trim, handsome man with sandy hair and a square, unsoft, lined Irish face. He has a brilliant, lopsided smile. When he is in New York, he shares an apartment with the publicist Gus Ober. It is in the East Seventies and looks out over the river from the twenty-fourth floor. Its small living room has a baby grand, bric-a-brac, oils, chinoiserie, a typewriter, gold draperies, and parquet floors, and it opens onto a vertiginous balcony that holds a wrought-iron table and four wrought-iron chairs. Shannon sat in his living room and talked. He talks very fast, sometimes gaining so much momentum that his words lock, blur, and become unintelligible. At one point, he talked for a solid hour. He sipped white wine, and, like Gertrude Stein, who felt that great views should be ignored to be appreciated, he sat with his back to the river. He is something of a dandy, and he was wearing a white lace shirt, a gold necklace laden with big gold coins, two-toned blue jeans, and red Moroccan slippers. This is what he said:

"Billie Holiday was my idol when I first came to New York, right after the Second World War. Meeting her changed my life. I was going with Marjorie Merwin, who admired Billie as much as I did, and Marjorie's mother would give me hundred-dollar bills. We'd go to the Downbeat Club, on Fifty-second Street, and I'd be so underfoot that Billie couldn't miss me. It got so she'd ask me to hold her dog, Mister, while she sang. One night, I persuaded her to go to a party Inez Cavanaugh was giving for Duke Ellington. She didn't want to, because she knew she'd be asked to sing. When she was, she said, 'If the kid will play for me.' After she'd finished, Inez made *me* sing. Well, I'd only worked weekends at college as a singer and pianist, but I did, and Billie said, 'Man, you don't sound like nobody! You *gotta* sing!' I could have burst. I was supposed to go into advertising, but instead I went to Provincetown for the summer of 1946. A whole bunch of us took a house in the dunes. It was miles from any-where, and it had a hot plate and an outdoor shower. Marlon Brando and Joy Cabot and Sydney Shaw and a radio actor came. Brando was not known yet, but he'd got good reviews in a show called *Truckline Café*, which lasted about ten days. I found a job almost immediately playing in a Portuguese bar that had a Bechstein upright. Gradually people knew I was there and started coming in, and it became almost chic. Then Julius Monk arrived in Provincetown with Imogene Coca and Daphne Hellman, and we did shows on Sunday nights in a room in the old Atlantic House. The ladies wore evening gowns—I think the Provincetown people thought they were nightgowns—and we filled the place. Maybe that's why we were raided out at our shack. I came home from work one night and Syndey Shaw was making tea and Marlon was playing his bongos and absolutely nothing was going on, when there was a rap at the door and there were the police. We were charged with disturbing the peace, and there was a hearing. The room was jammed and people were even leaning in the windows. The judge would ask, 'Where do you all sleep?' and we'd say, 'We have two pallets,' and he'd ask, 'How do you sleep on two pallets?' and we'd answer, 'It depends on who gets home first,' and so on. When the judge questioned him, Marlon got surly. In fact, he gave one of his better surly performances, and it all ended with our paying ten-dollar fines. Marlon used to accuse me of snobbishness, because I wore a dinner jacket when I worked. I told him he was a reverse snob, because he was always scratching and snuffling. But we did build a marvellous sand castle together.

"That summer, I met a girl from *Vogue* who had a wonderful apartment overlooking the Washington Square Arch, and when I got back to the city I bought a piano for eighty-five dollars and moved in. Ram Ramirez used to come up and there were always lots of Katherine Dunham's girls around. Julius Monk wanted me in Ruban Bleu, but I wasn't ready. I took a warmup job at a place in Jackson Heights, Queens, called the Blue Haven. We went back to Provincetown for the summer and Chemtoned the room in the Atlantic House dark blue and green and white, and we called it the Atlantic House Cabaret. Julius and I played two-piano duets, and Daphne Hellman had her harp and Schiaparelli gowns. Stella Brooks taught me 'West End Blues,' and Eileen Cook and Bibi Osterwald were there. Julius had a birthday party, and Stella Brooks banged Tennessee Williams' boyfriend's head against the wall. In the fall, I took another job in Queens, at the 22 Club, in Woodside. I alternated with a band every twenty minutes, but I had plenty of time to get my tunes together. M‚ first fan was a bus driver who'd park his bus outside the door every night and come in to hear me. After a while, the New York crowd, led by Faye Emerson and Elliott Roosevelt, showed up. I stayed at the 22 until January, when I went to Key West. Julius called and hired me for Le Perroquet, a new club on Second Avenue. In the fall, Stella Brooks came to Perroquet, too. She was most of all amusing, and she was a past-master of trivia. Truman Capote was so crazy about her—I think he was fascinated by her rudeness—that he took an apartment over Perroquet to be near her. He decorated it all in black. *Everything* was black but him. One late night, I ended up sleeping on the floor there, and when I woke up I thought, My God, I'm dead. There was no light. Nothing. Cy Coleman, who was very shy, came to Perroquet that winter and alternated with me. Then I went to the Empress Room, which had been opened for me, and Johnny Guarnieri was the other pianist. He loved to smoke cigars, and he wasn't used to Upper East Side supper-club types. By this time, I'd moved to the East Sixties, and I'd become a friend of Peggy Fears. She was a former Ziegfeld girl who'd married A. C. Blumenthal, who owned lots of theatres. Peggy gave five-o'clock soirées. Tallulah and Joan Bennett and Joan Crawford came when they were in town. Peggy'd been in New York when Lindbergh came back from France; she was always in the right place at the right time.

"One night at the Empress Room when I was playing 'Ballin' the Jack,' a voice said, 'Stop that tune!' It was Bricktop. I'd read about Bricktop everywhere—in Waugh and Fitzgerald—but no one had ever said whether Bricktop was a man or a woman. She came up and sang 'Ballin' the Jack' with me, and then we did a blues, a madeup blues. She was on her way from Mexico to Paris, and she told me she was going to take me with her as her new discovery. She was looking for a place to open a club, and I think Schiaparelli and Donald Bloomingdale were behind her. Julius Monk also wanted me for a place he planned to open in the South of France, and Peggy Fears wanted me to come over to Carrère, in Paris. I said yes to everybody, and I've since learned that this is what you must do to keep going in the saloon business: if you accept two or three jobs, one invariably works out. I had a little Pepsi-Cola stock and I sold that and went over on the Vulcania in steerage in a cabin with about eighteen other people. But I had my dinner jacket. When I passed up from the bowels of the ship into first class, I was properly dressed. We landed in Naples, and I took a fruit boat to Capri. It was unbelievable—villas perched like flowers on the rocks, which looked like sea horses, villas perched in the sky over the sea. I went to work in Numero Due. It was in an old wine cellar and had a beautiful grand piano, and I was an immediate success. They hadn't heard any American music for years, because f the war. Mussolini's daughter used to come in. She was very severe, and sometimes she stayed a short while and sometimes she stayed for hours. I finally found out she only liked one song I did—"Big Wide Wonderful World'—and when I'd done it she'd leave. I thought the whole situation was a lark, and had no idea I'd spend six or seven seasons there. So I quit in the middle of August, which was extemely bad form, and went to Cap d'Antibes. I had always travelled with letters of recommendation, and I had letters to Elsa Maxwell and Peggy Bainbridge. The bar in the Hôtel du Cap had a place for me for the rest of the season. Then I went to Paris, and Peggy Fears arrived and the five-o'clock soirées resumed. Carrère, which was done in yellow and white and was frighteningly chic, hired me. Doris Duke was back with Ruby Rubirosa, and I taught her to play blues on the piano. She had a light touch, like most women, and she was loaded with determination. I went to Montmartre one night and on the way back was in an enormous car crash and ended up in the hospital with twenty-seven stitches and a split front tooth. Someone sent a case of champagne, and the soirées moved to the hospital. I didn't want to go back into Carrère with my split tooth, so I hid in a tiny place, the Mars, where I was paid nine lavish dollars a night. I was practically anonymous at first, then everybody materialized—the Dunhams and Josephine Premice and Kitty Kitt and Brickie. They were in every night. If amusing people like each other, they'll see each other the next night and the next. That spring, Brickie opened a place in Montmartre with two pianos and a Chinese cook. There were limousines everywhere on opening night. The Windsors came, and Rosita Winston and Doris and Ruby, and it went on until eight in the morning, and soon Brick had put every other place like it out of business. It was divinely dark inside, but that didn't mean I could forget my manners—manners that have become ironclad. I never let on if I forget a name, because I never forget a face, and names invariably come back to me within three minutes. And I never move forward first when I greet someone. I wait for them to move. I went back to Numero Due the next season. Then back to Paris and on to London for the first time, where I sang in the International Club. I had some suits made and acquired a taste for oysters, which is what you do in England. And I met Betty Dodero. I had seen her yacht from afar that summer. She had just got a divorce from Alberto Dodero, who was an immensely wealthy Argentinian. She was Eva Perón's best friend. That winter, I took off for St. Thomas in the Virgin Islands, and became the first supper-club singer there. I had another season in Capri and for a short time was in Toni's Caprice in New York. It was all black and white, and it was quite stunning—one of the most beautiful rooms I've ever worked. They finally had to build bleachers behind the piano and cover them with cushions to handle the overflow. Betty Dodero appeared the next year in the islands. She would sit next to me all night and fan me while I played. We fell in love. She was Swedish and Irish and beautiful, and she had a marvellous sense of humor. And she never forgot a lyric. We lived together, and Betty never left me. We carried Benchley and Waugh and Dorothy Parker and Wodehouse everywhere, and Betty read them to me, over and over. She had a wonderful voice. Capri was magnificent that summer. Bea Lillie, Noël Coward—he and I playing four-handed piano—Judy Garland, Lena Horne, Ella Logan, Sophie Tucker, Gracie Fields, Patrice Munsel. One night, most of them appeared at once and they performed. It was the richest night of my life.

"I had already told Betty: You're very rich. You're very beautiful. You have everything I ever wanted. I love you. But I want *you* to tell me when we should get married. She finally did, and we had a civil ceremony in December of 1952, in New York. We were content. We needed no one else. Our lives took on a pattern for the next five years—the islands in the winter, Capri in the summer, and occasional jobs in New York and Nassau. Then the Germans discovered Capri, and it lost its chic. I worked part of the summer of 1957 in Westhampton, and it was my first time in the Hamptons. Henry and Anne Ford and the Southampton crowd came, as well as the Capri and Paris people. It is not braggadocio to say that I was becoming—indeed, have become—a kind of movable feast, a catalyst. People make their summer and winter plans according to where I go. Everybody has to go someplace, and they know that they will be safe where I am—that they will see their old friends, and that they will meet the right new people. Of course, it works both ways: I'm as happy to see them as they are to see me. But you must make the audience more important than yourself. When you outgrow your audience, or think you have, you're in trouble. In 1957, Betty began feeling unwell, and in January, 1959, we found out she had cancer. She was operated on and treated for six months. She had no pain. We were very quiet. We spent our last night watching TV. I think it was a 'Late Late Show.' I fell asleep, and when I woke Betty was gone. Patrice Munsel and her husband came and took care of me, and I lived with them a year. Julius Monk kept after me to go back to work, and finally I did, at Downstairs at the Upstairs, which was like working in Grand Central Station. Rose Murphy, who was there for a while, taught me that the way to handle noisy people is to look right at the spotlight and sing to it. That way, you look as if you knew something they didn't, and they quiet down in order to find out. I went to Rome— to Bricktop's on the Via Veneto—in the summer of 1960, and then to a villa in Stresa. I wrote a musical based on Betty's life, and it was terrible. And I wrote a sort of autobiography, which isn't too bad. I discovered I'm not a writer, and I rediscovered that I love playing the piano and singing more than anything else in the world.

"I don't know how many songs I know, but it must be in the thousands. I can immediately sing a song I haven't touched in twenty years. When I put my hands on the keyboard, it becomes a muscular chain reaction. The hands, the head, the voice—they all work together, and up come songs I thought I'd forgotten or didn't know I knew. There are certain tunes I don't like and will not sing, such as 'The Lady Is a Tramp' and 'Ebb Tide' and 'Tenderly.' 'My Ship' is a woman's song, and so is 'Love for Sale.' But I will sing songs that Mabel Mercer and Bobby Short won't touch— things from the Top Forty. My people request them because they want me to think they are with it. I never want anyone to leave when I'm play- ing—that goes back to my childhood—so I try to make my audience happy even if it kills me, and sometimes it almost does. Occasionally, I will sing four or five straight hours, and it takes something to keep control of myself. One July 4th at the Sea Spray, in East Hampton, I played with- out stopping from ten in the evening until three in the morning. The place had been doing a poor business until then, and suddenly hundreds of people arrived, so I played and played and played. If you are fair to the house, the house will be fair to you. It was a roasting night and the per- spiration poured down my nose and fell on my feet, which were bare, because I always play in bare feet in the summer, and the only way I kept going was by thinking, I'm getting thin, I'm getting thin, I'm getting thin. A lot of my people come in every night, and they become mesmerized. They begin to think they *own* me. They study every expression, every wrinkle. Then they tell me later they know I'm not feeling well when I'm feeling perfectly fine, or they tell me I look extremely happy when actually I'm miserable.

"When a tune has really become mine, I move around inside my head while I sing. I think brilliant thoughts, I think of places I've been and people I've known. I go to 470 Park Avenue, where Betty and I lived, or to Numero Due in Capri, and no one watching me has the least idea where I am or what I'm up to. I hear Betty reading Benchley or 'Vile Bod- ies' again. Sometimes I even go back to De Soto, where I was born. It's thirty miles outside of St. Louis, and it had a population of five thousand. It was built on seven hills, like Rome, and it had a creek going right through the middle of it. I'm exceedingly grateful to have been born and raised in a small town. How dreadful to be brought up in a city, thinking that people are evil! In a small town, you learn about friends and you learn about snobs. You learn stability and a sense of decorum and discip- line. I went to church four times on Sunday, and I was taught not to speak until spoken to, which is why I talk so much now. I was raised by my maternal grandparents, whose name was Stall. My mother died when I was born, and my father, who was just nineteen, deposited me with my grandparents when I was nine days old. I saw him only twice after that, but I don't blame him for what he did. How could a nineteen-year-old boy raise a baby? My grandmother, whom I called Mother, was a calm, strong, dignified woman. She taught me so well to be independent that I became a nonconformist. She always said two things: Play tennis with people who are better than you are, and never travel without a dinner jacket. I don't play tennis anymore, but I prefer being around people who are smarter than I am. My grandfather was one-quarter Sioux Indian, and he was very good to me. He was a conductor on the Missouri Pacific, and he grew roses. People came from miles away to see his roses. We had the first tennis court in town. My uncles built it themselves, and my grandfather put up chicken wire around it. When I got old enough, I raked it and watered it and rolled it. We did not have a lot of money, but we had a big house, with three floors and one bathroom. We used to sit on the porch summer nights with the crickets going, and people always stopped by and talked. Sometimes they told ghostly stories in that wonderful Missouri twang—stories that would make your spine ripple on a dark summer night, with the heat lightning behind the trees and the breeze beginning to smarten. I started taking voice lessons when I was five, from a Mme. Centorbi, and I also started piano lessons with Mme. Theobald. They were both very grand. I studied piano until I was seventeen, but all the while I went down to the sheet-music store and I learned every new tune that came out. I had a marvellous speech teacher, Martha Mae Boyer, who chose all the books I read—*War and Peace* and Thomas Wolfe and Benchley and Fitzgerald—and when I graduated from high school as valedictorian, she helped me get two scholarships to the University of Southern California. My grandparents wanted me to go to a Methodist college for a year and then to Yale, but I wanted to go where the pretty people were, where the convertibles and the blondes were. My grandmother was surprised when I told her, but no one ever raised a voice in our house, and I think she was even a little proud of my determination—even though she was never pleased at my becoming a saloon singer and hobnobbing with the Roosevelts. I took the Missouri Pacific out and got a job in a boarding house owned by a woman who treated me like a slavey. I served breakfast and dinner and cleaned up, ironed her two sons' shirts, and slept on a couch in the living room. But soon I moved into a house with a couple of classmates, and pledged Sigma Nu, and was the campus representative for Phelps-Terkel's clothing store—that meant wearing their clothes and being in the shop every afternoon, which was fine, because I already loved clothes. Then Joe Barbados and I opened a club just for students. We called it Barbados, and I played there every Friday and Saturday. I majored in advertising and merchandising and graduated in the top ten in 1941, and then worked as a movie extra. I joined the Navy, and they sent me to Harvard for six months. I went to dances at Pine Manor, where all the girls wore black lipstick, black nail polish, and black velvet. I asked for the Seabees when I finished Harvard, because I couldn't stand the stuffies I'd been with there, and it was the best thing that ever happened to me. I was in the 119th Battalion, Edwin C. Mackay commanding. I think he'd only gone through seventh grade, but he was brilliant. I became disbursing officer, which meant handling the payroll, and I was put in charge of the Officers' Club. The first thing I did was buy a piano, and we took it everywhere. We were sent to New Guinea, where we did a lot of waiting. I wrote letters and read *The Magic Mountain* twice. My God! Settembrini and Peeperkorn and the rest—how well I knew them! At night, everybody got drunk. I controlled all the liquor, and had I wished to I could have made two hundred dollars a bottle. An officer in my battalion was alcoholic, and one night he set fire to my mosquito netting with me inside because I wouldn't let him have booze when he wanted it. I'm crazy about Christmas, and I had brought four sets of Christmas-tree lights with me to the South Pacific. At Christmas, the Seabees raised a huge pole in which they had drilled holes and put branches from whatever trees were available, and I hung my lights, and we had a beautiful tree. Then we were sent to the Philippines. One Sunday, I went to a Catholic church and a local boy was playing a huge bamboo organ that the Seabees had put back in working order. It had a reedy, flutelike sound, and no bottom. The boy seemed to know only one song, and it was terribly familiar, but I couldn't place it. Then I got it. It was 'Don't Get Around Much Anymore' done as a dirge. When the war ended, all fifteen hundred of us took off our clothes and stayed drunk two days. In the middle of this, it suddenly came to me that here I was in the Philippines and this was my chance to see something of the Orient. I wasn't in any hurry to go home, because there was nothing in particular to go home for, so I asked Commander Mackay if I could have a couple of days' leave to go and see a friend of my grandmother's in Hong Kong, and insane orders were cut for me that said I could travel 'where verbally ordered.' I went to Hong Kong and then to Macao and finally to Shanghai, which was the most exciting city I've ever seen. I was mustered out on Staten Island.

"The Hampton years really began in 1962 with a wild summer at Francis Carpenter's Bull's Head Inn, in Bridgehampton. Pat Hemingway was there, the other, good Gardiners, Cordelia Duke Biddle Robinson, who thought 'Mrs. Robinson' had been written for her, Pat Havens Monteagle, Carlos and Joan Nadal, Betty Milliken, Frank Shields, Dorothy Fields, who had a steel-trap mind, all the Gabors, Bill Blass, and Cy Coleman, who wasn't so shy anymore. The next year, I worked at the Mid-Ocean Bath and Tennis Club and lived in a tiny cracker box on the dunes in Sagaponack. Truman Capote and I passed each other on the beach. Everyone stayed in my shack. George Frazier—dear George, who loved clothes so—and Carol Channing and Rona Jaffe and Julius Monk and Prince Michael of Prussia. Carol Channing got so sunburned one week-end that we had to take her back to New York in an ice pack to get her swollen eyes open so she could go to work the next night. I spent a season in East Hampton at the Hedges, and then I went into the marvellous Irving Hotel, in Southampton. I was there seven seasons. Formidable old ladies rocked on its veranda, and it had four enormous adjoining cottages and eleven acres of land and a beautiful garden where fashionable people got married. Bang-Bang Rutherford, who said she was going to marry me, hid a police car behind one of those giant Southampton hedges and it wasn't found for three days. I designed the room I worked in. It was called the Casino Library, and it had huge playing cards on the walls and fifteen hundred books and a fireplace and big dice cubes for tables. It was a great success. The Irving closed, and I went on for a year at the Sea Spray, two years at the Westhampton Bath and Tennis, and the summer before last I was at Zenda's, smack in the middle of Southampton. I still play winters in the islands, and occasionally I stop off for a few weeks in Palm Beach. This past summer, I went to Marbella, because I needed the change and the perspective Europe always gives me. All the Southampton people talked of committing suicide because I wouldn't be out there. A lot of my friends came over. We have pacts, little laws. One never mentions foolish or bad behavior from the night before. If you get drunk and fall down, you fall down among friends. One never talks about money. No one knows if I am rich or poor, and no one ever will. One never talks about illness. A wealthy woman I know said when a calamity occurred to a mutual acquaintance on Capri, 'We have no time on Capri for unhappiness. We are here to have fun'—which has its own undeniably wicked logic. During the day, my people have their boats and Meadow Club and cars. But I'm the night man, and from ten on they belong to me."

A Wholesome American Beauty Rose

Julie Wilson

Onstage, Julie Wilson is rarely still. Her eyes flash. Her head swings back and forth, lest she leave a listener untouched. Her arms are wings, and she often ends a song with one arm straight out, her long fingers curving up toward the ceiling. In the Oak Room of the Algonquin Hotel, where she often works, she sits on steps by the piano and sings; then, for her next number, she moves with unbelievable quickness from the steps to the top of the piano. In a blink, she is back on her steps—weightless, fleshless. She has a fine comic flair, and can rattle off nonsense songs, like Irving Berlin's "Snooky-Ookums," keeping her eyes at a laughing squint and her mouth in a big smile. She never sings a false note or makes a gauche move. She generally works with the pianist, singer, and songwriter William Roy, a small, neat, quick, immensely skilled performer, who does duets with her and supports her at every turn.

In conversation, Julie Wilson likes to sit close to her companion, and she leaves long pauses, like reflecting pools. She talks very quietly, but, always coiled and ready, she can let loose a jarring shout to make a point. She talked for several hours at the East Side apartment of a friend. She had on a head scarf and her hair was up, and she wore a navy-blue silk dress with white polka dots.

"I was born October 21, 1924, in Omaha, Nebraska. My dad's name was Russell Wilson and my mother's maiden name also was Wilson— Emily Bennett Wilson. He was a coal salesman, and he loved to work. Up at a quarter to six, breakfast at six, out of the house at half past six, at his office at six-forty-five. And it was more work when he got home—pruning trees, clipping bushes, painting. He was a beautiful housepainter. He died in 1980, and he worked almost to the end. He was tall and straight and slim, and he had white hair and blue eyes. It was hard for him to show affection. His way was to jab at you, be sarcastic—then send sentimental cards. He was impatient, and he swore a lot and had a hot temper. He was also a drinker—a mean drinker. He came from Stanton, Iowa, which was full of drinking Swedes. But he gave it up when he was sixty-four. Smoking too. And he was all right the rest of his life. My mother was from Missouri. She was the seventh of twelve children. She had black hair and a deep widow's peak, and she was very beautiful. She became a hairdresser when the popular hairdo was the marcel. She had the kind of look that made people who didn't know her think when they first came in the shop, Why, that skinny, pretty thing couldn't be any good. But she could really twirl that iron, and if there was any trouble it was 'Go get Emily.' She never had a wrinkle in her face, and her hair didn't turn gray until she was seventy-five. I had two brothers—Russell, who was eighteen months older, and Lawrence, who was eight years younger.

"During the Depression, we moved outside of town. We had a house and a little acreage. It was the only time my mother ever borrowed a penny. She went to the bank and asked them to lend her fifty dollars, and they said what did she want fifty dollars for, and she said to buy a cow. They gave it to her, and she bought a cow and some chickens, and we sold milk. Homeless people came to our door all during that time, and she never turned anyone away. Russell and I had a firecracker stand by the side of the road one summer. We'd order firecrackers by mail, and we each made enough to buy a bike. We stayed out there two or three years, and then moved into the little house my parents put up just outside the city limits. It's all built up around it now, but we still own it.

"After high school, I enrolled at Omaha University, where I had a major in drama and a minor in music. But I didn't last long. I had been singing with local bands since I was fourteen. One day, my Aunt Nora called and said Earl Carroll's 'Vanities' was in town. They were looking for someone to replace a girl who had pneumonia, and the girl they hired they'd take to Hollywood and make a star of. So I called and said, 'This is Mary Lou Wilson. I understand you are looking for someone,' and the man said 'Can you dance?' and I said 'A little,' and he said 'Can you sing?' and I said 'A little,' and he said 'Come on down.' I put on this black-cherry lipstick that was fashionable at the time, and went to the theatre. I sang a scale and did a time step, and was told to go and see Minnie and put on a costume and come back. It had a sketchy top and a little skirt. The man who had auditioned me said, 'You're a little hippy, but you'll do. The pay is forty dollars a week.' I was too embarrassed to tell anyone at the university what I had done, but when the dean of women called my mother, Miss Honest-Bones-of-the World told all. The troupe had comics who built houses and knocked them down, or played the piano and got their fingers stuck to the keys. There was a magician, too, and a funny ballet dancer. I was in a trio that sang songs like 'Morning Glory.' We stayed a week in each place, and I was with the company six months. I wasn't very popular with the girls in the chorus. They were seasoned, and I was a baby. So much so that I took off my makeup after every show, and there were five shows a day. It's a wonder I didn't wear out my face. We got to New York in the spring of 1943, and I gave notice at Loew's State Theatre.

"I met Wally Wanger, who did the hiring at the Latin Quarter. There were no openings, but he said he'd keep me in mind. I also met a sweet man named Al Buckner. Bucky, as he was known, was a bookmaker, and he made sure that I always had something to eat, that I didn't talk to strangers, that I was aware of the bad Broadway elements. I had heard about John Robert Powers' modelling agency, and one day I went there and waited four hours to get in. When I did, Powers said, 'My, aren't you a wholesome American beauty rose.' I was too heavy, and I had a face like a pie. I walked for him, and he told me I'd better go to modelling school. Of course, I had no money for that. I also met a man named Curly Harris, who did public relations for United Artists. He said Mary Lou was a corny name and that I should use Julia or Julie—my real name being Julia Mary Wilson. Wally Wanger offered me a job at the Latin Quarter in Chicago. I would be a production singer, which meant I would sing a number surrounded by the chorus. Seventy-five a week. I did three shows a night for seven days a week for three or four months. A rich old guy wanted to buy me a fur coat, and when I told my mother she came up to Chicago, took a look at him, and said, 'That coot is old enough to be your grandfather. Anyway, you should be back in college.' But the bug had bit. Wally Wanger booked me into a Detroit gambling club from Chicago, and I had my first bad experience. I was with a gent who used to drive the girls in the chorus from our hotel to the club. That was better than taking the bus. One night, he drove me home and said he'd buy me an ice-cream soda and take me to a party he knew about. Well, there wasn't any party, and he finally gave me five dollars for a cab. I packed up and went home.

"I was still too embarrassed to return to the university, so I went to Duchesne, which was a Sacred Heart school. The nuns didn't impose their beliefs on me, and they had tremendous empathy. Then Wally Wanger gave me a job at the New York Latin Quarter at fifty dollars a week. I took a little apartment in Forest Hills, and my mother and younger brother joined me. Curly Harris introduced me to Monte Proser, who did the hiring at the Copacabana. I made it into the chorus. I'd been there several months when I had the chance to audition for Johnny Long's band

and was hired. We went on the road, and I was fired on Christmas Eve. Monte Proser put me in a U.S.O. show that the Copa sent to Europe. I was still underage and had to have my parent's permission. We did Germany and France. I couldn't get over the bougainvillea on the Riviera. When I came back, things seemed to move faster and faster—sideways. I sang with Emil Stern's hotel band. I did a production number, 'The Coffee Song,' in a Copa show that had Peter Lind Hayes and Desi Arnaz in it. A job on Broadway opened up in *Three to Make Ready*, with Ray Bolger. I understudied Bibi Osterwald and was in the chorus. But the show suddenly folded, and I went into a room in the Hotel Duane, on Madison Avenue, and then into the Glass Hat, on East Fiftieth Street.

"I had three jobs and an almost during the next six months or so. The almost was a Broadway show Bob Hilliard was doing that had the song 'Civilization' in it, with those crazy lyrics 'Bongo, bongo, bongo, I don't want to leave the Congo.' I auditioned, but Elaine Stritch got the job. The first of the three jobs was at a beautiful place called the Beverly Country Club outside New Orleans, the second was at the Copa, and the third was at Copa City in Miami Beach. I was fired in Miami Beach—not because I wasn't any good but because the show's producer wanted the job for his girlfriend, as I found out later. I was only twenty-three, but I had already learned that it's not so much what is done to you as the way it is done—that people should have the guts to be square with you. I had also learned that getting fired is not necessarily a detriment. It can even be the reverse. It gets you energized and headed the right way again. So I moved into a place nearby, called Mother Kelly's, at half the pay, five shows a night, seven days a week. I was trying every sort of song. I was trying to find my way. I was sick of being ignored. I had discovered that being a nice girl from Omaha didn't make it. I decided to get mean, a little bitchy. I started sticking my chin in the air, and at the end of a performance I'd turn my back on the audience and walk out—and people began paying attention. One night, Kay Thompson's agent, Barron Polan, came in. He was a classy guy, and we talked three hours. The job at Mother Kelly's lasted seven or eight months, and then I went back to New York. I was broke. I knew a girl named Chris Kerrigan, who had worked at Mother Kelly's. She fell in love with Harry the Hipster Gibson, who worked at Café Society Uptown and on Fifty-second Street. He played the piano and sang wild songs about pot and drugs. Chris had a job at the Melody Club in Union City, New Jersey, doing a routine with a comic, and I got a job there as a singer. There was a pianist and a drummer, and I followed the stripper. Then Barron Polan told me he had lined up a screen test with Sam Goldwyn. Kay Thompson helped me buy a dress, and I took the train to California. I had my hair pulled back and was wearing earrings when I got to M-G-M, and Goldwyn's secretary said, 'Take off the earrings. He hates them.' I went in, and Goldwyn said, 'Is that your hair? Take it down so that I can see what you look like.' I did, and looked like a witch. He told me I could put it back up and go. I did the screen test with my hair down, and I could have been Gene Tierney's sister.

"Mickey Rooney had a program in Los Angeles—'Hollywood Show-case'—on which singers competed, the winner getting two weeks at the Mocambo. I won, with 'For Every Man There's a Woman.' At the Mocambo, I wore an elegant white gown. It was jersey, and it had lace, beading, a low neck, and long sleeves. Phil Moore had a group there, and he backed me and wrote some material for me, and it was a very successful engagement. It was the first time I had felt real electricity between an audience and me. From there I did Lake Tahoe, then the Mark Hopkins, in San Francisco, and the Maisonette, in New York. It was 1948. I must have gone into the Maisonette twenty times. It was my anchor, my jumping-off place. It was where I grew up. People sensed this and started giving me advice. Louis Sobol, the Broadway columnist, told me not to sing ballads. 'You're a nice girl,' he said, 'but don't sing a ballad.' Someone told me I was O.K. onstage as long as I kept moving. Arnold Weissberger, the theatrical lawyer, told me I had to be seen, I had to meet people, I had to make connections—when actually I would rather have stayed at home and baked pies. I auditioned for *Kiss Me, Kate*, and I had the lead for six months in the national company, and I did it in London. I also did *South Pacific* for a year in London. I started studying there with George Cunelli, a wonderful voice teacher. I had made up my mind I was going to improve my voice. I wanted to bridge the gap between chest singing and head tones. I wanted to be able to stop *pushing* when I sang. I took two lessons a day, and I also studied at the Royal Academy of Dramatic Arts. I was running out of money, though, and Barron Polan came to the rescue again. He wanted to know if I was interested in the lead in a new musical to be called *The Pajama Game*. But I was so involved with cultivating my voice that I said no. It was a terrible decision. It would have put me on the map. Instead, I went to Los Angeles to audition for Richard Rodgers' *Pipe Dream*. I used my new soprano, and Rodgers said it was the worst soprano he had ever heard, and what had happened to the voice that they had called me to California to hear? I didn't get the part, and that was the end of my soprano.

"That September, I opened at the Persian Room in the Hotel Plaza. Barron Polan and I were married, but it lasted only a year. He was the best friend I ever had. I finally went into *The Pajama Game*. Janis Paige opened the show, then Pat Marshall took over, and then I came in. I also did a couple of sleeper movies—*The Strange One*, with Pat Hingle and Ben Gazzara, and *This Could Be the Night*, with Jean Simmons and Paul Douglas. I was the only woman in the first picture and the blond saloon singer in the second. Then I was married for a short time to a man who owned a motel, and in 1959 I met a crazy Irishman named Michael McAloney. He produced *Borstal Boy* on Broadway. We were married in 1961. He wanted to run everything—me and my career—and I wasn't used to that. I even moved to Ireland with him to try and iron things out, to let him be the big cheese. I wanted a husband I could go in the same direction with, not one who was going in the opposite direction. My work is my life, and I need a lot of peace. When I go home at night, I go home to the stillness. But good came of the marriage—two sons, Holt and Michael. I was thirty-nine and forty when they were born. In 1976, when they were twelve and thirteen, I quit working to spend more time with them. Before that, I took them everywhere with me, school permitting, and we toured in *Company, A Little Night Music,* and *Follies.*

"I came out again in 1984. The way it happened was, like everything in my life, through luck and the intervention of other people. Barron Polan ran into Hilary Knight, the illustrator, and Hilary told him Gil Wiest was looking for a singer to do a Cole Porter show at Michael's Pub. Barron knew I wanted to come back to New York, and he told Hilary, who told Wiest, and I opened in early January. Since then, I have become a kind of fixture at the Algonquin, and I have bought a little place in Sullivan County and a little house in Jersey City.

"Only one singer has influenced me, and that's Billie Holiday. She is why I wear a gardenia in my hair every night. I used to listen to her on Fifty-second Street when I was with Johnny Long's band, and I finally met her and had dinner with her just a year before she died. No singer has ever moved me so much. No one has ever had such pain and emotion in her singing. There have been many better singers, but none as moving. She taught me that when you sing a song like Irving Berlin's 'Supper Time,' which has to do with a black woman whose husband has just been lynched, you picture him hanging, you think of what must be going through her mind, you think of her children and what she can possibly say to them. You keep all that in your mind while you're singing and it will come out in the words, in your vioce, in your face—and people will listen.

"For a long time, I was bothered by laryngitis. Either I didn't take care of myself—stayed up three nights in a row the way you do when you're a kid and think you can do anything—or I had a bad case of nerves. And I got typed into singing clever songs, double-entendre songs, saucy songs. I'd do a ballad and people like Louis Sobol would tell me not to compete with Peggy Lee or Ella Fitzgerald or Jo Stafford. But I couldn't stand being pegged. So I worked and worked until I could do what I do now—a Sondheim show or a Rodgers-and-Hart show or a Harold Arlen show, and follow all the different and marvellous avenues they move down. The great American songwriters all speak in their own tongues. Cole Porter can be affecting, funny, exciting. He had such style. The same is true of Rodgers and Hart. And Stephen Sondheim is incredible. He has so much depth and humanity, so much insight into feelings. Some songwriters you have to grow into. The first show I was ever in, in Omaha when I was a kid, was Kurt Weill's *Knickerbocker Holiday*, and I didn't understand 'September Song.' I wasn't old enough. I never thought I'd be old enough to sing 'September Song,' but now I am. I'm convinced that the great American songs will one day be like the Shakespeare sonnets. All they will have to do to be perpetuated is to be used. The songs will always be there. It will simply be a question—as it is even now—of where and how and when they will be performed."

Absolutely Pure

Blossom Dearie

Everything about Blossom Dearie is just right. Consider her singing. She is the youngest of the five consummate supperclub singers who rule the upper regions of American song. She has a tiny voice, smaller than Mildred Bailey's or Astrud Gilberto's or Wee Bonnie Baker's; without a microphone, it would not reach the second floor of a doll house. But it is a perfect voice—light, clear, pure, resilient, and, buttressed by amplification, surprisingly commanding. Her style is equally choice, and was once described by Rogers Whitaker as going from "the meticulous to the sublime." Her diction shines (she comes from a part of eastern upstate New York noted for its accent-free speech), and she has a cool, delicate, seamless way of phrasing that is occasionally embellished by a tissue-paper vibrato. Consider her songwriting. Few first-rate singers write music, and few first-rate songwriters sing. But she has produced well over thirty tunes, and they are affecting extensions of her singing. Some, like "Hey, John," written after she appeared on a British television show with John Lennon, are cheerful and funny ("Hey, John, look at me digging you digging me"); some, like "Home," are ruminative and gentle and pastoral; some, like "I'm Shadowing You," with lyrics by Johnny Mercer, are magic: even though one may never have heard the tune before, one immediately experiences a kind of melodic *déjà vu*. Consider her appearance and manner. She stands pole-straight, and is short and country-girl solid. Her broad face, with its small, well-spaced eyes, wide mouth, and generous, direct nose, has a figurehead strength. Her hands and feet are small and delicate. Angelic honey-blond hair falls well below her shoulders. When she is listening, she gives continuous, receptive, almost audible nods. There is no waste in her laughter, which is frequent and quick—a single, merry, high, descending triplet. And she has an almost prim manner of speaking; her sentences arrive boxed and beribboned. Consider her name. It sounds like a stage name or one of Dickens' hyperbolic inventions, but it is real. It is appropriately musical; her given name is soft and on the beat, and her surname is legato and floating. (Any other name—such as Tony Grey, which an overwrought agent once suggested—would be ludicrous.) It is also very old-fashioned; it calls to mind pinafores and lemon verbena and camomile tea. And consider her magnetism. Her old friend Jean Bach has said of her, "She is absolutely pure, and she will not compromise. She has this innocence that would take her across a battlefield unscathed. In a way, she resembles a Christian Scientist. If things go askew or don't fit in with her plans, they don't exist. She started getting under everybody's skin when she came back from Paris in the mid-fifties. I can't remember where she was working, but the place had Contact paper on the tables and out-of-work actors as waiters. It was funny when you'd take a new person to hear her. Her singing is so deceptively simple that at first there would be this 'What?' reaction, and then after a while a smile would spread across the person's face, and that would be it. You can be away from her for a long time and live your own life, and then she reappears and gets to you again. She's like a drug. She certainly has the English hooked. When she sings in London, they arrange all the chairs so that they face *her*, and there's not a sound. It's like church."

Blossom Dearie divides her year between a small Greenwich Village apartment; the family house, in East Durham, New York, where she was born; and London, whence she ventures into Scandinavia, Holland, Germany, and France. Part of her restiveness is due to economics, and part is due to an inborn need to keep on the move, to live light. Supper clubs have become almost vestigial in New York, and she is a demanding, even imperious performer who will not tolerate rude audiences. She subbed for Bobby Short at the Café Carlyle once, and, as is their wont, the swells who frequent the Café were often noisy and inattentive. Blossom Dearie repeatedly rebuked them by breaking off in midsong and announcing, in her teacup way, "You have to be a little more quiet. Some of these people are my friends and have come to hear *me!*" The swells responded by staying away, and business was poor.

   She lives in a one-room apartment on the third-floor front of an old building facing Sheridan Square. On nice mornings, the room is knee-deep in sunshine. It has a *pied-à-terre* look, is furnished with a convertible sofa, a couple of yellow director's chairs, a small round sidewalk-café table, an upright piano, a tiny white desk, a record player, and several shelves of records. Blossom Dearie brewed some Irish tea, and sat down with a mug. She was wearing black pants, a white turtleneck, and a patterned black-and-off-white cardigan sweater. She laughed, crossed her legs, and rested her clasped hands on one knee. "I've decided I want to live a long time," she said. "A very long time. So I'm very conscientious about taking care of myself. I read Carlton Fredericks and Adelle Davis, and I take vitamins, especially Vitamin E, which is the wonder vitamin and helps retard the aging process. And I go to bed early and get up early. I can't stand the all-night-club thing anymore, and anyway what reason is there for a single person like me to stay up late? So what I do at the Ballroom, where I am now, is give an early-evening concert. It starts at six-thirty and ends at eight. That way people can go out and hear me and have dinner and go home to bed. No drinks are served when I sing. I've been cracking since six this morning. I've transposed a new song into my key and nearly learned it, and I've practiced Billy Strayhorn's 'Lush Life,' which I've avoided for years because it has such poor lyrics. But it is a beautiful and quite complicated song. I've called London twice. I've written Norman Granz, asking if he can help me get the rights for the seven albums I made for him, so that I can reissue them. And I've written two of the eleven girl friends I regularly correspond with in foreign countries. I've had a business conference with my press agent. I'm trying to get my life beautifully organized, and I have several projects under way. One is starting my own place. I don't want to buy a building or anything, just rent a room. It's going to be *scientifically* done. I want perfect acoustics, so that people *can* talk but won't bother me. You'd be surprised what a performer can hear—every word, every whisper. There will be the right kind of ceiling and perfect ventilation, so that there won't be that horrible smokiness. And the lighting will not wear my eyes out. Another project is keeping my own record label going, in addition to reissuing the Granz things. And, finally, there are my songs, my composing, which has become very important to me. So important that I only want to collaborate with lyricists like Johnny Mercer. He sent me a marvellous letter not long before he died, celebrating our friendship, and saying that since we'd survived folk rock and soft rock and hard rock we'd go on forever. It really pleased me."

Blossom Dearie laughed, and abruptly stood up. "I'd make another cup of tea, but I have to tape part of the sound track for an industrial film for a friend of mine, and the date starts in twenty minutes. The studio is on West Fifty-second Street." She walked to Sixth Avenue and got into a cab. "I have a method now when I compose," she said on the way uptown.

"I write out the rhythms first, almost like a piece of drum music. Then I put the melody to that. Songs come to me in different ways. I've written quite a few of what I call tribute songs—songs for people I admire, like John Lennon and Tony Bennett. These songs are pure inspiration, pure communication between my brain and fingers and my admiration for the person, and generally they come to me quickly. Otherwise, I jot down ideas—three bars, eight bars, maybe ten—and work them out at the piano. I keep playing them over. I play them in the morning and I play them in the evening. I play them when I've had a drink and when I haven't. But I set myself a time limit. I'll work on a song for two weeks, and if it doesn't come out right I put it away for a year. But sometimes even that doesn't help, and the song never works. There's a lot of freedom now in writing songs. You don't have to follow the old thirty-two-bars-with-a-bridge pattern anymore. Songs can be any shape or length. They can be in sections or little movements. They can be a kind of string of ideas."

Two of the three accompanists Blossom Dearie had chosen for the industrial film—the reedman Hal McKusick and the bassist Jay Leonhart—were already at the recording studio and noodling away on opposite sides of the room. Blossom Dearie passed out lead sheets to them and sat down at the piano, which was wedged in a far corner of the studio. Only her pants legs and the blond top of her head were visible. The recording involved her playing and singing two choruses of Harold Milan's "Going Away." She ran through the tune once with McKusick, who played the melody on flute behind her. When she had finished, she peered at him over the sheet-music rack on the piano and said, "Does that sound right?"

"Very close," McKusick replied.

"All right, let's do it again," she said, in a commander-in-chief tone. "And maybe you should improvise behind me, Hal, instead of just doing the melody."

"I think I'll switch to the alto flute this time," McKusick said. "I brought it along because I suspect it will fit very well with your sound."

After the runthrough, Blossom Dearie said she was pleased with the alto flute, which has a smoky, enfolding timbre. She got up to greet her third sideman, the drummer Al Harewood. They embraced, and she laughed and told him the date would be heavy rock and roll. The A. & R. man, Gordon Highlander, appeared, and outlined to Blossom Dearie what he wanted in the first chorus—a medium tempo, quiet drums, and a strong beat. As soon as Harewood was ready, they played the tune again. Blossom Dearie's unamplified voice was being drowned out by her own accompaniment, and all hands put on headphones so that they could hear her. Two takes were made, and the second was played back. Her voice was sweet and exact, and the flute set it off like the ring around a rain moon. Two more takes were made, and Highlander said they had it.

"Take five minutes," Blossom Dearie ordered. She went up to the window of the control booth and, a little girl standing in front of a toyshop, said, "Have you got any tea or Danish in there?" There was no answer, so she went around the corner and into the booth. McKusick and Leonhart started a fast, light version of Charlie Parker's "Confirmation," and Harewood joined in, dropping contented bombs on his bass drum. The date resumed, but this time thirteen takes were needed before Highlander was satisfied. It was two-thirty. Blossom Dearie took down her musicians' addresses and filled out the necessary tax and union forms. McKusick told her how fine she sounded, and thanked her for the chance to work with her. He and Leonhart left together, and Harewood, after packing up his drums and embracing her again, followed.

"Al is a terrific drummer," she said, "I've worked off and on with him for years, and he can play any kind of drums. And with so much taste." Highlander reappeared and told Blossom Dearie that, after all, they would need some overdubbing—just the title of the song. She looked tired but nodded. She sat on a high stool in the middle of the studio, and, putting on headphones and raising her chin, sang five "Going Away"'s. Highlander asked her if she would sing them with a little more rubato. She did.

She took a cab to the Village, and said it would be nice to have some lunch. "I don't eat at night after work, but I do like a good lunch." She told the cab driver to stop at The Caffè da Alfredo, which is around the corner from the Village Vanguard. The Alfredo, which is on the parlor floor, looks out through big windows onto Seventh Avenue. It was crowded, and the only empty table was in the rear, "Oh," Blossom Dearie said. "I was hoping to sit right up front by a window, where there's lots of light and you can see everything. I hate sitting in the dark backs of places. I like light and sunshine and air." She sat down anyway, and then four people got up from a front table. "I'm going up there," she said. The table was loaded with glasses and dishes, and she asked the only waiter if she could move. He looked annoyed and shook his head. It appeared that she would sit there anyway. But all she did was let out a long "Well" and look at the menu. She ordered pea soup and a Niçoise salad.

"All I could think about up there in that studio was my mama. She passed away a while ago. In fact, I've just come back from the country, and tonight will be the first time I've worked in several weeks. My mother was in her late eighties, and she was a wonderful woman. She came over as a little girl from Oslo, where she was born. Her father was in the merchant marine, and she was raised by a grandmother. She married a rich man in New York, and they lived on West Twenty-second Street and had a house in the country—the same house she died in. It was a two-day trip in those days—up the Hudson by steamboat and twenty more miles by horse and buggy. After her husband died, she moved to the country for good. She met my father up there. When I think of my daddy—well, he was just one of those people who never seem to find their way, who never get into the niche meant for them in life. He was in the First World War, and then he was a bartender for the rest of his life. He was a lovely man. He was from Irish and Scottish parents. The name Dearie goes back in Scotland to the sixteenth century. People ask me over here if it's my real name, but everybody over there knows it. My daddy had the Irish wit— he could mimic anybody—and he was musically gifted. He could sing and dance, and he wanted to be in show business, but I guess he just didn't know how, and anyway he was not aggressive and was very much involved in his families. He had been married before, and both he and my mother had children in their earlier marriages. She had three boys, and he had one. I was their only child. It was he who named me. I was born in April, and the day I arrived a neighbor brought over some peach blossoms, and when my father saw them he said, 'That's it. We'll call her Blossom.' My mother liked Victor Herbert, but she wasn't musically inclined. She'd take me on her lap when I was two or three, and I'd pick out real tunes on the piano. I took my first piano lessons when I was five, from a Miss Parks, who lived three or four miles up the mountain. She taught me how to read. Later, I spent some time down in Washington with one of my brothers, and I studied there with a Mrs. Hill. For a year. She'd play Bach and Chopin, and if I liked it she'd tell me to learn the piece. Too many piano teachers force-feed their students. She wanted me to be a classical pianist, and thought I should study at the Peabody Conservatory, in Baltimore, when I got old enough. But I went back to the country, and I didn't study after that. I played with the high-school dance band, and I listened and listened—to Count Basie and Duke Ellington and Art Tatum. The first singer that made a real impression on me was Martha Tilton.

"After I graduated from high school, I came to New York. I had spent a little time here before, and I'd met Dave Lambert, the singer. It was the late forties, and I lived in a midtown hotel with a bunch of girl singers. I started to sing for the first time in New York. I hung out with Dave, and we rehearsed and talked a lot about singing. And I hung out in that basement apartment Gil Evans had on West Fifty-fifth. I don't know how he ever got anything done, because there were people there twenty-four hours a day. Charlie Parker lived there for a while, and you'd generally find Dizzy Gillespie and Miles Davis and Gerry Mulligan and John Lewis. Or George Handy would be there, or George Russell or Barry Galbraith or Lee Konitz. I'd go over to Fifty-second Street, and hear Bird and Diz." She hummed the most famous version of Charlie Parker's "Embraceable You" note for note—a feat, considering that it is also one of the most subtle and difficult improvisations ever recorded. "Then I began getting jobs around New York. I was in the Show Spot, which was underneath the Byline Room, where Mabel Mercer was singing. I played piano and sang and accompanied other singers. I still like to accompany friends who sing."

The salad arrived, and Blossom Dearie dug in. "In 1952, when I was working at the Chantilly, I met Nicole Barclay. She and her husband owned Barclay Records, and she asked me if I'd like to work in Paris. I said yes, and took the boat. I stayed with Nicole's grandmother and studied French at Berlitz. I worked in the Mars Club in Paris, and with Annie Ross at a club in London. I formed a group called the Blue Stars of Paris; the Swingle Singers eventually grew out of it. There were four boys and four girls. The boys played instruments and sang, and the girls just sang. We had Christiane Legrand, Michel's sister, and Bob Dorough, who was in Paris accompanying Sugar Ray Robinson. We had a hit record—'Lullaby of Birdland' sung in French. There was a marvellous ambience in Paris then, an easy, hanging-out-in-cafés ambience. Bud Powell was around, and so was Don Byas. I met Norman Granz, and he recorded me there. And I met my husband, Bobby Jaspar. He was playing flute and tenor saxophone where I was working, and we became friends right away. He came from a wealthy Belgian family, and he had a degree in chemistry and spoke three languages. His father was a well-known painter. We were married in Liège, in 1955, and came back here the following year and lived in the Village. He worked with Miles Davis and J. J. Johnson. Then we separated. He had a heart condition and became ill, and he died. It was all very sad.

"For the next several years, I worked around New York, at the Village Vanguard, opposite Miles Davis, who became a great friend, and the original Upstairs at the Downstairs. Then I heard the album of 'Beyond the Fringe,' with Dudley Moore and Peter Cook and Jonathan Miller and Alan Bennett, and I was crazy about it. I met Dudley Moore at the Vanguard one night when he was working there, and he asked me if I was English, and I said no, but that it was a great compliment that he had thought so. We talked until five in the morning at the Vanguard, and it was through Dudley that I eventually got back to England. The English audiences seemed to take me in and like me, and I've been going every year since.

In 1966, I started working for a month every summer at Ronnie Scott's club. The only thing I don't like about it is that the first show isn't until *eleven-thirty* and I don't finish until two. But I just sleep a little later in the morning to make up for it."

It was five o'clock. "Oh, my," Blossom Dearie said. "I'll just run home and get dressed and put on some makeup. I like to get to the club real early."

A Living, Breathing, Flexible Thing

Carol Sloane

Carol Sloane is short and broad-shouldered. Her hair is light-colored and bouffant, and she has a strong, slightly beaked nose. Her eyes are wide and ready for anything. She has stubby hands and tiny feet. She is cool about clothes and sometimes has a come-as-your-are look, even onstage. She performs easily. She sits on the edge of a stool and waves her microphone vaguely in front of her, bringing it closer when she wants to change dynamics. She talks to the audience as if it were made up of chums, and her singing is conversation put to music. She closes her eyes and tilts her head when she sings, sending her music just over her listeners' heads, so that it rains on them rather than beats against them, as is the case with many singers. The melodies that she invents constantly curve, and they move between her words, under her words, over them. So her diction sometimes sounds careless and a little unclear, but it doesn't matter. She has made a new *song,* and we know the gist of most of the words she sings. She talked one afternoon in the West Side living room of her friend Richard Rodney Bennett, the English composer, arranger, and pianist.

She said, "To my way of thinking, Louis Armstrong is the best male singer and Carmen McRae is the best female singer. When I first heard her, the light broke. That diction, that intonation, that edge of salt in her voice. She sounded *human.* She sounded like she could make a mistake— where Ella Fitzgerald and Sarah Vaughan never did. When I watch her sing, I take notes. She's a teacher. Sometimes she calls me and complains about the room she's singing in, or the dressing room, or the manager, and I just laugh, I'm so pleased to hear her. Jazz singing is a living, brea-thing, flexible thing. The same song should change every night. I love to sing Duke Ellington. I think, Can I get those fat Johnny Hodges sounds, those fat Ben Webster sounds? Can I swing them? I'd rather sing 'Prelude to a Kiss' or 'In a Sentimental Mood' or 'Sophisticated Lady' or 'Some-thing to Live For' than anything else. They're perfect songs.

"I've always sung. When I was fourteen, I got a job not far from where I lived, in Rhode Island, in one of Ed Drew's bands. He had bands all over southern New England. The band played at a big ballroom called the Rhodes-on-the-Pawtuxet. It was full of balconies and white latticework. I sang there every Wednesday and Saturday for scale, which was nine dol-lars and eighty cents a night. At first, I didn't know anything. The band used stock arrangements, and there were a lot of key changes. The first time I sang with them, the musicians modulated, and I went along in the same key, and they cracked up. I didn't even know what four bars or eight bars meant. I'd sit in my ruffles and petticoat at the end of the bandstand with the boy singer, and get up every once in a while and sing a song like 'Wheel of Fortune,' and pretend I was Kay Starr. My Uncle Joe would drive me over and back. After I'd been with Drew two years, a couple of local guys, Jim Howe and Jim O'Neill, asked me if I'd record a song they had written. Howe knew me because I had done some babysitting for him. We drove down to a studio in New York. The guitarist George Barnes was one of the accompanists and there were four singers ooh-aah-ing behind me. The song was called 'So Long,' and Howe and O'Neill filled my head with what a great future I had and how the recording would send me on my way. I listened to the radio constantly. I'd call disk jockeys and ask them about what they had played. Or I'd ask them if I could visit them and watch. One who said yes was Carl Henry. He also had a record shop—Carl's Diggins. It was in the black section of Provi-dence, and I bought Stan Kenton records there with the first money I earned with Ed Drew. Later, Carl would ask me when I came in, 'Have you ever heard Art Tatum?' Or 'Have you ever heard Ben Webster?' I began to take their recordings home, and I learned about improvisation. During high school, I got a job as a legal secretary in Providence, and when I was eighteen I married a disk jockey. What else? He's with WBZ in Boston now, and he's married for a third time. He got drafted after we were married, and we went to Germany. It was 1957. I touched base with the Special Services Club where we were stationed, and the first thing I was involved in was a hurry-up production of *Kiss Me, Kate*. A general who was about to be sent home asked if we could put together some sort of production of the musical, because it was his favorite show. We did. We made our costumes, and we painted the sets. Eventually, we took it all over Germany in an old school bus.

"We came back to the States at the end of the year, and I went to work for another law firm. We lived in Providence, on Waterman Street, not far from Brown University. I got a part-time job singing in a club in New Bedford, and one night this substantial-looking man came in and listened and gave me his card. His name was Bob Bonis, and he represented the Les and Larry Elgart band, which was playing at an amusement park in Fall River. Bonis asked if I'd go for an audition. There was no pianist, but Turk Van Lake was on guitar. I decided on ' 'S Wonderful,' in the key of G. I set a very fast tempo, and the musicians gave me a this-will-put-her-in-the-soup look. But I did it, and Larry Elgart said he'd like to take me on the road with the band. My marriage was breaking up, so I agreed, and stayed two years. I was born Carol Morvan, but I was calling myself Carol Vann. Larry didn't like the name, and he'd introduce me as Carol Rogers or Carol Price, or something like that. Finally, he hit on Carol Sloane. I left the band in 1960 in New York. The singer Jon Hendricks, of the vocal trio Lambert, Hendricks, and Ross, wanted to know if I would be able to fill in for Annie Ross should the occasion arise. I said yes, but I knew how complicated their work was, so I bought all their records and studied them. Then I got a call from Pep's, a night club in Philadelphia, saying the trio needed me. I rode down on the train with Jon Hendricks' brother Jim, and all he did was ask me if I knew this tune or that tune the group did, and by the time I got there I was having fits. There was no rehearsal, and the first number was Duke Ellington's 'Cottontail,' very fast. I got through it, and I worked on and off with the trio for a year. Early in 1961, Max Gordon offered me two weeks opposite Oscar Peterson at the Village Vanguard, and I almost fainted. Oscar was the first jazz musician I had ever seen in the flesh. It was at the Celebrity Club in Providence, and they let a bunch of us underage kids in and put us in a corner. Oscar did a marvellous thing for me at the Vanguard. Every night, he would ask me to sing Kurt Weill's 'My Ship.' I had been doing fancy things to that heavy, beautiful song, but I slowly began to relax, and by the time my gig was almost over I was doing the song as it should be done, and Oscar was smiling. I also did the pop festival that replaced the jazz festival in Newport that year. I was part of a group of new stars. The new stars all stayed on too long, and by the time I came out everybody was starting to leave. I wanted to do 'Little Girl Blue,' but my piano player didn't know the verse, so I sang the verse by myself, and people turned around, and I got a terrific reaction when the song was over.

"I recorded for Columbia later that year, and things took off. I did the hungry i in San Francisco and Mister Kelly's in Chicago and the Blue Angel in New York. I did Arthur Godfrey's radio show. I worked with people like Stiller and Meara, and Woody Allen, and Bill Cosby, and Godfrey Cambridge, and Lenny Bruce, and Richard Pryor. I had a lot of work in the sixties, but it began to taper off around 1968. I took to writing record reviews for *down beat*, and I sang once in a while at the old Half Note. The trombonist Bob Brookmeyer and I became very close. Then he moved to California. I had a miserable time. I was broke, and I wanted to get out. It wasn't a good time for singers in New York. I got an offer from a new club in Raleigh, North Carolina, named the Frog and Nightgown, and I went for a week. I couldn't believe it. It was winter in New York, but it was balmy and beautiful down there. People said hello in the elevators. I gave up my apartment in New York and moved to Raleigh in April. I found a job in the law offices of ex-governor Terry Sanford, and I worked there seven years. I also sang off and on at the Frog, which was owned by Peter Ingram, who had a Ph.D. in biochemistry and was a drummer. The Frog closed in 1975, and I put out my first record since 1962. Gil Wiest, of Michael's Pub, heard it on Jonathan Schwartz's radio show and offered me a couple of weeks at the Pub. I was so excited it was terribly hard to control my energy. Everything I did seemed to fly away.

"One night after work, George Mraz, my bass player, said, 'You better come to Bradley's to hear Jimmy Rowles'—he said 'Rowles' as if it had a row, a fight, in it. I knew who Jimmy was, but I had never heard him live. I went down every night, and I met him, and we fell in love. We moved into an apartment in SoHo, and we were together almost four years. Many singers think Jimmy is the best accompanist in the business, so there must have been a lot of jealousy among them—'Boy, I bet she sings with him every day.' Actually, we only worked together three or four times, and he only played for me once or twice at home. After a while, I began worrying about his drinking and his emphysema, which had just been diagnosed. Jimmy worried about himself, but in strange ways. To save breath when he went upstairs, he'd go up backward, a step at a time, even though he was probably using twice as much breath and strength doing it that way. Then Norman Granz asked him if he would accompany Ella Fitzgerald. I thought it would be good for him, that it would keep him closer to the straight and narrow. And it did for a time. I toured with them twice, and I never saw him when he couldn't find the piano. He was with her two years. Jimmy's destructive side was beginning to spill over on me. When I found myself pouring a drink first thing in the morning, I knew things were getting bad. I had gained a lot of weight, and I was looking ugly. We broke up, and I moved in with some friends in Brookline, near Boston.

"The first business day of 1981, I began looking for a job and was offered one in a law firm where all the lawyers sat in wing chairs. I told them I couldn't start for a couple of weeks, because I had a commitment to sing in a new club a friend had opened in Chapel Hill. The same thing happened to me when I got down there that had happened in the late sixties. It was balmy and beautiful, and everybody said good morning in the elevators. The new club was the handsomest night club I had ever seen. The owner wanted to make me the artistic director, and I had to tell the Boston people I couldn't take the job. I called Jackie Cain and Roy Kral, and Joe Williams, and Carmen McRae, and George Shearing. Then I discovered, the club owner was terribly in debt, and the whole wonderful thing fell through. In 1982, I started my own radio show. I played records by singers, and I talked about them. I'd do an hour of Mark Murphy, or Helen Humes, or George Shearing and Mel Tormé, or Mabel Mercer and Bobby Short. But slowly a sense of failure took me over, and in the summer of 1985 I hit bottom. I had no money. My phone was cut off. The bank took my car. I knew the electricity would be next, and I had no idea how I would pay my rent. A powerful thought came to me one Friday night: I want to live. I very much want to live. I picked up the phone and, miraculously, the dial tone came on, and before they cut it off again I started calling clubs where I had worked. I had forgotten that if you don't do things for yourself no one will do them for you. I've worked ever since, and I've moved back to Boston. I got married in 1986. My husband is the entertainment director for a big chain of motels in the Boston area. He's supportive, and he's honest. He's been married before and has grown kids. Now I'm near my family in Rhode Island, and I go to Fenway Park, and I'm tuned in to the Celtics.

"I grew up surrounded by a sense of family. I was born in Providence in 1937, and I have a sister, Lois, who's two years younger. My parents are Canadian-French. My mother's family was from Halifax, but she was born in Rhode Island. My father was born in Manchaug, Massachusetts, a few miles from the Rhode Island border. They were from large families. We lived in Georgiaville, about twelve miles north of Providence, and my parents worked in a textile mill in Esmond, which was a couple of miles from us and was famous for its blankets. My father's name is Frank Morvan. He's a simple man with twinkly eyes and a great smile, and he's got an Indian nose—like the face on the old nickel. He always looks as if he's about to tell you a joke. He likes the Red Sox, and a cold beer on a hot summer day, and the *National Geographic*. He used to bring home Glenn Miller and Johnny Desmond and Frank Sinatra records and sing along with them in a sweet voice. Sometimes I'd stand on his feet and he'd dance me around the room. He's seventy-six and fragile, and he hears what he wants to hear. He and my mother have moved to a little house in a town up near the Massachusetts border. It's immaculately maintained—everything inside and out just so. My sister lives next door. My mother's name was Claudia Rainville. She's seventy-nine. She's round-faced and petite and a live wire. She wanted to be a writer, but she was the oldest of nine and had to quit school to take care of her brothers and sisters. She couldn't get away to marry my father until she was twenty-eight. She loves politics. She loves to laugh. She loves to write letters. She's had a couple of pen pals from New Zealand and Japan since she was a teen-ager. During the Second World War, she would send my father in to Providence to the U.S.O. to pick up as many soldiers as the car would hold and bring them back to our house for a meal. Now she volunteers at the library and listens to talk shows.

"We grew up in a house that had a barn and four huge shade trees and was near a lake. My grandmother and two aunts lived in three houses down the hill from us. My grandmother was always there if we wanted to stop in after school. A lot of summer Sundays, the whole family would assemble at our house for a barbecue. There would be horseshoe pitching, and when the sun went down and the fireflies came out and the kids quit running around and were leaning against their mothers Uncle Charlie would tune up his ukulele, and everybody would sing 'On Moonlight Bay' and 'Shine On Harvest Moon.' Most of us sang in the church choir, and there were a lot of good natural voices and some good harmony. When Lois and I were around eight and ten, we decided to repaint our old 1942 Chevy, which was a hideous green. Our parents were at work, and we took some black paint and brushes and started on a front fender. We had just about finished it when they arrived home. They took one look, fell down laughing, and joined in. That's the kind of great childhood we had. It was also a reading one. I spent a whole summer on the screened porch reading Nancy Drew, and later there was Keats and Conan Doyle and Ibsen. My mother never took a book away, never said a book was too old. I went to parochial grammar school, even though I could have walked to public school. But I learned to diagram sentences, and I learned to spell, and I have pretty handwriting. I switched to public high school after one year of parochial high school, and I mastered Gregg's shorthand. I was sorry I never finished parochial high school. The freshmen wore green ribbons on their uniforms and the sophomores wore blue, but the seniors had beautiful red ones."

Betty Bebop

Betty Carter

Alec Wilder was a passionate listener, and he used to turn his head and shut his eyes at musical performances. He even did this when he listened to recordings. He once explained why: "I discovered a long time ago that the human eye and the human ear are constantly at war—that when you're listening *and* looking your eyes win out. That's why musical audiences tend to 'listen' with their eyes, thereby missing most of what they came to hear. The only way I can listen to music properly is with my eyes closed—as rude as it might appear to the performers onstage." Wilder would have been surprised by the surrealist jazz singer Betty Carter, for she must be seen to be heard. Her onstage presence—a kaleidoscopic series of facial expressions and Martha Graham plunges and slides and arabesques—is a visual extension of her singing. It is sound made three-dimensional. She forces her audience to look and listen with equal intensity, and it is an almost cathartic experience: eyes and ears are sated. Betty Carter comes in four consummate and indivisible parts—clothes, face, body, singing. In a large hall, she will wear a white snood or turban, a gold lamé caftan, and white silk pants. On television, she will wear a multicolored fillet and a three-quarter-length pale-red silk dress with a loose décolleté top. On the street, she will wear a white silk blouse, a chocolate cotton skirt, boots, a long tan coat, and a brown fedora, its crown rounded and its brim down. Her clothes are handsome vessels that set off her singing and her motions and her extraordinary face. She has a wide mouth, and large eyes that tip up at their outer ends. Her teeth are square and very white, like Louis Armstrong's. She has a ski-jump nose and freckles and small, pretty ears. Hers is a rubber face, an actress's face, and it is almost never still. Smiles slide in and out of grimaces. Her eyes close slowly, then suddenly pop open. Her eyes close suddenly and her eyebrows shoot up. Her lips pout and her chin sinks stubbornly into her neck—naughty-child fashion. She is a lithe, medium-sized woman who moves weightlessly. She calls to mind the encomium that tap dancers used to lavish on one another after a particularly fine performance: "I saw you dance tonight, man, and you never touched the floor."

Betty Carter begins a song standing slightly stooped, with the microphone in her right hand, and her right leg slightly crooked. Her left arm is horizontal, and her left hand is just so—the thumb cocked, the index finger and the little finger out straight, and the middle fingers folded flat. At the end of her first eight bars, she slowly lowers the left hand, keeping the thumb cocked, and, in an unbroken motion, sways back and forth, turns, and straightens, so that she is facing to her right. A smile moves across her face and becomes a grimace. The bridge of the song begins, and she swings her head back and forth to emphasize the words. Her brow furrows, her eyes shut, then open, and she looks sharply over her left shoulder. She shifts the microphone to her left hand, puts her right hand on her right hip, and swings her head until it is directly over her right arm—Egyptian queen. Midway through the last eight bars, she hunches her shoulders, looks forward and down, and, shutting her eyes, moves her head up and down in half time. She abruptly raises her right hand and chops it to stop the rhythm section, and goes into a coda. Her eyes flash and slowly close, and she drops into sotto voce. She purses her lips and lowers her chin into her neck. Her voice sinks into its lowest register. Her eyebrows go up, her forehead wrinkles, her right hand comes to rest on her right hip, the fingers splayed. She holds this pose and falls silent (her chin still sunk, her face contorted). The drummer hits a rimshot, and the pianist goes into a fast tempo. Her head snaps up, and she smiles brilliantly, and bows. Only half of Betty Carter comes through on recordings. More comes through in concert halls and night clubs. But the best place to watch and hear her is on television. She makes the medium exhilarating.

Betty Carter lives in three floors of a brownstone, which she owns, near the Brooklyn Academy of Music. Her seventeen-year-old son, Kagle, is in high school and lives with her, and her twenty-two-year-old son, Myles, is studying communications at C. W. Post College, in Brookville, Long Island. She talked about herself one day in Brooklyn. Her voice has a contralto tint, and she talks in gusts. A sentence will come out tight and fast, loosen into everyday speech, and balloon into a shout. The shout falls into silence, and she laughs—a round, tumbling arpeggio—and explodes again. There is no pretense about her.

"People are always talking about my age, so there's no secrets about it," she said. "I was born Lillie Mae Jones, on May 16, 1929. We lived on the west side of Detroit, but my mother went to Flint, to her sister's, to have me, because I was the first and she was scared. She stayed out there nine months, then went home. Later, when she had my sister Vivian and my brother James she stayed home. They're still in Detroit. James is a sheriff, and Vivian works in a hospital. My mother's name was Bertha Cox, and she was born in Arkansas. I don't think she was a very happy woman. She was stocky and brown-skinned, and I resemble her. My father was James Jones, and he came from Arkansas, too. He and my mother were married there, before they moved to Detroit. He was about five foot eleven, and lean and fair and rather handsome. There were moments during the thirties when we were on welfare, but it never came to our being destitute. My father and mother both worked in defense plants during the war. Then, when I was fifteen, my father died, and we lived on his pension. My mother stayed sad a long time. There was no talking to her, no getting her out of it. She finally remarried and moved to Flint to be with her family and stayed there until she died. My parents were religious. My father was director of the senior choir in the church he belonged to. I played piano in church, and did some arranging. I think my father sensed something in me before he died, some gift, even though he didn't know quite what it was. My mother always looked down on what I did. Jazz music to her was a mortal sin. There was no 'Go get 'em, kid!' from her. When I was in high school, the word 'college' was never mentioned.

"By the time I got to Northwestern High, I was having my little ins with jazz music. There was a soda bar near school that had a jukebox, and we hung out there and listened to Charlie Parker and Dizzy Gillespie and Billie Holiday and Woody Herman. We learned the melodic lines of all the solos. We learned the changes. Bebop was the sound that was hitting the streets, and we were all on it. I had had a little piano training, and I had a pretty good ear, so I was the assembly person in school—playing selections up there before the program began. Everyone loved Avery Parrish's 'After Hours' and Eddie Heywood's version of 'Begin the Beguine,' and if you could play eight or ten bars into either of them you were a social success. When I was sixteen, I auditioned for the black amateur night they had every Wednesday at the Paradise Theatre. I sang 'The Man I Love,' and accompanied myself, and I won second prize. I did well enough for a couple of Detroit booking agents to pursue me for Sunday-afternoon cabarets and for appearances at the Elks Hall and at fashion shows. I was listening to singers. I liked Billie Holiday and respected her, but the music was headed toward a different level—toward Sarah Vaughan and Dinah Washington. I listened to Big Maybelle and to a Detroit singer named Alberta Adams, who nobody knows about. And there was a singer in my school, Rachel Babcock, who was better than I was. I had p-e-r-s-o-n-a-l-i-t-y, but she had a better voice. About that I never had any illusions. I couldn't have been a lead singer in church. Gospel singers have great pipes, and I'm weak in that department. I started working at night in clubs when I was seventeen. Cincinnati, Dayton, Lima—places like that. They hired singers for the weekend, and I'd work with a local trio. Then a boyfriend asked me to go hear Lionel Hampton's band, and the kids we went with told Hampton I was a singer. He said 'Do you sing, gates?'—which is what he called everybody—and I said yes. I did some scatting, and it worked out. His singer, Wini Brown, was leaving, and Hampton offered me a job. His wife, Gladys, travelled with the band, and she was my savior, my model. She used to sew for the movie stars—slips and underclothes, everything cut on the bias, which takes some skill. She was well dressed and well read, and she was a shrewd businesswoman. She was the force behind the band. Hampton and I fought a lot. He'd ask me whose band I liked best—his or Dizzy Gillespie's, which I loved. I'd tell him Gillespie, and because he was kind of jealous of Diz and Charlie Parker he'd tell me I couldn't sing that night, or he'd fire me and Gladys would rehire me. Because I loved Dizzy's music and because I was a scat singer, Hampton called me Betty Bebop. I had taken the name Lorraine Carter, since it sounded good, and, of course, what finally came out was Betty Carter. Hampton had Charlie Fowlkes and Benny Bailey and Milt Buckner and Charlie Mingus. Once, when we were playing the Strand Theatre in New York, Charlie Parker turned up and tried to put the touch on Hampton for fifty dollars. Hampton said, 'All right, gates, but you play a show for me.' He put Charlie Parker in the second-saxophone chair, and Parker borrowed an alto saxophone and did the show, reading all the parts and taking solos, and you never heard anything like the reaction in that band. All the soloists thought they were in heaven. They played *way* over their heads. That was the effect Charlie Parker always had. When word came that he was on the scene, musicians started *thinking* about what they were doing. Even Hamp was thinking that afternoon. I had met Charlie Parker once before, in Detroit. I was hanging around a club I sang at, waiting for him to rehearse with the chorus line. He was four hours late, and when he came in all he said was 'I'm hungry. Where can I get something to eat?' I was sitting at the end of the bar near the door, and I told him across the street. He grabbed my arm, and we went across the street and he ate a huge meal of soul food. At the rehearsal, it turned out that the girls couldn't dance to what he played, so there wasn't any chorus line that week."

Betty Carter is the last of a sixty-year succession of women singers who have moved American nonclassical singing from its relatively straightforward beginnings to its adventurous present. (The half-dozen or so great male jazz singers—Louis Armstrong, Jelly Roll Morton, Joe Turner, Jimmy Rushing, Jack Teagarden, Leo Watson—have helped, but they have been a minority.) Bessie Smith came first, and she was a jazz singer only in that she used blue notes and jazz timbres and had an elastic, swinging rhythmic sense. Billie Holiday picked up where Bessie Smith stopped. (She made her first recordings three days after Bessie Smith made her last.) She had listened to Bessie Smith and to Louis Armstrong, and she improvised almost constantly. The melodies she sang were recognizable, but she dropped notes, and she played hob with rhythm. She lifted each song out of its rhythmic frame and placed it within her own, which, alternately legato and on the beat, moved in its own graceful time zone. She and the tenor saxophonist Lester Young, loosening the stays of jazz rhythm, prepared the way for the beboppers. A host of admirers immediately appeared (they are still appearing), and the best was probably Anita O'Day. She moved closer to the sound and techniques of a horn player, sometimes letting her lyrics go by the board and singing in a brittle, jumping way. The earliest jazz players had been affected by the human voice, and now the circle closed: jazz singers imitated instruments, and out of Anita O'Day came such horn singers as Mavis Rivers, Annie Ross, Jackie Cain and Roy Kral, Sheila Jordan, Morgana King, and Betty Carter. (During the forties and fifties, Mahalia Jackson and Dorothy Love Coates headed a majestic group of women gospel singers. They did not consider themselves jazz singers, but, of course, they were, and out of them came Dinah Washington and Aretha Franklin.) Betty Carter is a shock at first hearing. She abstracts her songs. She converts her melodies into strangely shaped fragments made up of long-held notes, many of them bent; clusters of eighth notes; quick, diving arpeggios; and variety of hums and moans. Capacious silences often separate her phrases. The melody, viewed through the heavy scrim of her style, is sometimes there, sometimes not. She stretches time even father than Billie Holiday. She will sing a song like "Spring Can Really Hang You Up the Most" in a very slow tempo. This allows her to rocket in and out of double, and even triple, time, to wallow luxuriously along in the chosen tempo, and to engage in a kind of staccato parlando. Her voice is not big—she has about two and a half octaves—but, like Billie Holiday's, it does everything she asks of it. Her low register has a lot of room, and she can even manage a vibrato when she hits a low C. She has in recent years begun to scat-sing a great deal, and she has no match among the living—or, perhaps, among the dead. She has pulled just about even with the Joycean scat singer Leo Watson, whom she resembles but whom she says she has never heard. Most scat singing, as it has been developed in the past thirty years by Ella Fitzgerald and Jackie and Roy and Mel Tormé, is rubbery and one-dimensional. It is made up of "b"s and "d"s and "ooeeyop"s. It repels you—it fends you off. Once in a while, Betty Carter will scat non-stop for twenty or thirty minutes. She passes through half a dozen tempo changes, ranging from slow to very fast. She fashions beautiful slow passages of sounds that fall between hums and moans. She scats at top speed, using mostly vowels, and winding around and up and down with astonishing swiftness. And she drops into medium tempos, making her meaningless words loaf and sway and strut. Her scat singing has nothing to do with trying to jam the entire alphabet into each measure. It is an exercise in free-floating, free-associating melody.

Betty Carter is unique, and she proclaims it. She once told the jazz writer Michael Ullman, "In that time we dared not imitate. It wasn't easy for us as black people to imitate other great stars and make it. It didn't settle with us. A second Sarah Vaughan would never have the respect of the black community. In the white world, they imitated each other. Stan Getz had a lot of tenor players sounding like him, while he sounded like Lester Young. . . . There were never two Sarah Vaughans, or two Billie Holidays, or two Ella Fitzgeralds. Even in our dancing acts, we all strived to be our own person. That was my whole background, my whole foundation."

Betty Carter left Lionel Hampton in 1951. After a short stint at home, she settled in New York, moving into the Hotel America, on West Forty-seventh Street. "There was a lot of work uptown, at places like the Apollo," she said. "I spent much time there in the fifties and sixties, and at places like Wells' and Smalls' Paradise, and at the Baby Grand, here in Brooklyn. You could still walk safely on the streets and travel safely in the subways, and everybody had a good time working. Money didn't matter. It was the fun of being out there on the scene, digging all the singers and musicians and having them dig you. And the club owners were different. Some of them would go under rather than not have someone like me. The Showboat in Philadelphia—it's now called the Bijou—has always been like that, and I still work there twice a year. In 1956, I moved to an apartment in East Orange. I couldn't afford New York anymore, and I wanted a little distance between my singing and my personal life. I worked in Jersey in places like Teddy Powell's Lounge and the Key Club. I married a man named James Redding in 1960, and in 1965 we moved to Newark. The Beatles knocked us all for a loop in the sixties, but in 1969 I did manage to start my own record label, and I've done four albums so far. And I've started doing dates at white colleges, and in night clubs with mostly white audiences. I crossed over, and the reason is that black people are not supporting their own music. In the early seventies, I had a backup trio made up of Danny Mixon and Buster Williams and Louis Hayes. Danny inspired me on the energy level. I had left my husband, and I was down. Danny proved to me that I wasn't completely dead musically. His example told me I still had somewhere to go, and I even started writing tunes of my own, which I sing now. Things have been changing and growing ever since. I have a lot more confidence in me. People might say 'Who's that?' when I go on a network television show, but I've made it musically and I'm doing all right monetarily. I'm getting on, and I'm preparing myself to survive. If you really care, if you really love your music, you can't help but improve. Everything I do now has just evolved naturally. I've learned there's an intelligence line that makes you able to communicate with your audience and still maintain your integrity. I don't look at the television shows I've done, and I don't listen to my records. If I did, I'd run the danger of imitating things I might like about what I do. I don't want anything planned. I want everything fresh and new. I want what comes out in my singing to be the result of my whole personality. Each time I sing a song, I sing it differently. I hear the chords in my head, but not the melody. That's left behind. The young kids I sing for now, a lot of them have never heard the songs I sing, so the melody means nothing, and the older folks know the melody and don't need to hear it again. They can hum 'The Trolley Song' and 'Can't We Be Friends?' and 'My Favorite Things' and 'Everything I Have Is Yours' without my help. I'm trying to make my lyrics clear. I *want* people to understand what I'm singing, and I think you can if you listen closely. I know that some of the composers I sing don't like what I do with their songs, but the songs are full of available music. They're full of inventions if you have the ear. If you don't do anything but sing the melody straight, how can you improve it?"

New American Songs

Dave Frishberg

It no longer matters whether you describe Dave Frishberg as a songwriter, a pianist, or a singer. All three skills have become indivisible. Indeed, he has become a Blakean cottage industry. First, he thinks of a song title. Then, in the course of a month or two, he writes the lyrics and the enclothing melody, usually concurrently. He performs the song publicly, and if both he and the public like it he records it, often supplying his own liner notes. Last, his publishing firm prints the song. Frishberg started as a pianist. He talked in the mid-eighties about his beginnings. He was sitting in his music room—a high-ceilinged converted garage, furnished with a grand piano, a word processor, a flat-topped oak desk, a sofa and several chairs, a huge Sempé poster, and a floor-to-ceiling wall of books, records, and tapes. The music room was part of a one-story wooden California house, built forty years ago in the San Fernando Valley. The house wandered to the right and left as you entered, and had three bedrooms, a split-level living room, a kitchen, a new enclosed back porch, and a skirting back yard. The living room contained a small collection of baseball memorabilia and of early Robert Benchley books. Most of the baseball artifacts were in a glass cabinet, and they included "Babe Ruth's Own Book of Baseball" (1928); two books by Christy Mathewson, "Pitching in a Pinch" (1912) and "Won in the Ninth" (1910), which is "the first of a series of stories for boys on sports to be known as the Matty books;" and a 1911 copy of *Baseball Magazine*, with an article by one Richard W. Lardner on the first baseman Frank Chance, which Frishberg believes may be Ring Lardner's first magazine piece. On the opposite side of the room, on top of an upright piano, were his Benchleys, among them "The Early Worm," "Of All Things," and "Love Conquers All." Frishberg mentioned that he might seem jumpy, because he was trying to quit smoking a second time, having stopped the first time for eight years.

"I was born in St. Paul, Minnesota, on March 23, 1933," he said. "I was the youngest of four children—three boys and a girl. We all get on. Miriam lives in Seal Beach out here, Arnold's in St. Paul, and Morton's in Minneapolis. My father, Harry Frishberg, came over from Russia during the pogroms. He sold Philco radios in Minnesota and the Dakotas, and he was apparently a world-champion salesman. But he gave up the road around the time of the Second World War and went into the retail clothing business in St. Paul. When I got to know him a little, he was already in his fifties and getting portly, but he was still handsome and had a lot of charm. From the first, I knew he was considered to be very funny. People always laughed when Harry was around. Legitimate music was his thing. He sang in the temple, and he loved cantorial music. I never saw things his way musically, and he never saw things my way. The first time he heard me play professionally was in 1960, when I was Carmen McRae's accompanist. He was amazed. He had no idea I had any sort of profound skills. It had always been 'This piano playing is very nice, but when are you going to do something serious?' My mother was Sarah Cohen. She was from St. Paul. She had snapping brown eyes, and she was waspish and had a tongue on her. She was a good critic of life. She not only cooked; she kept the books at my father's store. She was a little woman, and she must have had a nice figure when she was young.

"I was eight or nine when I started playing piano. My sister and my brothers had left home, and I was a child by myself. My parents enrolled me with a classical teacher. I didn't like it, but I could tell I had natural ability. I learned the simpler Mozart and Schumann pieces. Then one day I put a Mozart piece into conga rhythm—da da da-dum, da da da-dum. I played it at my lesson, and I was bawled out. I couldn't believe that doing such a thing was wrong, so I quit practicing, and eased out of the lessons. My father was so upset he sold our grand piano. Later, he relented and bought a Kimball upright. By this time, I was listening to the blues and boogie-woogie pianists—Pete Johnson and Jay McShann and Albert Ammons. I used to play some of their stuff for Jimmy Rushing years later, and he'd call me "Home." Our house was rich with records. We had *Pinafore* and *Iolanthe* and *The Mikado* which I loved and studied endlessly. I also listened to the Goodman small groups and to Count Basie—and to Frankie Carle, who killed me. I was an insufferable purist. When I was fifteen or sixteen, I met a piano player named Jimmy Mulcrone. He gave me lessons Saturday mornings for five or ten dollars. I could play in C, F, or G. He showed me the minor-seventh chord, and a whole new musical universe opened up to me. 'That chord doesn't sound like Joe Sullivan, does it?' I'd say to him, and he'd say, 'No, it doesn't.' He'd make me practice a tune like 'Just You, Just Me' in five keys. He got me listening to bebop. By the time I was a junior in high school, I'd found other kids who liked bop, and we formed a band. My first decent job was in the house trio at the Flame in St. Paul in the early fifties. When I started, the main act was the Art Tatum Trio, with John Collins on guitar and Slam Stewart on bass. Collins lives out here, and I see him every so often, and for some reason he still remembers that gig and me playing there. Billie Holiday came through, probably with Bobby Tucker on piano, and so did Johnny Hodges' little band, with Lawrence Brown and Emmett Berry and John Coltrane.

"I went to the University of Minnesota and majored in journalism. To be a music major, you had to play an instrument, classically, and that wouldn't have worked for me. So I took every music elective I could—orchestration, counterpoint, theory. I learned to deal with written music, to write it, although I didn't become a good sight reader until later. I didn't think I'd be a professional pianist. I thought I'd be a columnist. I guess at the time I had bought my dad's philosophy that music is fun, not a job. Then I heard Jimmy Rowles on those Woody Herman Columbia small-band sides—'Pam' and 'Steps' and 'Igor' and 'Fan It'—and it was the best jazz-ensemble piano playing I had ever heard. I had never heard anyone bend notes on the piano, and he had a way of rolling a chord, of clouding a chord, and of constructing these skipping melodic lines. I wanted very much to sound like Rowles. A bell rang inside me: You better be a professional piano player."

Frishberg the pianist is an unclassifiable creation. The blues pianists he once aped lie at the bottom of his style, particularly in his strong basso-profundo left hand. A level or two up are traces of Fats Waller, Jess Stacy, and Earl Hines. Art Tatum comes and goes on the next level, and so does Nat Cole. At the top, like a meadow sprinkled with rare wildflowers, is Jimmy Rowles. Frishberg's singing, pitched in the low tenor register, is bold, declarative, and unencumbered by such trappings as vibrato, chest tones, and dynamics. It is the kind of utilitarian singing that was meant to get lyrics across to the listener as pleasantly and clearly as possible. When Frishberg sings, the words file by, face you long enough to sink in, and move on. Most singer-pianists skimp on their piano playing (Blossom Dearie doesn't, and neither does Shirley Horn), but Frishberg is a superb self-accompanist and a good soloist. He swings constantly, and he has learned Jimmy Rowles' trick of surreptitiously squeezing odd single notes and offbeat chords into the cracks between a singer's words. Frishberg is of medium height and size—he could lie under his grand piano and keep dry—and he has a strong, many-planed face. His mother's snapping brown eyes shine like headlights through his metal-frame glasses, and he has a vigorous Roman nose, a wide mouth, and a leading chin. His brown hair is loose and plentiful over his ears but is receding between. He smiles a great deal when he talks, and he talks carefully.

Frishberg got up and went into the kitchen for a cup of tea. Just as he returned, his wife, Sam, entered the music room from an outside door, her arms full of groceries. She is a pretty, cheerful brunette, who was born Cynthia Wagman and nicknamed Sam. Frishberg went out and brought in more bags, and Sam asked him what kind of sandwich he'd like for lunch. He said Swiss and salami on rye, and she said it would be ready in a little while. He sat down and, in the way of new ex-smokers, tried to find things for his hands to do. Then he described the circuitous route he had taken from St. Paul to California. "I graduated from the University of Minnesota in 1955. I had joined the Air Force R.O.T.C., and part of the deal was that you had to go into the service for two years. I was stationed in Salt Lake City. I had a lot of spare time, and I helped start a little company called Notable Ads, and we made jingles. We had a cadre of local musicians and a vocal group. I stared writing music and lyrics. I must have done fifty jingles. I had already decided that I would go to one coast or the other when I was discharged, so I went to New York and got a job at WNEW, writing continuity and spot announcements. The station still had live music, and I spent most of my time with the musicians or copying out arrangements for them in my office. At night, I was a wild man, making every loft and sitting in. I was at WNEW for about six months, then with RCA for six months. I wrote promotional material there. I also got a job as solo pianist at the Duplex, on Grove Street. There was an upstairs and a downstairs, and at first I was downstairs, playing a piano with sixty-six keys. The upstairs had theatrical singers and comics, and pretty soon I was doing the show upstairs, too. So I worked without a break from nine to four every night, for seventy-five dollars a week. I had an apartment on Greenwich Street, and I felt I was really sailing. I stayed at the Duplex several months, then went on the road with Kai Winding and his four trombones. When that trombone sound got to me, I went on the road for a year with Carmen McRae. When that got to me, I went back to New York and began working at Eddie Condon's, which was downstairs in the Sutton Hotel, on East Fifty-sixth Street. I also played at the Metropole, on Seventh Avenue. I made a lot of connections with the older musicians. I liked them, and I began to find myself immersed in their music. I played with Bud Freeman and Pee Wee Russell and Rex Stewart and Buck Clayton and Wild Bill Davison. In 1962, I worked with Ben Webster at the Shalimar, in Harlem. Richard Davis was on bass and Mel Lewis on drums. We also played at the Vanguard and Birdland and the Half Note. By the time I knew Ben, he was in his mid-fifties, and the fabled brawler had disappeared. He was just an excessively sentimental guy. He cried every time he mentioned his mother. But he really took charge on the bandstand. He never told us outright what he wanted to play. He'd hum a bar and start, or he'd just go 'BLAM! BLAM!' and we were supposed to know what he was going to do. I made some mistakes at first, but after a week or so I learned to translate the hums and blams. When we were at the Shalimar, Ben took us to a little grocery store next door, and we'd hang out there between sets. The man who owned it told us that if we ever needed to hide we would find a home in his store. I had no idea what he was talking about, but a couple of months later, when we were with Ben down at the Half Note, the riots broke out in Harlem. Ben cried when he heard about them. Musicians came in to hear Ben all the time, and people like Billy Strayhorn and Johnny Hodges and Paul Gonsalves would sit in. Al Cohn and Zoot Sims came in, too, and they listened to me and asked me to join their band. There was nothing in the world I wanted to do more. Eventually, we became the house band at the Half Note, and we worked there off and on for four or five years. But I did a lot of things in the sixties besides play jazz choruses. I went on the road with Odetta. I conducted for Dick Haymes and Fran Jeffries. I conducted for a country-and-Western singer named Johnny Tillotson. I played with various rehearsal bands. All in all, I think I played the piano somewhere every night for fifteen straight years. In 1971, I was hired to write funny songs for a weekly television show called 'The Funny Side,' with Gene Kelly as its host. I had put out an album called 'Oklahoma Toad' that had some of my songs on it, and the producers of 'Funny Side' had heard it and wanted me. The show was produced in Los Angeles, so I moved out here."

Sam summoned Frishberg to lunch. She talked about her first child, which was due in a couple of months. Sam said she hoped that their German shepherd, Bix, wouldn't be jealous of the baby. Bix came in from the porch and stood in the living room like a pony. Frishberg started his sandwich, then put it down and said that on his most recent trip to New York he had ordered a club sandwich at the Carnegie Delicatessen that turned out to be about a foot and a half high. He told the waiter it was a vulgar sandwich, and asked him how he was supposed to eat it. The waiter suggested he take it apart. Frishberg said it wouldn't be a sandwich anymore. The waiter shrugged, and Frishberg told him to take the sandwich away, and he left in what he said was "a cold fury." Sam said they were thinking of moving—maybe to Oregon, maybe to Minnesota. Frishberg nodded, and said he didn't want their child to be a child of the freeways. (The baby was a boy—Harry Nicholas—and in the summer of 1986 the Frishbergs moved to Portland, Oregon.) Frishberg thanked Sam for lunch and went back to the music room. He talked about songs.

"When I was at the Duplex, I became aware of the great world of songs," he said. "I found myself looking analytically at these songs as pieces of art, instead of as vehicles, which is what they generally are for the jazz improviser. I'd listen by the hour to Bob Corwin, the intermission pianist at Condon's. He knew a million tunes, and he wrote music, and I began to write lyrics to his songs. I started thinking about being a song-writer. I met Johnny Mercer through Corwin, and Mercer introduced me to Bob Dorough, who's a deep musician. I met Blossom Dearie. They became my songwriting friends. Dorough and I wrote one song together—'I'm Hip.' I wrote 'Peel Me a Grape' for Dick Haymes and Fran Jeffries in 1962. I sent 'Wallflower Lonely, Cornflower Blue' to Frank Loesser, and he called me in and talked to me for a couple of hours, show-ing me what was right with the song, what was wrong. For me, it was like talking to Babe Ruth. There was dignity in everything Loesser wrote—no cheap lines, no cheap rhymes. He made the vernacular classy. I loved *Guys and Dolls* and *How to Succeed*. Each of his shows had its own personality, and I think he got better and better. Anyway, six different recordings were made of 'Peel Me a Grape' in the first few years after it was published, and I thought, This songwriting business is a snap—you just write a song and it's recorded all over, and in come the royalites. But none of my songs were recorded again by anyone but Blossom for eight years. I had been singing privately for quite a while, and I didn't sing in front of people until I was out here and doing gigs with Jack Sheldon, the trumpet player, who would suddenly announce, 'And now Dave Frish-berg will sing you one of his songs,' and I would. I began to sing regularly in public, and got a good response. In 1977, I opened a Bing Crosby show in front of six thousand people at the Concord Pavilion, in northern Cal-ifornia. Bing was one of my heroes, and when I came off he shook my hand and said I had done a good job, and I was on air. During his part of the show, which was a medley of forty of his biggest hits, the sound went off, and he gave one of the great exhibitions of professionalism. He just stood there, his hands at his sides. He didn't make any wisecracks, he didn't put anybody down. By sheer force of personality, he quieted the audience and held them in silence for the five minutes it took to get the sound back. It was only when he came off the stage after the show that he blew up.

"After 'The Funny Side,' I worked in the studios doing jingles and mov-ies. I was either bored or panicked. I'd talk to myself about it: 'You don't enjoy this. You're not temperamentally suited to it. You're not even a good sight reader.' Besides gigs with Jack Sheldon, I worked with Joe Pass and Bill Berry and Irene Kral, and I spent two wonderful, funny, first-class-all-the-way years with Herb Alpert and the Tijuana Brass. The time of the Crosby show was when I began to appear with my own trio and sing my own stuff. All along, I had been writing songs for other people. Now I began to write for myself, with my own voice in mind. Then I took jobs as a solo singer and pianist, which is where I am now. I'm on the road three or four months of the year, and the rest of the time I try to work locally."

Frishberg's songs, like his piano playing, are multilayered. One can find Sir William Gilbert in them, and Hoagy Carmichael and Johnny Mercer and Frank Loesser. But only in small amounts. They are new American songs. Some are extremely witty, some are extremely funny. Some are fits of nostalgia. Some are lamentations. Some are cautionary. Some are highly satirical. Some are love songs in disguise. Frishberg's lyrics drive his songs, but his melodies are their wheels. (Melodies by others that Frishberg has put words to rarely work as well as his own songs.) Most song lyrics die on the page, like sails without wind. But Frishberg's generally don't. Here is the second stanza of "Blizzard of Lies," a hilarious catalogue of the awful fibs we pass off on each other every day:

> You may have won a prize,
> Won't wrinkle, shrink or peel,
> Your secret's safe with me,
> This is a real good deal.
> It's finger lickin' good,
> Strictly by the book,
> What's fair is fair,
> I'll be right there,
> I am not a crook.
>   Marooned, marooned, marooned
>   In a blizzard of lies.

His early, brilliant "Peel Me a Grape," which has long been one of Blossom Dearie's anthems, laughs at social ennui in the seventies and eighties in the way that Cole Porter laughed at it in the thirties:

> Peel me a grape, crush me some ice,
> Skin me a peach, save the fuzz for my pillow,
> Start me a smoke, talk to me nice,
> You gotta wine me and dine me,
> Don't try and fool me, bejewel me,
> Either amuse me or lose me,
> I'm gettin' hungry—peel me a grape.

"Van Lingle Mungo" is simply a list of older baseball players' names set to a loose Brazilian rhythm. It has no verbs or adjectives or adverbs. It has no story, no moral. But the way the words are stretched or telescoped, the way the melody is speeded up or slowed down, as in the mournful two-note "Mun-go," gives the song the motion and weight of a good standard ballad. It becomes a kind of cheerful threnody.

"Sweet Kentucky Ham" is both a love song and a dirge about the sorrow and longueurs of being on the road:

> It's ten P.M.
> They're rolling up the
> sidewalks in Milwaukee,
> And the only place to eat
> Is just across the street.
> So you sit there with a bowl of navy bean,
> And you turn the pages of your magazine,
> And you feel you want to quit while you're
> behind—
> 'Cause you've got sweet
> Kentucky ham on your mind, on your mind,
> Nothing but sweet Kentucky ham on your mind.

"Slappin' the Cakes on Me" is built around an expression given Frishberg by Sam, who was born in Kentucky. A girl who slaps cakes on a boy is one step ahead of him—already knows his line, and is making a fool of him in the kindest way:

> I was mute, I was mum,
> I was trying not to look too dumb.
> I said, "I certainly hope you won't misconstrue.
> But perhaps we could have a little drink or two."
> I said, "What's your pleasure?" She said, "Guys like you."
> She was slappin' the cakes on me, my friend.

"Dear Bix" is addressed to the legendary cornettist Bix Biederbecke, who died of alcoholism at twenty-eight in 1931. It is addressed to him as if he were still alive, and, cognizant of his problems with drink and of his various aesthetic frustrations, it wishes him well and cheers him on. It is full of affection and gentleness. In its strange way, the song steps completely around time. This is how it ends:

> I wonder, Bix old chum,
> When you reminisce in years to come,
> Will you ever hum that someday song
> You've been looking so long to find?
> So, do what you got to do—
> And may the years be good to you—
> 'Cause you're one of the favored few,
> Dear Bix, you're one of a kind.

Frishberg had had a beer with lunch, and he got himself another. Then he talked about songwriting and about songwriters he admires. "I've written a hundred or more songs, and recorded about forty of them," he said. "A lot of them are just lying there. They're finished, but I don't think they'll be used again. I don't have any regular work pattern. I'm not a workaholic, although I wish I were. It's easier to write songs to order than for myself. 'My Attorney, Bernie' was written for a friend who was celebrating twenty-five years as a lawyer. 'Listen Here' was done for Mary Tyler Moore. 'Dodger Blue' was written for the Dodgers, and tears came down Walt Alston's cheeks when he heard it. I'll write a song a month in a hot year, and four or five songs in a cold year. I work at the piano, and I start with the title. Then I think of a lyric premise that will fit the title. I try to figure out how the song will end, where the payoff—which is generally near the end—will be. The music comes along with the lyrics. I design the music as best I can to make the words happen. They have to be presented, they have to be understood. You can't do this if people are bored by the music. If you put a two-chord melody to one of my songs, it would sound terrible. Often the comedy element in my songs is pointed up by the melody. I set 'Van Lingle Mungo' to a romantic, Brazilian-type tune, and I think the contrast is what makes the song funny. When I sing, I want the audience to understand every syllable. Hoagy Carmichael heard me do some of his songs once, and he told me, 'You don't have a real good voice, but I understood every word.'

"I admire Frank Loesser and Yip Harburg and Johnny Mercer as much as I admire anyone. Leonard Bernstein is a wonderful songwriter—the songs in *West Side Story* are triumphant. And Stephen Sondheim must be a very proud guy. Hal David is a terrific lyricist. When he first heard that quirky, fearless Burt Bacharach music, he must have reeled. Cole Porter and Larry Hart were playing with language, it seems to me. Mercer and Loesser were working on meaning, on communicating. They knew that good lyrics don't sound like poems. They knew that good lyrics should be literate speech that says something in a lyrical way. They knew that good lyrics come up to the edge of poetry and turn left."